THE CRITICAL LINK:
ENERGY AND
NATIONAL SECURITY
IN THE 1980s

**THE CENTER FOR
STRATEGIC AND INTERNATIONAL STUDIES**

Georgetown University
Washington, D.C.

THE CRITICAL LINK: ENERGY AND NATIONAL SECURITY IN THE 1980s

CHARLES K. EBINGER, Project Director

foreword by:
Henry A. Kissinger

Energy and National Security Staff

Wayne Berman
Richard J. Kessler
Eugenie Maechling

A report of the
International Resources Division
Amos A. Jordan, Executive Director

BALLINGER PUBLISHING COMPANY
Cambridge, Massachusetts
A Subsidiary of Harper & Row, Publishers, Inc.

International Standard Book Number: 0-88410-645-4

Library of Congress Catalog Card Number: 81-8065

Printed in the United States of America

Library of Congress Cataloging in Publication Data

Project on Energy and National Security (Georgetown University)
    The critical link.

    Includes index.
    1. United States—Energy policy.   2. United States—National
security.   I. Ebinger, Charles K.   II. Title.
HD9502.U52P77 1981   333.79'0973   81-8065
ISBN 0-88410-645-4   AACR2

DEDICATION

To my mentor, Mel

CONSULTANTS

Yonah Alexander
Tom Barger
Sevinc Carlson
Melvin A. Conant
Charles Jepsen
John Lichtblau
Francis X. Murray
G. Henry M. Schuler
Dillard Spriggs
Jonathan Stein
Ellen Stein
Kenneth Steuer
Penelope Hartland-Thunberg
Murray Weidenbaum
Edward Wonder
William Young

CONTENTS

LIST OF FIGURES

LIST OF TABLES

FOREWORD

The imperative need to reduce the nation's (and the West's) vulnerability to energy supply disruptions led my colleagues at the Georgetown Center for Strategic and International Studies in March 1980 to embark on a major examination of the linkages between energy and national security during the decade of the 1980s.

The project staff have focused their inquiry on three broad issues: (1) the use of market forces and government policies to encourage domestic energy production and influence patterns of energy consumption; (2) the need to work closely with our allies to plan for emergencies and avert crises, and, failing that, to manage an energy crisis effectively; and (3) the implications of the energy crisis for our national security. As the study shows, the changing terms of commercial access to energy in world trade have significantly diminished the market's natural ability to cushion another oil shock. The authors examine the threat posed to international energy trade by international terrorism. There is a section on the threat to the stability of the international financial system. The last chapter traces the effect of the global energy crisis on United States foreign policy.

This Foreword draws upon testimony before the Senate Committee on Energy and Natural Resources, July 31, 1981.

The link between energy and national security is of enormous importance. Nowhere is this truth more stark than in the Middle East and the Persian Gulf.

In the last three decades we have become so increasingly dependent on imported energy that today our economy and well-being are hostage to decisions made by nations thousands of miles away.

The energy crisis has placed at risk all of this nation's objectives in the world. It has mortgaged our economy and made our foreign policy vulnerable to unprecedented pressures; it has weakened the industrial democracies economically and undermined the political unity that is basic to the security of free nations. It has curtailed world economic growth and frustrated the hopes for progress of most of the developing nations.

The energy crisis touches the lives of Americans in many direct ways: in the constantly increasing price—and sometimes unavailability—of the fuel to heat our homes or drive our cars and in the seemingly endemic inflation and recession to which it has contributed. But it has also profoundly affected our national security by triggering a political crisis of global dimensions.

THE MIDDLE EAST AND THE PERSIAN GULF

Apart from the crucial role it plays in the world oil drama, the Middle East is a cauldron of political and strategic conflict. The region's political turmoil can be viewed from three aspects: as a major factor in the shifting balance of global power; as a contest between the moderate and radical forces in the area; and as an Arab–Israeli conflict. As the authors of this book note, it is not possible to deal with the region's problems by addressing any of these aspects in isolation—even an issue as important as the Arab–Israeli dispute. They must be understood and dealt with concurrently or the chaos will only multiply.

First, *the global balance of power.* Both history and personal experience endow Middle East leaders with a highly developed instinct for the nuances of the global balance of power. They may proclaim the conventional litany of nonalignment, but they understand perfectly well that their security depends on an overall equilibrium of military strength. A global imbalance of power enables expansionist countries to blackmail them, to interfere with diplomatic efforts for peace, to subvert domestic structures, or in the final analysis to repeat the pattern of Afghanistan: military intervention. They know that the only counterweight to these pressures is American power. Understandably, some leaders who cannot themselves contribute to a global balance might wish to keep aloof from the day-to-day diplomacy by which the East–West contest is played out. They would be horrified, however, if the West took their statements of self-reliance at face value.

The degree to which American power and influence have waned in the Middle East is best exhibited by the lack of enthusiasm with which the Carter doctrine was received in the Gulf. Our past vacillating policies engendered the pervasive conviction that we lacked the means or perhaps the will to implement it. Leaders in the area, from centuries of national experience, do *not* believe that their countries' security can be maintained by declarations of nonalignment or of solidarity with other countries equally unable to protect themselves. Their dissociation from us reflected, rather, their dismal assessment of the trend in the global balance.

These shifting strategic realities are bound to have their effect on the price of oil. Even with the production cutbacks dictated by OPEC, some moderate oil producers in the Middle East are still producing more oil than their own economic necessities warrant and absorbing more revenues than their development programs require. The present exorbitant oil price would thus be even higher were not some OPEC countries willing to produce beyond their purely economic needs—as the price for Western and particularly American political and military protection. However, to the extent that the global balance of power is perceived to shift against us, our persuasiveness or even seemingly purely economic decisions such as the price of oil is also profoundly eroded.

For all these reasons it is imperative for the United States to move urgently to restore its overall military strength. President Carter was correct to declare our strategic stake in the security of the Persian Gulf. Now that he has done so, it is essential that President Reagan win broad bipartisan support to create rapidly the forces needed to give effect to this inescapable commitment.

The second dimension of the instability in the Middle East and the Gulf is the *contest between the moderates and the radicals* in the area. From Pakistan to the Sahara, the region has seen a decade of turmoil and upheaval.

We are often told that domestic change is inevitable and irrepressible, that we have to get on the side of the forces of change. There is merit in these propositions. But we must never lose sight of a crucial distinction: We have a vital stake in the *nature* of that change, and in the success of those who support peaceful change and ties with the industrial democracies. We must *not* attempt to appease anti-Western radicals who are driven by ideology and will not be charmed out of their hostility to us by professions of our goodwill. At stake in the contest between these two groups is, among other things, the world's energy future. For example, the disintegration of the pro-Western government in Iran was the principal cause of the oil crisis of 1979. Radical countries sought to drive up the price of oil to obtain resources to achieve their international objective of undermining American and Western influence. Moderate regimes had the paradoxical incentive to *reduce* production, since they feared the disruptive consequences of the process of modernization that destroyed the shah. Both developments pushed up the price; together they spell disaster for the West.

Governments that have traditionally relied on us know that the various radical regimes, however different their origins and motivations, all agree in their all-out opposition to peaceful evolution, Western values, and the survival of the present world economic system. The inevitable result of radical ascendancy—regardless of its origins—would be to threaten the survival of all pro-Western governments that remained in the Third World, and especially in the Middle East, with obvious geopolitical consequences.

The West has so far supplied no serious answer to this challenge. Clearly we have fully analyzed neither the dynamics of political change nor our interest in relation to it. We must be clear in our minds what our own survival requires, the scope of change we can responsibly advocate, and what countries we must defend in our own interest.

The Arab-Israeli conflict is without doubt a principal factor in the turbulence of the Middle East. But its solution is closely connected with the military balance and the relationship between moderates and radicals in the area. If the Soviet Union emerges as the dominant outside power, moderate countries will be reluctant to support peace processes that displease it. In the face of a dominant radicalism, even more friends will disavow schemes that are in fact in their own best long-term interest.

A dangerous escapism has developed in the West. The illusion is widespread that solving the so-called Palestinian problem is the *deus ex machina* that will defuse all the region's other tensions. A West Bank solution is important, but whether it contributes to the solution of other problems depends on the nature of the settlement, the auspices under which it is achieved, and who benefits from it.

I do not believe that the status quo on the West Bank can or should be maintained. But I am not impressed, either, by the many fashionable proposals that amount to finding some way of introducing the PLO into the negotiations on the optimistic assumption that it would then moderate its goals and contribute to stability in the entire region.

Any effort to solve the West Bank issue in one grand negotiation, defining all frontiers and all relationships, is almost certain to fail. And a prolonged inconclusive effort is bound, in its turn, to compound the tensions in the area. If negotiations based on the Camp David autonomy scheme do not produce the desired outcome, I hope other avenues will be attempted. It is in the common interest that we not chase abstractions but begin a process that can lead to rapid results. In this manner progress can be made in the West Bank that contributes to political stability in the area and contains, rather than unleashes, radical pressures.

RESPONSE TO THE ENERGY CRISIS

Since the first price explosion of 1973, we have learned that the energy crisis is not a mere problem of transitional adjustment; it is a grave challenge to the political and economic structure of the free world. The world's postwar financial institutions and mechanisms of cooperation were never designed to handle so abrupt a price rise in so vital a commodity or such massive shifts of wealth. The problem will not go away by simply letting inflation proceed; on the contrary, runaway inflation is part of the vicious circle that drives oil prices up. Nor can the financial imbalance be overcome by permitting the debt of consumers to expand indefinitely, even though this is what has been happening. The gradual impoverishment of the industrialized world is certain to end in financial catastrophe, with grave political consequences. Finally, for a consumer/producer dialogue to be effective, certain objective conditions must be met, which do not now exist.

There is no secret about what we must do. As my colleagues note in their report, the industrial democracies must adopt stringent conservation measures, develop new supplies of oil and alternative sources of energy, strengthen collaboration among the consumer nations, address the plight of the developing nations, and seek a more reliable long-term relationship with the producers. These objectives are easy to state in the abstract. It is devising programs to implement them that has proved to be the obstacle. I will not get into the domestic side of the problem here, except to point out the disastrous international political consequences of our continuing vulnerability and to urge that the problem be dealt with as a matter of highest urgency. Aside from our military defense, there is no project of more central importance to our national security and indeed our independence as a sovereign nation.

The response to the energy crisis, of course, itself has an international dimension. For finally its solution depends on our fortitude and bold leadership. We have been subjected to political pressures, not only in the 1973 embargo but even more recently, when we were threatened by OPEC with production cutbacks if we sought to build up a strategic oil reserve. But we cannot tolerate being forced into a state of permanent vulnerability. No country has a right to demand that we remain eternally subject to blackmail. Building a strategic oil reserve is a sovereign decision of the United States and an essential matter of survival; outside attempts to interfere with our filling the reserve demonstrate its importance. We should fill our strategic reserve promptly, and any country taking retaliatory steps must know that it does so at the cost of its good relations with the United States.

No area of policy has been more disappointing than consumer cooperation. Since the establishment of the International Energy Agency in 1974, cooperation among the industrial democracies has not been adequate to the challenge. Instead of bold concerted action, too many of the industrial democracies have preferred currying favor with the OPEC countries, competing for some transitory special position or dissociating themselves from our negotiating efforts in the Middle East conflict. But any special position gained by one country can be rapidly transferred to another that outbids it. Such a course is in fact against the interests of the moderate oil producers, the claimed beneficiaries. Once the principle is established that a political price can be exacted, the moderates will become the target of radical pressures to raise the political price. The moderates cannot stand fast if the industrial democracies do not.

A subject on which it is urgent for the industrial democracies to develop a common approach is the plight of the developing nations. These countries are caught in an impossible bind. Higher oil prices absorb all their aid and export earnings; the bill for other imports mounts because of the global inflation fueled by the energy crisis; and their own capacity to export is reduced because of the recession in the industrialized countries, which is another result of the energy crisis. Thus a reexamination of the development needs of the new nations is imperative. The devastation of the developing world's hope for progress is a grim omen for a world of peace.

Another subject requiring urgent concerted attention by the global community is the recycling of financial surpluses. By 1983, the financial claims of the oil producers on the OECD countries will reach one-half trillion dollars. That amount cannot be recycled by the commercial banking system; it will lead to the bankruptcy and instability of many developing nations; it will overtax the financial institutions even of developed nations. Recycling is easiest precisely into those countries that need it least; it will not abate the devastating impact of current prices on nations whose export earnings and foreign assistance now go largely toward paying their energy bills.

As I have urged consistently since 1973, the need for solidarity among the oil-consuming nations is plain. I do not accept the proposition that it is proper for the producers to organize but confrontational for the consumers to seek to cooperate with one another. To reduce our common vulnerability research into alternative sources of energy could be pooled, and major resources could be allocated to joint programs to develop alternative energy sources with clear target dates. Above all, a joint approach should be worked out for a comprehensive dialogue with the producing nations.

Eventually the solidarity of the industrial democracies will provide the secure basis for a dialogue between consumers and producers. There is in fact a congruence of interests. The consumer countries have a political stake in the independence of the producer nations, even those whose domestic policies are repugnant to us, such as Iran. The producers in turn have a stake in a stable and growing world economy because many of them depend on it for their technology, for their development, and in a deeper sense for their independence. Both together must find means to enable the developing nations to fulfill their aspirations. But this cannot take place in an atmosphere of chaos and blackmail. The producers cannot continue the practice of periodically announcing, in a series of unilateral proclamations, decisions affecting the economic future of the entire world without any consultations or any apparent concern for their impact. The industrial democracies must form a more coherent group if a consumer-producer dialogue is to give expression to the reality of interdependence.

President Reagan has before him the challenge to lead the way out of these dilemmas. The United States is better able than other countries to regain some mastery over events. We have the domestic resources, the technological skills, and the creative genius to transform the world's energy market. Therefore, decisive American efforts to implement an energy policy would transform the internal environment—reducing the cartel's stranglehold on the world economy, restoring world prosperity, dispelling the clouds of political demoralization, and strengthening our security.

Henry A. Kissinger
Counselor
The Center for Strategic and
International Studies
Washington, D.C.
June 26, 1981

PREFACE

Stalking the United States of the 1980s is an illusion that threatens the economic stability and security interests of this country and indeed the world far more than the global aggrandizement of Soviet power. The illusion has touched all regions of the country and all socioeconomic classes, transcending partisan politics and reaching into the highest levels of the executive and legislative branches of government and the boardrooms of domestic and international corporations. It is the illusion that the energy crisis is essentially behind us and that we can relax and let market forces solve our energy dilemma.

The illusion is based on several beliefs: first, that parochial interests can be allowed to continue to hamper the formulation of a coherent national energy program; second, that the nation has the luxury of postponing the tough economic, political, and social decisions that could begin to reduce this country's dependence on imported oil; and, third, that failure to act, on the part of the United States and its industrial allies, will not affect the prospects for a brighter future for the mass of mankind, especially in the Third World.

This book does not reexamine in detail the familiar story of how the energy crisis emerged at the time of the 1973–74 embargo by the Organization of Arab Exporting Countries (OAPEC); rather, focus is on the implications of the energy situation confronting the United

States and the global community in the wake of the 1978–79 Iranian revolution and the outbreak of the Iran-Iraq war in September 1980.

These events, resulting in the loss of perhaps 5–6 million barrels per day (mmbd) of Iranian and Iraqi oil that would normally have entered the world market, demonstrate the critical link between energy and national security and, with the Western world dependent on the Persian (or Arabian) Gulf region for about 40 percent of its total oil supplies, the fecklessness of continued reliance on the politically volatile region. The national security risks posed for the United States and its major industrial allies by this dependence must be reduced as rapidly as possible. It is here that the politics and economics of domestic and international energy become inexorably linked. The failure to enact a comprehensive energy program to alleviate oil import dependence ensures continued vulnerabiity to international oil shortages.

The links between energy and national security are several. First, international competition for oil, especially in times of a real or perceived shortage, as in the case of the 1979 Iranian crisis, strains political and diplomatic alliances as nations move unilaterally rather than in concert to secure access to vital energy supplies. One of the reasons that this beggar-thy-neighbor policy reigns is that actions the United States may perceive as necessary to preserve access to the Persian Gulf nations' oil supplies may be viewed as confrontational by one or more members of the European community, Japan, and the key oil states.

This difference in perception arises not only because our allies are far more dependent on Gulf oil than is the United States and hence reluctant to support U.S. policies they believe may threaten their own supplies, but also because some of our major allies believe that other American policies—namely, concerning the Arab-Israeli dispute and America's "special relationship" with Saudi Arabia (and formerly with Iran)—are at variance with broader European and Japanese interests in the region. As a result, since 1973 there has been a lack of solidarity on energy and Gulf issues among the major oil-importing countries, preventing the development of an effective concerted strategy for dealing with oil-import dependence.

The nature of the allies' differences on energy problems are discussed in detail in Chapters 1 and 8; here it suffices to note that these differing perceptions and views of the best means to ensure access to oil resources threaten to weaken the global strategic balance of the industrial world vis-à-vis the Soviet Union. Only when deterioration of the alliance becomes a central concern of the allies will the industrial world be likely to generate a unified energy policy capable of an adequate response.

Reliance on insecure oil supplies impinges on the military security of the United States and its allies in several other areas. First, safeguarding major oil producing states against external attack or internal subversion necessitates difficult strategic choices. The military must have the bases and operational mobility it needs to move quickly to protect against the threat of sabotage the energy logistics systems inside the major energy-exporting countries and on the high seas. The military must also position adequate fuel supplies that might be needed for the defense of Europe, Japan, and the United States as well as to support allied interests in other conflict areas. The West's ability to support sufficient military forces in an era of fiscal austerity and high energy costs is another link.

The security of the United States and its allies is also threatened by skyrocketing oil-import bills, which strain the ability of the international banking system to recycle petrodollars from creditor to debtor nations, thus raising the specter of severe worldwide economic depression if not global economic collapse. Oil payments represent a massive transfer of real wealth from energy-deficient countries to energy-surplus countries. This raises questions concerning future growth in the deficient countries, their prospects for more equitable income distribution, and their political and economic stability. Major defaults by one or more major less-developed countries (LDCs), say Turkey or Brazil, would send shock waves throughout the entire international financial system, including in the U.S. banking community. For this reason alone the United States cannot turn a deaf ear to the economic and political problems of critical Third World states.

Energy and national security policy are linked in a third way: Political, economic, and environmental conflicts over energy development, conservation, and end use endanger uncertainties over future economic conditions and the supply and cost of energy, thus constraining investment and the prospects for enhancing industrial productivity. To the extent that the "regulatory" climate emanating out of Washington, D.C., the state capitols, or local public service commissions constrain energy supply fuel switching or hinder efforts at greater fuel efficiency, the nation's reliance on expensive foreign oil is perpetuated and our national security is impaired.

Parochial interests must not be allowed to continue to thwart the formulation and implementation of a coherent national energy program. In order to effect a change in the status quo, it is first necessary to understand that the conflicts over energy policy go to the very heart of the American political system.

Among the impediments to an effective national energy program are the following: the different economic interests of energy-producing versus energy-consuming states; tensions between environmental and production concerns; policy differences both within each sector of the energy industry and between proponents of each fuel type; conflicts over the allocation of scarce resources like water, which are needed both for energy development and other vital economic interests, such as ranching and farming, and finally competing institutional and industrial interests.

It is a central thesis of the analyses in this book that unless these interests are reconciled and policy measures enacted to accelerate domestic energy production, to improve the efficiency of energy consumption, and to enhance conservation, the United States will be in grave danger and the consequences will be potentially devastating not only for the United States but also our major industrial allies.

Although record inventories of both crude oil and most petroleum products, falling spot-market prices for oil, sagging U.S. oil imports, and apparently sizable savings from conservation may temporarily seem to belie the need for a sense of urgency on the domestic energy front, it is the belief of the Energy and National Security Project (ENS) staff that such a view is extremely shortsighted and neglects not only possible oil cutoffs arising out of hostilities in producing areas but also the increasing politicization of international oil supplies that has occurred since 1973–74 and especially since the Iranian crisis.

One of the areas of greatest concern is that although the United States has moved (slowly) to end the political impasse on the domestic energy front in order to reduce dependence on imported oil, no effective short-run contingency plans have been formulated to meet oil supply cutoffs that might be militarily or politically induced. In Chapters 1–4 of this book various emergency fuel measures are examined in detail; these include provisions for energy demand restraint, accelerated domestic energy production and electricity generation, and massive liquid fuel conservation. No adequate domestic oil allocation and rationing program exists. Neither in the first oil crisis of 1973–74 nor in 1979 did the supply shortage last for more than four or five months, it should be noted.

In order to implement effective contingency programs without inordinate delay, it is important to remove conflicting regulatory and allocation procedures and to establish before any emergency arises the legal and institutional mechanisms that would be needed to cope with it. Moreover, as part of any effective emergency planning program, it is essential that similar measures be enacted multilaterally in the International Energy Agency (IEA), the North Atlantic Treaty Organization (NATO) and other appropriate forums.

Although conservation, fuel substitution, mechanisms for restraining demand, the development of new liquid and gaseous synthetic fuels, and the implementation of effective emergency allocation procedures should all be pursued, there is no substitute for the accelerated build-up of a major strategic petroleum reserve (SPR).

The ENS project staff believes what William S. Paley first argued in *Resources for Freedom* in 1952, that the creation of a strategic petroleum reserve both nationally and privately should form the cornerstone of an energy contingency policy designed to protect the nation's security.

Although the details of the policy recommendations delineated in this book may be criticized, the project staff believes that when the analysis and recommendations are viewed in total, the policy options recommended provide the framework for an energy program that will, as far as possible, protect U.S. national security during the 1980s.

It has not been the investigators' purpose to attack either specific interests or the policies of particular administrations on a partisan basis. Rather, the goal has been to gain distance from the partisan fray in order to assess the larger national interest as it has been affected by the geopolitical events that have dramatically transformed the international petroleum market since 1973–74.

The policy choices before the nation are stark. Either we, as a society and as part of the global community, move forward in a concerted manner to secure access to vital energy supplies, or we remain at the mercy of more parochial interests, both at home and abroad, and thus lose control of our economic, political, and strategic destiny.

Charles Ebinger
Director, Project on
Energy and National Security
The Center for Strategic and
International Studies
Washington, D.C.
July 16, 1981

ACKNOWLEDGMENTS

The completion of a manuscript after many months of work gives time for reflection and an expression of gratitude for all those who helped through the long research and publication process. Without the foresight and sponsorship of David Abshire and Amos Jordan at the Center of Strategic and International Studies (CSIS) of Georgetown University, this project would not have been possible. Their generous mandate to conduct the study as I and the members of my staff deemed fit, was an expression of support and trust few authors have the good fortune to enjoy.

Likewise, a note of very special thanks must go to all those in industry, government, academia, and private consulting, without whose help this study could never have been completed. Although it is impossible to single out all those who deserve to be mentioned, the unswerving support of Ted Eck, Melvin Conant, Clyde Wheeler, Henry Schuler, Jack Evans, Art Callaghan, Connie Shields, Bob Ebel, Sam Schwartz, Harry Williams, Doug Hartman, Clem Malin, Dick Fisher, and Tom Barger deserve special recognition.

For the seminar sessions that were held as part of our research efforts, gratitude is owed to all those specialists who gave generously of their time. These sessions formed a vital part of the research process and John Bernard of the CSIS staff deserves praise for all his efforts in ensuring that the sessions ran smoothly and efficiently.

It is hard to believe that it was over two years ago that the idea of an Energy and National Security study was first conceived. Since that time, only the unflinching efforts of the CSIS fund-raising staff saw the publication through to its conclusion. While many helped in this endeavor, Etta Pollock deserves very special thanks for her long hours of effort on our behalf. Christa Dantzler is also owed a special note of recognition.

However, it is to my immediate staff and those other CSIS specialists that I owe the deepest gratitude. Both Eugenie Maechling and Richard Kessler were invaluable associates in helping to delineate the direction, form, and conclusions of the study. Eugenie Maechling was the principal author of Chapters 2, 3, 6, and 8, and responsible for integrating the work of consultants. Their substantive contributions reflect the wide diversity and depth of their backgrounds, and their untiring oral and written review and revision not only of their own work but also my own were invaluable. Michael Sharzynski and Susan Agusti were instrumental in the preparatory work on the project. Penelope Hartland-Thunberg deserves special thanks for her chapter on the financial consequences of import dependence, while Frank Murray and Bill Young deserve mention for their invaluable input on the coal and nuclear power sectors. Jonathan Stein deserves special praise for his analysis of the Soviet energy situation, and Edward Wonder, an outside consultant, provided expert analysis of the Canadian energy scene. G. Henry M. Schuler deserves special recognition for his insights into changes occurring in the international energy market.

However, it is to Wayne Berman that I owe a note of very special recognition. As the original member of my staff, it was Waynes's unceasing efforts both as a consummate fund raiser and as planner and executor of our substantive seminar sessions that moved our project off the drawing board to final completion. Not only was he an invaluable associate throughout the study, but he also became a close confidant and friend.

Finally, a note of commendation is owed to Pat McNess for her editorial assistance and to my associates Pauline Younger and Bill Harris who provided invaluable help in the preparation of the manuscript and to my wife for never tiring in her role as a sounding board for my ideas.

Charles K. Ebinger
Project Director
Washington, D.C.
September 1981

1 THE ROOTS OF THE ENERGY CRISIS

Contrary to popular belief, the energy crisis unleashed by the oil embargo of 1973-74 was not the first to threaten the national security of the United States. A world petroleum shortage was acutely feared between 1918 and 1924 because of the rapid spread of the automobile after World War I, rapidly rising demand for petroleum, and the adoption by Mexico's government of nationalist policies that threatened American oil interests. By the late 1920s and throughout most of the 1930s, concern shifted as increased production in Venezuela, the Middle East, and East Texas, combined with the deepening depression, sent domestic U.S. oil prices plummeting. With the outbreak of World War II, oil experts grew alarmed that wartime fuel requirements would deplete U.S. reserves enough to threaten aviation fuel supplies. By 1942-1944, experts feared a shortfall as high as 128,000 to 746,000 barrels per day (bd)[1] despite the fact that the United States was producing 3.9 million barrels per day (mmbd).

The oil supply crisis receded as the war ended but not before profound structural changes had occurred in the international oil market that would greatly affect future oil supply. By 1945 the locus of world oil production had shifted from the western hemisphere to the Middle East owing to the availability of lower cost crude oil; in 1947 the United States became a net oil importer for the first time in its

1

history. Before the war crude oil had represented only one-third of the total volume of oil traded on the world market; oil products had become more important. By 1950 crude oil accounted for 50 percent of the total market; on the eve of the 1973 embargo by the Organization of Arab Petroleum Exporting Countries (OAPEC), it would be 84 percent.[2]

During the 1950s and 1960s the United States and its major allies experienced three more supply crises. Iran's nationalization in 1951 of all foreign assets posed the first direct threat to the international oil companies. Only surplus productive capacity allowed the world to cope until the crisis passed in 1953 with the overthrow of the Mossadeq regime and the restoration of the shah. At the time, world petroleum trade was only at 2.9 mmbd, but the crisis sent shudders through the system.

In October 1957 another supply crisis loomed when Egypt closed the Suez Canal to oil traffic, effectively cutting off two-thirds of Western Europe's supply (2.1 mmbd at the time). No major shortfalls occurred, because production in the western hemisphere was increased, petroleum stocks were heavily used, and pipeline shipments from the Middle East to Mediterranean ports were increased. The main reason a supply crisis was averted was that the United States was able to act as a marginal supplier, to offset the impending European shortfall. This U.S. capability was important again during the oil crisis set off by the 1967 Arab-Israeli war, when by increasing domestic production and diverting supplies previously intended for itself, the United States was able to make almost 1 mmbd additional oil available to Europe.

By 1970 the international petroleum market had changed drastically. With inexpensive foreign oil increasingly available, consumers in the non-Communist world had increased their dependence on oil from 9 mmbd in 1950 to over 30 mmbd in 1970, an average compounded growth rate in oil usage of over 7 percent a year.[3] Because after 1968 the United States no longer held reserves that could serve as a buffer for Western Europe in times of crisis, the oil-consuming nations became vulnerable to a supply disruption.

The easy availability of cheaper imported oil during the 1950s and 1960s undercut domestic oil prices so much that some segments of the petroleum industry cited national security as the main reason for enacting the Voluntary Oil Import Program (1957–1959) and the Mandatory Oil Import Program (1959–1973). The intent of the latter program, according to two of its enabling provisions, was to protect military and essential civilian demand against reasonably possible foreign supply interruptions for which emergency replacement steps were infeasible and to prevent damage to domestic industry from excessive imports that would weaken national security.[4]

Despite this program to reduce dependency, oil imports continued to climb; the reason is the many exemptions: overland imports from Canada and Mexico, petrochemical products from Puerto Rico, oil products processed in the Virgin Islands, and, after 1966, residual fuel oils.

By 1970 the danger signals were visible to anyone who looked for them. Shortages of natural gas and heating oil occurred during the winter of 1969-70 and in the summer the East Coast experienced brownouts. Shortages continued the following winter. The Organization of Petroleum Exporting Countries (OPEC) members were disenchanted with the oil companies, the Suez Canal remained closed in the aftermath of the 1967 Arab-Israeli War, marginal oil demand was met more and more by the Arab oil producers, Venezuelan reserves fell, and Colonel Qaddafi's new radical regime in Libya took advantage of a ruptured pipeline between the Persian Gulf and the Mediterranean to force a major confrontation over prices with U.S. companies operating in Libya. In the ensuing crisis, Libya cut production by 850,000 bd, setting the stage for the Teheran agreement of 1971 and price leapfrogging that continues to this day. As Melvin Conant, a leading international petroleum consultant has noted, Libya demonstrated to other oil producers that price changes could be imposed unilaterally on oil companies without being challenged by consumer governments, particularly the United States.[5] After the Libyan crisis, access to energy became crucial to U.S. national security.

The world energy situation by April 1973 gave little reason for optimism. Between 1950 and 1970 world consumption of petroleum had risen from 9 mmbd to 40 mmbd; by mid-1973, it had risen to 48 mmbd. OPEC oil production, which grew at an annual rate of 2 mmbd between 1966 and 1972, accounted for most of the increase.

Crude oil production in the United States, which had peaked at 9.6 mmbd in 1970, now declined to 9.4 mmbd. Oil imports had shot up to 6.2 mmbd, divided almost equally between crude oil and petroleum products. Consumption of natural gas, which cost less than one-third its energy-equivalent in oil, escalated at twice the rate of new discoveries, causing shortages during the winter of 1973-74.

Coal's share in the U.S. energy balance fell from 23 percent in 1960 to 18 percent in 1973. Because of environmental objections no federal lands had been leased for strip mining since 1971; nuclear energy, which produced only 5 percent of electricity in the United States remained a pipedream.[6] Finally, U.S. energy policy was determined by a myriad of agencies, commissions, and departments, many of which worked at cross-purposes or duplicated one another's efforts.

In an attempt to alleviate growing gasoline shortages, President Nixon abolished the Mandatory Oil Import Program in April 1973, replacing it with a system of license fees that allowed companies to import as much as they wished. Although the fees were small, those on imported products were higher to encourage domestic refinery construction. The president also proposed a number of other measures designed to accelerate domestic energy production.[7] By May, when the crisis had intensified and independent refiners and jobbers were charging that the large oil companies were manipulating the crisis, the government enacted a complex allocation program, which created new shortages. In July, as part of Phase IV of the administration's price stabilization policy, a complicated two-tier crude oil pricing system went into effect, under which "old" oil was placed under price ceilings while new oil (that produced above 1972 production levels), was exempt. This was the situation that existed in the United States on the eve of the OAPEC oil embargo and price crisis of 1973–74.

U.S. RESPONSE TO THE OIL EMBARGO

When the United States resupplied Israel with weapons after the outbreak of the 1973 Arab-Israeli War, the OAPEC oil ministers retaliated on October 20, 1973, by imposing an oil embargo on the United States, the Netherlands, and Canada. Although other nations were exempted from the embargo, they too experienced shortfalls, because the embargo affected the Dutch port of Rotterdam, Europe's largest oil refining and transshipment center. Western Europe and Japan, which were hardest hit by the embargo because they are so dependent on oil imports, saw U.S. policy toward Israel as having jeopardized the flow of oil—a perception that would later complicate formulation of U.S. domestic and international energy policy.

Responding to the oil embargo, President Nixon stated in an address to the American people on November 7, 1973, that the national goal by the end of the decade should be to meet U.S. energy needs without any dependency on foreign oil. By the time President Ford released the *Project Independence* report in November 1974, U.S. energy policymakers were aware that under no political circumstances could the United States become totally self-sufficient in energy at reasonable economic costs. President Ford's motto, "reasonable self-sufficiency," was heard more and more. Although the *Project Independence* report reflected this new mood in concluding that it would be difficult for the United States to reduce its dependence on imported petroleum substantially before 1980, the report's energy supply projections were wildly optimistic.[8]

President Ford advocated bold initiatives, designed for the most part to encourage development of domestic energy supplies: creation of a 300 million barrel strategic petroleum reserve (SPR), a tariff on imported crude oil, attempts to decontrol domestic oil and natural gas prices, the authority to order major power plants to convert from oil and gas to coal. President Carter warned the nation early in his term of office that resolving the energy crisis was "the moral equivalent of war."[9] Meanwhile domestic regulatory policies, regional politics, and infighting among special interest groups prohibited the enactment of a comprehensive energy program. Despite a declared policy of reducing oil imports, U.S. dependence on oil imports increased by 2.6 mmbd between 1973 and 1977, with imports of crude oil alone jumping from 3.2 to 6.6 mmbd. OPEC's share of total imports increased from 48.7 to 70.4 percent during the same period, while OAPEC's share escalated from 14.7 to 36.1 percent. Moreover our dependence on OPEC and OAPEC was in reality greater than the figures suggest, because we imported so many petroleum products from Caribbean refineries, whose purchases of crude oil feedstocks from OPEC and OAPEC, although difficult to measure, were considerable.

The main reasons for this increased import dependency were a fall in U.S. production of about 1 mmbd; plummeting exports (1.2 mmbd) from Canada and Venezuela as both countries reduced production out of concern over the level of their oil reserves; and a reduction in the real price (indexed for inflation) of oil between 1974 and 1978 in comparison with escalating costs for alternative fuels.

To deal with the crisis President Carter in April 1977 unveiled the first National Energy Plan (NEP),[10] the basic objective of which was to reduce reliance on oil imports from projected levels of 16 mmbd in 1985 to 6 mmbd. This was to be accomplished by greater use of coal and energy conservation until renewable energy resources could be developed. Nuclear power was seen as an energy source of last resort. The SPR was to be expanded to 1 billion barrels.

The U.S. Congress, which feared incurring the wrath of its constituents if it supported higher energy prices, did not share the president's sense of urgency about the energy crisis. Most members of Congress, like most citizens, believed either that the energy crisis would pass with time or that the crisis had been manufactured by the energy industry to bolster its prices and profits. While Congress, the administration, the media, and the energy industry traded charge and countercharge about who was to blame for the energy crisis, little progress was made formulating a national energy program.

The problem that President Carter's National Energy Plans 1 and 2 encountered in Congress was, that although legislators agreed that higher domestic oil and natural gas prices were needed to encourage conservation, they could not agree on how high oil prices should go or who should benefit from the increases. They debated: Should oil be priced at the world price as determined by OPEC? Would the appropriate price be the replacement cost of a depletable resource? What is a valid measure of replacement cost? Is price based on production cost plus a fair rate of return more appropriate than price based on replacement cost? These questions formed the cornerstone of the domestic policy debate.

NEP 1 focused more on reducing energy demand and improving energy efficiency than on providing major incentives to increase energy supply. Debates on proposals for a wellhead tax and continued oil price controls focused on the fundamental question of who should benefit from oil prices. The Carter administration argued that the uncontrolled price of newly discovered oil provided enough incentive to foster new exploration and production and that the oil industry should not be allowed to recoup windfall profits from existing reserves, which had cost them little. The oil industry argued that part of the tax should be returned to industry to provide revenue for investment in new, more expensive oil exploration and to foster the development of high-cost alternative energy sources by the oil industry.

Debate over the wellhead tax led to an impasse between 1976 and 1978, with representatives from energy-producing states opposing the tax, while those from energy-consuming states favored it since it would help offset the effects of higher energy prices.

Oil prices were not the only subject for argument. President Carter's opposition to the decontrol of domestic natural gas prices led to a rancorous debate in the Congress, delayed the construction of the Alaskan pipeline (thus retarding development of 10 percent of the nation's reserves), and caused a serious confrontation with Mexico, which subsequently reduced the volume of gas it had agreed to send to the United States. Debate on the National Energy Plan failed both to increase domestic energy production and to diversify U.S. energy imports through accelerated pipeline and liquid natural gas (LNG) imports from Mexico, Canada, Algeria, and Indonesia.

While the political debate on energy policy raged between April 1976 and December 1978, when the National Energy Act was passed, filling of the strategic petroleum reserve was halted at 91 million barrels; the Continental Shelf Leasing Bill was shelved for two years; a proposal for a coal slurry pipeline was attacked by the railroad industry, farmers, and landowners concerned about its impact on their property and by some environmentalists and representatives of Western states who were fearful that the pipelines would deplete scarce water supplies; the Alaskan gas pipeline remained in limbo; no pipeline system was constructed or retrofitted to allow surplus Alaskan oil on the West Coast to be moved to the central part of the nation where it was vitally needed; President Carter's opposition to the breeder reactor and his vacillating position on nuclear energy helped delay enactment of a bill to expedite nuclear licensing and to resolve the problems of nuclear waste storage.

The December 1978 passage of the National Energy Act, which included the National Gas Policy Act, the Powerplant and Industrial Fuel Use Act, and the Energy Conservation Policy Act, was heralded as a major step toward reducing U.S. dependence on imported oil. In reality most of the provisions had only a marginal impact on the way Americans produced and consumed energy, while others, particularly the Powerplant and Industrial Fuel Use Act (PIFUA), actually served to increase oil imports by limiting the use of natural gas by electric utilities.[11]

By the time of the Iranian crisis in late 1978–79, it was apparent that most government leaders did not really understand (1) how the energy industry is structured, that it is not monolithic and that segments of it are major adversaries and competitors; (2) the degree to which deep seated regional, economic, political and social issues are affected in the process of energy policy implementation; and (3) that enactment of an energy program requires serious trade-offs in terms of other social goals, such as protection of the environment and equitable distribution of income regionally.[12]

Although oil imports fell from 8.8 mmbd in 1977 to 8.2 mmbd in 1978, the U.S. energy situation had improved very little since 1973. Indeed much of the decline had occurred because of rising domestic Alaskan oil production, a drawdown in oil stocks that had been built up to historically high levels in the fourth quarter of 1977 when a national coal strike had been feared, enhanced conservation in response both to rising OPEC prices, and fear that the 1976–77 gas shortage would be repeated. By late 1978, the U.S. oil import bill hovered around $3 billion per month.

INTERNATIONAL RESPONSE TO THE OIL EMBARGO

The quadrupling of oil prices between 1973 and March 1974 generated fear in international financial circles that ever-escalating oil prices combined with the inability of the oil producers to spend their surplus petrodollars could lead to a collapse of the international financial system. Fortunately the system proved more resilient than anticipated. But by 1978 a combination of unprecedented military and development expenditures by the oil-producing nations and three years of declining world oil prices had brought the OPEC current-account balance down to $1 billion.

Once the immediate financial crisis receded, disagreement on a number of issues made it impossible for Western Europe, Japan, and the United States to form a unified response to the challenges posed by OPEC. A number of problems strained alliance relations:

- NATO members except for Portugal and briefly the Federal Republic of Germany refused to let the United States use their territories to resupply Israel during the 1973 Arab-Israeli War for fear of retaliatory curtailments of oil supplies.
- Some nations, especially France, opposed U.S. leadership of a united negotiating position for oil-consuming nations.

- Japan and members of the European Economic Community (EEC), notably France, sought bilateral deals with the Arab oil producers to ensure access to oil supplies—possibly to the detriment of other consuming states.
- A European-Arab dialogue began in June 1975 without the participation of Japan and the United States.
- Participants in the 1975–77 Conference on International Economic Cooperation disagreed about policies that would ensure access to oil supplies at reasonable prices.
- Europe and Japan became suspicious of U.S. motives in seeking a special relationship with Saudi Arabia at the very time (June 1974) the United States was urging allied cohesion and formation of the International Energy Agency (IEA); Europe and Japan feared the United States was moving to protect its own interest at their expense.
- Europe, Japan, and the United States differed about international nuclear policy, especially the development and export of enrichment and reprocessing facilities that could be utilized to manufacture nuclear weapons.
- Europe, Japan, and the United States disagreed about what policies to adopt in the Arab-Israeli dispute.
- The United States failed to adopt an energy policy to reduce its accelerating dependence on oil imports and thereby alleviate pressure on world energy supplies and prices. With only 6 percent of the world's population, the United States consumed about 40 percent of the world's energy and about 33 percent of its oil.

Western Europe and Japan were gravely concerned about the direction of U.S. policy and the degree to which U.S. political and economic interests might diverge from theirs, especially on the subjects of the Middle East, energy, and nonproliferation.

Between 1973 and 1978, imports met 70 percent of Western Europe's oil requirements and a staggering 99 percent of Japan's. By 1978 European and Japanese dependence on crude oil supplies from the Persian Gulf and North Africa had risen to 14 mmbd or over 80 percent of their oil imports. In contrast, the United States received only 30 percent (3 mmbd) of its oil imports from the region. In view of their greater dependence on Middle Eastern oil, it is not surprising that Japan and Europe did not want the United States to adopt policies toward Israel that would antagonize the Arabs and thus jeopardize their access to the region's oil supplies.[13]

By Fall 1978 oil analysts who focused on the short-term balance of oil supply and demand were failing to recognize the dangerous state of the world oil market. During 1977 many experts had forecast a "tight" oil market between 1980 and 1985. In 1978 leading energy groups declared the energy crisis an event of the past, citing new, more optimistic estimates of global and domestic resources and the time needed to exploit them, new developments in enhanced oil and gas recovery technology, and enormous potential for energy savings through more efficient use of energy.[14]

These optimistic forecasters did not seem aware of how the major oil producers viewed the world energy scene in late 1978. The major OPEC nations were alarmed at how their bargaining power had eroded since 1973-74. Although the United States and other consumers had increased their dependency on OPEC oil, the OPEC nations saw their financial surpluses eroded as a result of declining real oil prices, rapid inflation, and the consequent rapidly escalating price of manufactured goods imported from the major industrialized nations.

By the third quarter of 1978, OPEC production was 10 percent below the peak level of 1973, while non-OPEC production was up about 11-12 percent. The current account surplus of the OPEC countries, which had risen from $5.7 billion in 1973 to $66.7 billion in 1974, had fallen to $1 billion by 1978[15] despite previous forecasts that it would be $28 billion.[16]

By late 1978 wide variations in medium- (1985-1990) to long-term (1990-1995) forecasts of global energy supplies had left the public confused and suspicious.[17] Differences in projections generally stemmed from different projections or assumptions about world gross national product (GNP) growth rates, the price elasticity of energy demand, the availability of oil and gas reserves, discovery rates for new reserves, oil-flow rates (reserve/production ratios), the impact of regulatory policies on the timing of energy resource development, and the speed with which enhanced oil recovery technology would develop.[18] Experts also disagreed about whether the development of new conventional oil resources in China and Mexico and unconventional resources in Venezuela and Canada could diminish the power of the OPEC cartel and alleviate pressure on energy supplies.

Concern about supplies was intense in late 1978. Rumblings in Iran, uncertainty about whether high prices would depress burgeoning Third World energy demand, and concern that the industrialized nations might have to compete increasingly for oil with countries of the Communist bloc and the rapidly developing OPEC nations themselves intensified worries about how much oil would be available for export during the 1980s.[19]

Analysts who ignored the warning signals and emphasized that OPEC had excess production capacity of 6 to 8 mmbd, committed the cardinal error of believing that a shortfall in one region would be made up elsewhere. Many of them failed to grasp the political motivations that affected the production decisions of the major producers, especially Saudi Arabia.

Although Saudi Arabia had restrained oil prices between 1975 and 1978 to alleviate pressure on the world economy, the United States had demonstrated little sensitivity to Saudi interests. Riyadh was dismayed by the failure of the United States and Egypt to consult Saudi Arabia before Egyptian President Anwar Sadat's visit to Jerusalem in December 1977, the refusal of the United States to transfer Saudi-financed arms to Somalia in response to the Soviet-Cuban military build-up in Ethiopia in 1977–78, the failure of the United States to oppose the Communist-backed coup in Afghanistan in April 1978, the anti-Saudi and pro-Israeli tone of the U.S. congressional debate in May 1978 on the sale of F-15 fighter planes to the kingdom, the lack of an effective U.S. response to the assassinations of the presidents of North and South Yemen in June 1978, the attendant drift of the new South Yemeni regime of Abdul Fattah Ismail into the Soviet orbit, and U.S. inaction in the unfolding 1978 crisis in Iran. These events suggested to the Arabs a fundamental erosion of American influence in the region and raised questions about whether the United States would honor its implicit security commitment to Saudi Arabia.

Because the U.S. government believed Saudi outbursts against Israeli intransigence were for intra-Arab consumption and did not reflect the more moderate stance conveyed in behind-the-scenes Saudi diplomacy, Washington ignored the burgeoning crisis in Iran, granting the shah carte blanche between 1974 and 1978. Washington would learn the improvidence of this policy in early 1979.

THE 1979 IRANIAN CRISIS: THE
GEOPOLITICAL ENVIRONMENT

The removal of 5 mmbd of Iranian oil from the international market between December 27, 1978, and March 4, 1979, generated shock waves in the industrialized world. Overnight, 3 mmbd of surplus oil production was eliminated and world oil reserves were drawn down at the rate of 2 mmbd. The fall in Iranian oil production set off panic in the spot market as large independents, small refiners, and other new market entrants rushed to buy oil, sending prices soaring. In a portent of the future, many producers abrogated existing contracts, diverting more oil into the higher priced spot market. Producers began to accumulate large financial reserves once more.

These events were of particular concern in Western Europe and Japan, which both depended so heavily on supplies of Iranian crude.[20] Countries like Sweden and Ireland that relied on imported oil products and third-party sales from the international oil companies rather than direct purchases of crude oil experienced drastic shortages as spot prices soared above official prices and the major companies curtailed the volumes of oil available to nonaffiliated customers.

The Iranian political crisis generated alarm not only in the industrialized world but also in the countries surrounding the Persian Gulf, especially Saudi Arabia. Already dismayed by the Middle East policies of the Carter administration, Riyadh now found itself challenged as the spiritual leader in the fight against Zionism. Yasir Arafat's visit to Teheran and the pro-Palestinian policies of the Khomeini regime made it impossible for Riyadh to adopt a public policy on the Egyptian-Israeli peace accord favorable to U.S. interests. To have done so would have been to risk isolation from the Arab world and the possible overthrow of the House of Saud either by elements in the Saudi royal family that opposed the pro-American policies of Prince Fahd or by militant factions of the Palestine Liberation Organization (PLO) or the dissident Popular Front for the Liberation of Palestine (PFLP).

All of the Gulf States shared Saudi Arabia's concern about the policies of the Khomeini regime. The United Arab Emirates and Iraq were particularly disturbed by the ayatollah's power over Iran's Shi'ite masses. Since they both had sizable Shi'ite minority populations, even veiled threats of a pan-Shi'ite *jihad* (holy war) chilled the ruling elites of both countries. More generally Khomeini's attack on the modernization process itself and its corruption of fundamental Islamic values generated uneasiness throughout the Middle East. Khomeini raised a basic question: Why should the Middle Eastern oil-producing nations produce more oil than they needed locally to meet the needs of the industrialized world?

While OPEC production levels fluctuated widely in 1979 in response to gyrations on the spot market, world petroleum production rose from 60.2 mmbd in 1978 to 62.4 mmbd in 1979 despite withdrawal from the market of sizable volumes of Iranian oil during much of the year. Meanwhile oil prices rose by 140 percent.

Evidently uncertainty about the availability of petroleum supplies sparked off panic buying on the spot market by small and independent refiners. Fearful that deepening shortages would put more pressure on prices, buyers moved to protect themselves, sending demand and prices climbing.

OPEC members realized they could make tremendous profits by unilaterally raising official (long-term contract) prices and diverting more oil into the higher priced spot market. These actions unleashed new upward pressure on price, bringing even some of the major oil companies into the spot market. Increased stockpiling of oil, in anticipation of further price hikes, boosted demand until finally consumers began to top off their gas tanks for fear of gasoline shortages. Woefully inadequate U.S. government allocation further exacerbated the gasoline crisis.

Intemperate remarks by the chairman of the U.S. Senate foreign relations committee and others as to the benefits of a special U.S. relationship with Riyadh, not only demonstrated a disturbing parochialism but also showed that some U.S. political leaders still viewed energy policy outside the framework of wider geopolitical consideration.

The fall of the shah of Iran profoundly affected the Saudi ruling elite. If the United States failed to support the shah, whom only a year earlier President Carter had toasted as "an island of stability" in a sea of chaos, Riyadh queried, could the United States be counted on to protect the kingdom? The dispatching of unarmed F-15s to Saudi Arabia, Secretary Harold Brown's untimely request for a U.S. military base in Saudi Arabia, and U.S. sponsorship of Egypt as a potential base to substitute for its Iranian bases left the Saudis doubtful about how well U.S. leaders understood Middle Eastern political realities. The Saudi governent could not believe that after it had raised production to help offset the Iranian shortfall (a policy opposed by a significant element of the royal family) President Carter not only failed to express his gratitude but also personally intervened in the Egyptian-Israeli peace talks without informing the Saudi's of his intentions and with no apparent concern for the isolated position in which his intervention placed them. Saudi Arabia was not the only OPEC nation to raise oil production in 1979. Output increased substantially in Iraq, Kuwait, Nigeria, Venezuela, Mexico, the North Sea, and Canada.

The Iranian crisis rendered the supply and demand projections of the International Energy Agency obsolete, and raised new fears of a world oil shortage. In 1978 the IEA had projected that OPEC oil production through the 1980s would be around 37 mmbd and that world oil supplies would meet demand until 1985. Admitting the possibility of a supply crisis in the late 1980s, the IEA had argued that there was enough time to develop alternative energy sources, especially coal and nuclear power, if key decisions were taken soon.

By late 1979 many IEA specialists were projecting that OPEC oil production through the 1980s might be closer to 30 mmbd, with the result that the time available for making structural adjustments in energy supply and demand had been telescoped in a manner that threatened the stability of the international economy. The pessimism of the IEA was borne out when 1979 OPEC production was only 30.9 mmbd. This put tremendous pressure on the United States. If the United States, as the largest energy consumer in the IEA, had failed to reduce its oil imports to the level pledged at the 1978 Bonn summit, other major oil-consuming nations had cause to wonder if there would be oil enough to meet their needs.

THE IRANIAN CRISIS: THE DOMESTIC POLICY RESPONSE

Responding to the long gas lines in California and on the East Coast that had been precipitated by curtailment of Iranian oil shipments, President Carter admonished the nation in April 1979 that the nation's energy problem was serious and getting worse. "Our national strength is dangerously dependent on a thin line of oil tankers stretching halfway around the earth to the Persian Gulf," warned Carter. "We must produce more. We must conserve more."

Carter's April 5 energy message could not have come at a worse time. On March 28, 1979, the country experienced the most serious reactor incident in its history. The events at Three Mile Island in Pennsylvania evoked doubts about the nation's policy of promoting nuclear energy and bolstered the resolve of nuclear power's critics. The report in October 1979 of the presidentially appointed Kemeny Commission called for fundamental changes in the country's system of operating and regulating nuclear power.[21]

Meanwhile Congress in October 1978 had rejected the thrust of the first National Energy Plan, approving instead a complex phased decontrol of natural gas but doing nothing about oil price decontrol for fear of alienating voters. Because of congressional inaction, six years after the first oil embargo the nation's economy was not prepared for the effects of tumultuous price increases that occurred in the remaining months of 1979. By April 1979 the landed cost of OPEC crude was between $18 and $19 per barrel. By December it would be $24-31 per barrel.

The key provisions of President Carter's April 1979 energy package[22] were the phased decontrol of oil (to induce conservation) and a windfall profits tax on oil company earnings, with proceeds going to an "energy security fund" to help low-income families pay their energy bills and to accelerate development of synthetic fuels, such as shale oil, coal liquids and gases, and alcohol from farm wastes.

Carter enunciated his April 5 energy message at a time of shifting crosscurrents in U.S. energy policy. Between April and June 1979, the inadequacies of the U.S. Department of Energy's allocation system made a minor gasoline crisis worse. In response to rising energy prices, average daily consumption of petroleum products in this country fell from 18.8 mmbd in 1978 to 18.4 mmbd in 1979. This was the first drop in consumption since 1975, when the economy was still recovering from the price hikes of 1973-74.

It was difficult to know in early 1979 to what extent high energy prices were structurally changing U.S. dependence on oil. Oil consumption fell partially because of the economic slowdown and partially because Americans were driving more fuel-efficient cars, homeowners were switching from oil to natural gas and installing insulation and storm windows, and industry was embarking on major improvements in energy efficiency.

Conservation became more attractive as energy prices continued to rise. Indeed, three major energy studies published in 1979 recommended conservation as a quick and relatively inexpensive way to reduce the nation's use of foreign oil.[23] In one, *Energy Future*, conservation was heralded as a key energy source for the rest of the century.[24]

Despite increased advocacy of conservation, there was little consensus among policy analysts about how much conservation measures would affect energy demand over a period of several years. Even in the midst of the Iranian oil supply crisis, Congress refused to mandate any drastic changes in consumer habits. Industry, which was equally skeptical about the possibilities of conservation but generally applauded the decontrol of oil prices, was puzzled about why the president had reversed his position on oil decontrol yet had not proposed measures to accelerate the development of natural gas, coal, and nuclear power. Clearly, no consensus yet existed on the difficult energy policy choices confronting the nation.

In mid-July as gasoline lines lengthened, inflation soared to 11.3 percent and Congress remained silent about energy problems, President Carter released National Energy Plan 2 and the Solar Bank initiative. Under NEP 2, projected 1990 oil imports of 13–17 mmbd were to be slashed to 4.5–8.5 mmbd through accelerated residential and commercial conservation, crash development of synthetic fuels, greater use of heavy oil, development of unconventional gas, conversion to coal, enhanced automobile efficiency, and development of mass transit. Synthetic fuel development was to be directed by a new Energy Security Corporation, financed by the windfall profits tax, and empowered by an Energy Mobilization Board to expedite issuing of permits for and construction of critical energy facilities. Stating that the United States "will never use more oil than it did in 1977," President Carter imposed an 8.2 mmbd oil import ceiling.[25]

In shifting his emphasis from energy conservation toward development of new energy supplies, President Carter encountered serious problems, problems that continue to block implementation of an effective national energy program under the Reagan administration.[26] Before we can develop reasonable energy policy, we must reconcile conflicting environmental, economic and energy policies, as well as the competing claims of consumers, business, government, and various regional interests. Moreover we have to define the proper roles of government and industry in the formation of domestic and international policy.[27]

Little had been done to resolve our national energy problems when President Reagan assumed office in January 1981. Oil prices were being decontrolled in phases, and oil import levels had fallen, but in 1980 the United States had still imported 37 percent of its oil and 5 percent of its natural gas, at the staggering cost of about $100 billion a year. OPEC prices for oil had escalated to between $34 and $41 per barrel.

Since November 1974 and Project Independence, the United States had pursued an import reduction strategy based on coal use, but in 1981 no market existed for almost 100 million tons of the coal produced. There had been no new orders for nuclear power plants since 1974. Seven years after the embargo a Roper poll concluded that more than half of the American people believed no energy crisis had ever existed and that the OAPEC oil embargo had been manufactured by the oil companies.[28]

INTERNATIONAL RESPONSE TO THE IRANIAN CRISIS

In 1974 the major industrial countries had established the International Energy Agency as an independent "oil consumer cartel" within the Organization for Economic Cooperation and Development (OECD). (The IEA is discussed more fully in Chapter 5.) Responding to Iran's curtailment of oil shipments, the members of the IEA agreed in March 1979 to institute voluntary measures to cut oil consumption by 5 percent, or 2 mmbd. The United States pledged savings of 1 mmbd, but the failure of Congress to enact the president's April energy package by May raised doubts about the seriousness of U.S. policy, although U.S. conversions from oil to natural gas had eliminated 400,000 bd of oil dependency since 1978.

In May 1979 the oil market was thrown into further turmoil when Nigeria, which supplied 1.1 mmbd to the United States, threatened to block exports if the United States did not adopt forceful policies against South Africa's apartheid system. The threat passed, but the fact that it occurred in conjunction with continued uncertainty about future levels of Saudi production sent spot prices soaring.[29]

Despite a stressed market, the United States sparked recriminations from Western Europe and Japan when it asked American refiners in May to enter the spot market to build up distillate stocks above 1978 levels. This unilateral action, which escalated official and spot market prices about $5 a barrel,[30] was difficult to reconcile with the U.S. pledge to cut oil demand by 1 mmbd and raised the specter of dangerous competition for oil among the major industrialized countries. It was against this backdrop that the Tokyo economic summit convened on June 28, 1979.

Two issues dominated summit deliberations: the role governments should play in regulating spot market prices and the establishment of firm oil import targets for the IEA countries. There was no agreement on the first issue. France favored controlling the spot market in Rotterdam, whereas Germany and the United Kingdom supported a free market. As for setting oil import targets, France assailed the United States for not even beginning to conserve oil. In June 1979 U.S. imports were 26.6 percent above pre-1973 Arab oil embargo levels and Japan's had risen 1 percent. In contrast, the European Economic Community (EEC) had cut oil imports by 5 percent. However, U.S. imports in 1978 were 6.9 percent below 1977 levels and had dropped another 2.5 percent during the first half of 1979. Energy consumption per unit of GNP had declined each year after 1973.[31]

Participants in the Tokyo summit agreed to cut oil consumption and imports but could not agree on how best to do it. Washington and Tokyo advocated strict targets for import cuts in 1979 and 1980; the Europeans wanted a freeze on import levels until 1985. The United States, Canada, and Japan objected to the European proposal that EEC oil imports be frozen collectively, the imports of the non-European participants individually. The United States felt that 1978 was not a good base period as U.S. imports had fallen that year because of new Alaskan oil, not because of structural changes in the U.S. market. Japan opposed a freeze on imports because it would stifle Japanese economic growth. The non-European states were angered by Europe's insistence that the rapid development of North Sea oil should not reduce Europe's share of oil imports.

Finally the participants at the Tokyo summit reached no consensus on whether to reactivate the producer-consumer dialogue initially launched by the Conference on International Economic Cooperation. Some of the European countries categorically refused to engage in any dialogue that did not address all of the world's economic problems, especially those of the developing nations.

Meanwhile, spot prices for Arabian light hit $41 a barrel during June and some U.S. refiners paid $49 a barrel for high-quality Nigerian crude. Then spot prices fell back to $32–35 a barrel, with

Arabian light oil selling officially for $15.67. By the end of the month, however, there was little reason to doubt that prices would rise further.

Throughout the summer of 1979 the international energy market was buffeted by forces that each generated new fears of cataclysmic price rises and petroleum shortages. After the sabotage in July of a crucial 600,000 bd Nigerian export terminal, Lagos decided to reduce oil production 10 percent, thereby partially offsetting the effect of a Saudi decision on July 1 to increase oil production by 1 mmbd. Iran's decision in August to terminate its triangular gas export deal with the USSR and Europe intensified concern in Western Europe about the security of energy supplies from the Persian Gulf. Coming at the time of Algeria's reevaluation of its natural gas export policy, the Iranian decision sparked further price rises on the spot market. As many companies rushed to the spot market to rebuild stocks, uncertainty over the future level of Iranian oil production made the oil market even more volatile.

By mid-August Congress's failure to enact President Carter's July crash program for U.S. energy development before the summer recess and the loss by British Petroleum of 9 percent of its total crude oil supply following Nigerian nationalization threatened to plunge the world oil markets into chaos.

The surge in OPEC prices during 1979 generated fears in international financial circles that OPEC's balance-of-payments surplus might rise to $75 billion in 1979, a staggering increase over its $1 billion surplus in 1978. At the same time, the OECD, which because of falling real oil prices had had a surplus of $6.5 billion in 1978, was projecting a $40 billion deficit by the end of 1979. The plight of the Third World nations (discussed more fully in Chapter 7) raised fears about the stability of the international financial system. The current-account deficit of the developing nations, $40 billion in 1978, was expected to reach $50 to $55 billion by August 1979, an incremental increase that effectively offset all economic development assistance and eroded the positive benefits of a decade of development.

Many analysts recognized the danger in constantly rising oil prices, but few as clearly as James Schlesinger. In his farewell address as energy secretary, Schlesinger stated that the vortex of the crisis between the superpowers was no longer on the central European front but in the Persian Gulf and that NATO could not protect Western security because it could not protect the "energy resources on which our collective survival depends."[32] Warning that "the energy future is bleak and is likely to grow bleaker in the decade ahead," Schlesinger expressed incredulity that the American populace doubted the reality of the energy crisis and accepted the fantasy that their country had enormous proven reserves of oil hidden and unreported. "Without greater utilization of coal and nuclear power over the next decade," said the secretary, "this society may just not make it."

By Fall 1979, despite falling spot market prices, there was little reason for the major industrialized countries to be optimistic concerning their energy situation. Debate continued in the IEA and the EEC over how to implement the decisions taken at the Tokyo summit. The problem was especially vexing in Europe, since the EEC's own forecasts demonstrated that, while imported oil's percentage share of gross energy consumption would decline during the 1980s, all of the EEC countries like Denmark and the United Kingdom would become more dependent on imported oil, in terms of absolute volume.[33]

By September the fall in oil prices had made enactment of President Carter's energy program seem less urgent. It became apparent that instead of the 30–40 synthetic fuel plants the Carter administration wanted to "fast track" under the proposed Energy Mobilization Board (EMB) there would be only 6–8 prototypes. As a result, the administration reduced its July 1979 estimates of how much energy synfuel plants could produce by 1990 from 2.5 mmbd to 1.75 mmbd. By compromising on the scale of the synfuels program and reduced legislative powers for the EMB, Carter got congressional passage of a "windfall profits" tax on decontrolled domestic crude oil, the proceeds of which were to provide investment risk guarantees for companies developing synfuels.

With only a small drop in U.S. oil imports and an increase in Japanese oil imports projected for 1979, the industrialized nations remained acutely vulnerable to another oil shock. A report issued by the Central Intelligence Agency in September 1979 predicted that OPEC sustainable producing capacity would be 35 mmbd in 1985, not the 43–47 mmbd the CIA had projected in 1977.[34] Even more disturbing, the CIA concluded that the oil-consuming nations would be increasingly vulnerable to "unpredicted" oil supply interruptions during the 1980s. According to the agency, an OPEC decision to use oil as a political weapon, political instability in the oil-producing countries, a severe winter, or a national coal strike could be enough to create another major oil crisis.

The report went on to say that while the world is not running out of oil, if consumption continued to greatly exceed new discoveries, output would fall within a decade and the major industrialized countries would not necessarily have first claim on or continue to receive their current market share of OPEC exports. In the CIA's view both Communist bloc and Third World nations would increasingly become claimants for Middle Eastern oil.[35] Shortly after the CIA report came out, an explosion and fire at the giant Ras Tanura facility in Saudi Arabia demonstrated the susceptibility of energy supplies to unanticipated events.

Though little noted at the time, the same month the CIA issued its report Ali M. Jaidah made an important speech at the Oxford Energy Seminar on how the events of 1979 had transformed the world oil market.[36] Because there was less flexibility about output, said the former secretary-general of OPEC, short-term crises were now almost "unavoidable," and any future supply squeeze would be worse than ever, because excess capacity previously available for emergencies would no longer be available. Postulating that for political, technical, and economic reasons the OPEC countries were no longer able or willing to act as a buffer between world supply and demand, Ali Jaidah made the chilling observation that economic adjustments to tight energy supply had been accomplished largely through economic stagnation rather than by structural and technological changes in energy use patterns. "This may imply that every attempt at economic recovery, every upswing of the business cycle, would inevitably produce an imbalance between growing demand and constrained supply." According to Jaidah, the world's most pressing problem was how to prevent short-term supply crises from becoming major catastrophes. He warned of the threat to oil supplies posed by mounting sociopolitical tensions in producer countries, intraregional political disputes, and tensions between superpower blocks.

Neither the oil-consuming nor the oil-producing nations seemed eager to stabilize the oil market during the last months of 1979. Despite Saudi Petroleum Minister Ahmed Yamani's warning that "we are losing control of everything," the OPEC price ceiling of $23.50 a barrel dissolved in October, setting off a two-tier system that seriously alarmed the international petroleum market. The official price remained $23.50 a barrel, but surcharges and other levies sent spot prices up to $45 a barrel. Existing contracts were abrogated at will, as were new contracts as soon as they were signed.

One reason for the surge in spot prices was the declining power of the international oil companies to control global oil supply and demand (a subject discussed further in Chapter 6). As crude oil surplus companies such as British Petroleum and other traditional sellers exercised *force majeure*, those crude oil refiners and other firms that usually relied on third-party sales had to enter the market to survive. When companies, especially end-use refiners with no crude oil supplies of their own, approached the OPEC oil producers for supplies, they were told that no oil was available for the foreseeable future. Countries that did have oil to sell added surcharges of $8–10 per barrel on 1980 official contract sales.

The industrialized world did not react realistically to the volatile oil market and the deteriorating situation in the Middle East. In December 1979 the International Energy Agency projected a shortfall in 1980 of 900 mmbd, rising to 6 mmbd by 1990 if current trends continued.[37] To meet the challenge, the United States proposed four measures: individual country oil import quotas, close monitoring of oil imports (especially products), sanctions against countries exceeding their quotas, and a reduction of 1 mmbd in the previously set quota for 1980.[38] Despite U.S. support for a binding agreement to cut 1985 oil imports to 24 mmbd, members of the IEA reached no consensus. Because of EEC support, they did agree to binding country import ceilings for 1980 of 24 mmbd after subtracting 310 mmbd of Norwegian oil exports, but including 1.4 mmbd of bunkers (oil used by oil tankers). More important, the IEA established in principle a new oil-sharing mechanism for mini-shortfalls.[39]

The IEA's decisions in December 1979 were remarkably tame considering the threat posed by a 6-mmbd shortfall in 1990. Clearly supply and demand would always balance at some price, but the IEA's complacent attitude toward the energy crisis suggested to some observers that the industrialized nations would accept economic recession, lower rates of economic growth, and higher levels of unemployment, rather than enact bold legislation that emphasized increased production, more efficient use of energy, and effective emergency standby programs—all measures that would require difficult political trade-offs on the questions of inflation, employment, and the environment.

While the IEA negotiated the United States ended two years of acrimonious debate with Mexico by agreeing to adjust the base price of Mexican gas by the same percentage as world oil prices changed. Despite the final consummation of an agreement, the net effect of these negotiations was to embitter U.S.-Mexican relations, reduce the amount of gas Mexico originally offered from 2 billion cubic feet per day to 200 million cubic feet per day and to commence the process of granting oil and natural gas energy price equivalency on a Btu basis. Clearly the protracted negotiations with Mexico did nothing to enhance the security of U.S. energy supplies.

By early 1980 the financial community was growing apprehensive about the adequacy of existing internal mechanisms to recycle petrodollars, particularly for the Third World nations. OPEC financial surpluses were now projected to reach $120 billion (up $45 billion from forecasts issued only six months earlier). The 1980 current-account deficit of the OECD nations was expected to reach $95 billion, while that of the developing countries was climbing toward $70 billion. Experts feared that the cumulative foreign debt of the Third World might reach $440 billion, up from $150 billion in 1975.[40] Ten developing countries were paying 40 percent of their total export earnings simply to finance the existing debt on their oil-import bills.[41]

Most alarming in early 1980 was the fact that the global economic situation had been transformed. Whereas between 1974 and 1978 massive economic development programs and military purchases by the OPEC countries had recycled petrodollar wealth, by 1980 the fall of the shah of Iran and the outbreak of demonstrations in several oil-producing states made them begin to worry about the side effects of large infusions of petrodollar wealth: high inflation, unsound urbanization, the waste of financial resources accruing from lack of effective planning, the fall of traditional agricultural and industrial production, and the accelerating maldistribution of income between societal groups. Leaders of oil-producing nations wondered whether these side effects might not pose such serious threats to political stability that their economic development programs and hence oil production should be drastically cut back. As a result of these fears the OPEC nations announced production curtailment of 2.8 mmbd in 1980.

As 1979 waned the international petroleum market was further buffeted by the Soviet invasion of Afghanistan. (The foreign policy implications of the intervention are discussed in Chapter 9.) The Soviet action transformed the geopolitics of the Persian Gulf. Coming in tandem with the November seizure of the American hostages in Iran the attempted takeover of the Grand Mosque in Mecca, the assault on the Mohammed tomb in Medina, riots among the Shi'ite workers in the Aramco oil fields of Saudi Arabia, Israeli intransigence on the West Bank settlements issue, and the deterioration of Iran-Iraq political relations, these events threatened to set the Middle East ablaze.

In this disturbed political climate, a surge in official OPEC oil prices in January and February 1980 threatened the stability of the international oil market. Despite Saudi efforts to restore market equilibrium, the chasm between Saudi prices and prices elsewhere widened to the point that Gulf prices were $7 a barrel and North African prices $10 a barrel higher than Saudi prices.[42] As prices escalated demand declined. Several countries slashed production to alleviate the resulting oil glut. According to a February 1980 issue of *Petroleum Intelligence Weekly*, OPEC could curtail production to 40 percent of its 1978 output and still earn revenues equal to those achieved in 1978.[43]

By early March 1980 expectations that the glut of petroleum would increase rather than diminish had removed any sense of urgency about implementing forceful policy initiatives. Despite U.S. pressure the other members of the IEA opposed convening in March to lower 1980 oil-import ceilings still further. However, they did agree to meet in May to consider establishing 1981 limits, and on April 1 they enacted a decision made at the earlier Tokyo summit to register refined-product imports. This would provide the IEA secretariat with better information about patterns of product trade.

In defense of the IEA countries that resisted taking action we should note that most OECD countries had adequate to large oil stocks by March 1980, oil demand in the non-Communist bloc countries was expected to decline from 52.8 to 51.4 mmbd because of high prices, and non-OPEC (Mexican, North Sea) oil supplies were expected to increase about 1 mmbd. The IEA assumed that demand for OPEC oil outside the Communist bloc would hover at 29 mmbd, down from 31 mmbd in 1979. Then, OPEC announced production cuts of 2.8 mmbd to be implemented in 1980.[44]

The optimistic forecasts that began to emanate from leading financial institutions and international oil companies revealed that little had been learned from the events of 1979. If nothing else, those events had taught that the world could no longer count on OPEC automatically increasing oil production to meet its energy needs. This is true in both a technical and a political sense. In the wake of the fall of the shah and rising concern over the dangers of too rapid modernization, the OPEC nations began to develop their own internal agenda that increasingly governed the rate at which they made oil available to the rest of the world. No longer would OPEC automatically set its oil production rates at a level sufficient to meet the industrialized world's marginal demand for oil. Most observers failed to recognize either the implications of the fact that OPEC could no longer be counted upon to meet incremental energy demand or the impact that high energy prices would have on elasticity of energy demand. The structural shifts in demand that were occurring were pronounced. OPEC oil production, 29.5 mmbd in January 1980, had fallen to 27.8 mmbd by April. In January 1979 at the height of the Iranian crisis, OPEC had produced 28.4 mmbd. Even such industry giants as Exxon were slow to recognize the market changes. In its March 1980 *U.S. Energy Outlook*, Exxon forecast the U.S. oil imports would continue to rise, from 8.2 mmbd in 1978 (44 percent of total supply) to 9.3 mmbd in 1990 (57 percent of supply). Exxon's major assumption was that oil imports would have to rise to fill the gap between declining domestic production of conventional oil and the production starting in 1990 of from 700,000 bd to 1 million bd of synthetic fuel. Exxon warned that U.S. production of conventional crude oil and natural gas liquids could drop from 9.9 mmbd in 1979 to 6 mmbd in 1990, and that if synfuel production were held up, oil imports might rise dramatically. Exxon also projected that U.S. natural gas imports would double by the turn of the century.[45] By December 1980 Exxon had revised its estimates. It predicted domestic conventional crude oil and natural gas liquids production of 7-8 mmbd in the 1985–2000 period; oil imports, it predicted, would peak at 8.5 mmbd, barring delays in synfuel development.[46]

The IEA was equally shortsighted. In trying to determine to what extent governments should intervene in the spot market to curtail excessive stockpiling in times of crisis, the IEA secretariat decided in Spring 1980 that what had caused the surge in crude oil prices during the 1979 supply crisis was not a shortage of oil but panic buying and a woefully inept allocation system in the United States. In fact, the situation was more complex; the chief problem was the major oil companies' loss of control over the international supply system.

As prices climbed the large international oil companies witnessed the further erosion of their guaranteed access to crude oil supplies. In 1969 the seven major oil companies—the so-called Seven Sisters (British Petroleum, Gulf, Royal Dutch-Shell, Exxon, Mobil, Standard Oil

Co. of California, and Texaco)—had had a near monopoly on world oil trade. By 1979 the seven companies extracted only 45 percent of OPEC crude, or about one-half what they had extracted in the late 1960s. With less crude oil at their disposal, the "majors" curtailed third-party sales to protect their affiliates, thus placing independent refiners who had depended on them in a desperate financial position. As control by the majors declined and the number of state-to-state deals and destination restrictions increased, it was uncertain whether the IEA's industry advisory board would be able to allocate crude oil supplies if a severe supply emergency occurred or whether the IEA oil-sharing mechanism would work if activated. The seriousness of the situation was demonstrated by the fact that over 42 percent of the oil sold in international trade by late February 1980 was sold direct. In one year direct sales had increased by over 3 mmbd.

As late as April 1980 the Seven Sisters still had to purchase about 1.5 mmbd, or 7 percent of their total energy needs, on the spot market. Of course, some companies were more dependent on spot purchases than others. Two of Aramco's partners, Standard Oil of California and Texaco, purchased almost no crude oil on the spot market, but Exxon, which was about 7 percent dependent on spot purchases, bought 330 mmbd on the open market, and Mobil, which was about 1 percent dependent, bought 30 mmbd. The levels of dependency for Gulf, Royal Dutch Shell, and British Petroleum were 12 percent (175 mmbd), 9 percent (500 mmbd), and 19 percent (600 mmbd), respectively.[47] The companies most dependent on spot sales had to pay premium prices even though demand was falling or risk losing their crude supplies. As demand fell, however, product prices plummeted, so the companies could not recover their crude costs in the marketplace.

Not only did the costs of crude oil vary, but the allocation system in the United States also affected various companies differently. As a result, some firms were able to sell gasoline at lower prices than others. The reasons for this were easy to understand if you knew how the market worked, but they were never explained to the gasoline consumer. As a result, the public came to see the oil companies as exploiting them. Press reports focusing on huge inventory profits rather than the oil industry's rate of return on capital invested further distorted the public's perception. As long as people believed the energy crisis was contrived to increase company profits, there was no political constituency powerful enough to push through a vigorous domestic energy program.

Despite the OPEC oil ministers' announcement that OPEC production capacity would not exceed 35 mmbd in 1985,[48] and the CIA's prediction that OPEC oil production would decline during the 1980s and that the Communist bloc would need 1 mmbd of OPEC oil by 1985,[49] the IEA members continued to wrangle about firm ceilings on oil imports.

At the May 1980 IEA meeting, the United States asked the group to establish an automatic method of setting short-term per-country ceilings on oil imports, and to set import ceilings for 1990. Bonn, most of the other European members, and Japan argued that current petroleum supplies were not tight enough to mandate adoption of the U.S. proposals. Japan noted that before the meeting it had agreed to hold its oil imports to 6.3 mbd, a level below that agreed to at Tokyo (6.3–6.9 mmbd in 1985). The United States pointed out that this was almost 1 mmbd above projected imports for 1980.

The fact that a federal court struck down the Carter administration's oil import fee on the eve of the meeting, thus eliminating the tax of 10 cents per gallon on gasoline, did little to convince the other IEA members that they should pursue more aggressive energy conservation policies. Nor was this U.S. "signal" lost on OPEC. Before OPEC's ministerial conference adjourned, its long term pricing committee predicted that oil would cost "at least" $60 per barrel in real dollars by 1985–87.[50] To OPEC this implied that oil was still underpriced in the international market.

West Germany was somewhat justified in thinking that no immediate crisis loomed. In mid-May Saudi Arabia announced that it would maintain crude oil production at 9.5 mmbd through 1980. One week later Riyadh raised its prices for crude oil from $26 to $28 per barrel, but most analysts focused on Saudi supplies rather than prices. Although the Saudi action set off a new sequence of price leapfrogging, which added $20 billion a year to the oil-import bill of the consuming nations, the industrialized world remained paralyzed by inaction.

By the time of the Venice economic summit on June 22, 1980, German, British, French, Canadian, Japanese, and American leaders were ready to focus their deliberations on energy. Many countries had been forced to draw on their reserve inventories because of high energy prices and radical changes in the commercial terms of access to oil, especially the politically restrictive contract the Saudi National Oil Company (Petromin) had asked Denmark to sign.

The summit participants paid special attention to the effect high energy prices were having on the economies of the less-developed nations and urged the World Bank and the oil-exporting and industrial countries to give high priority to spurring the exploration, development, and production of both conventional and renewable energy sources.

The summit leaders were not specific about how to meet the main energy goals they had delineated for their countries: reducing oil's share in total energy use from 53 to 40 percent and developing nonoil energy supplies equivalent to 15–20 mmbd by 1990. To meet these goals the summit leaders proposed a "large" increase in coal use and "enhanced" use of nuclear power in the medium term, and, in the longer term, synthetic fuels, solar, and other forms of renewable energy.

To the distress of many observers, the summit leaders acknowledged the need to rely on nonoil fuels for future economic growth but did not discuss how to overcome legal, institutional, environmental, political, social, and economic obstacles to their development. The failure of the Venice summit to implement concrete actions, together with the scaling-down of President Carter's synthetic fuels program, sparked new OPEC price rises in July. The OECD projected that for the first half of 1980 inflation would be 12 percent, that OECD's current-account deficit would increase $100 billion a year, and that OECD unemployment would average 7 percent.[51]

By mid-summer of 1980, the United States had some reason to feel more optimistic. In July, the Canadian government gave its long-awaited approval for prebuilding the southern sections of the $30–40 billion Alaskan gas pipeline, therefore increasing the prospects for a near-term increase in Canadian natural gas exports to the United States and, later, for making available natural gas from the North Slope of Alaska, which represented 10 percent of U.S. natural gas reserves. In addition some international oil companies had resumed signing third-party crude oil contracts because spot prices had fallen to near official levels. Furthermore the synthetic fuels program enacted on June 30, 1980, although considerably less ambitious than what President Carter had proposed, signaled that the United States had begun to move, however slowly, toward reducing its dependence on imported oil. In June 1980 OPEC output was lower than it had been in four and one-half years (and nearly 3.9 mmbd below the June 1979 level) because of declining demand.

By September 1980 increases in non-OPEC (North Sea and Mexican) oil production, rising oil inventories, and the U.S. decision to resume filling the strategic petroleum reserve gave the industrialized world not only short-term relief from rising OPEC prices but also the false impression that they were insulated from further oil shocks well into 1981.[52]

The surge in oil inventories made the major industrialized countries dangerously complacent. With OPEC oil production at 27.1 mmbd in August 1980, oil supply and consumption were roughly in balance. Reserve stocks afforded some protection against production curtailments, but if these stocks were drawn down OPEC could simply hike prices dramatically whenever the oil companies had to reenter the market to rebuild their inventories.

The 400 million barrels of commercial inventory that existed as a cushion in October 1980 was nearly equivalent to the surplus oil Saudi Arabia had placed on the market after it had raised its production level in mid-1979 from 8.5 to 9.5 mmbd. Although Washington never acknowledged it, surplus Saudi production was the key factor in the fall in spot market prices in 1980. There was little reason to hope, however, that supplies would expand to meet world demand in the 1980s. Prospects were great that OPEC oil production might be curtailed, that the Soviet Union or Eastern Europe might require 1 mmbd of OPEC's oil production by 1985 and between 2 and 3 mmbd[53] by 1990, that rising Third World demand might offset new non-OPEC sources of oil production and that OECD demand might continue to grow albeit at slower rates.

In 1980 world oil reserve/production ratios continued to decline. It is not well understood that simply to maintain existing global oil reserve/production ratios, it is necessary to discover new oil reserves the size of those in Kuwait or Iran every three years or those in the North Slope or North Sea every six months. Such reserves have been found in only one year out of the past thirty.

Rapidly increasing domestic consumption in the OPEC nations will also affect the amount of oil OPEC makes available on the world market during the 1980s. In September 1980 the OPEC secretariat projected that the group's internal oil product requirements would rise from 2.4 mmbd in 1980 to 3.9 mmbd by 1985 and 6.3 mmbd by 1990.[54]

The implications of these projections are staggering. If OPEC oil production stabilizes at about 27 mmbd, the volume available for export will at best be about 23.1 mmbd in 1985 and 20.7 mmbd in 1990.

If the Communist bloc gains access to at least 1 mmbd of OPEC oil by 1985 and 2 to 3 mmbd by 1990, it is apparent that even with no growth in current levels of OECD energy consumption, the amount of OPEC oil available to the free world might be around 22.1 mmbd in 1985 and 17.7–18.7 mmbd in 1990. This is assuming that OPEC production will not decline below an average 27 mmbd a year by 1985. But there is good reason to believe that OPEC production will decline.

Clearly, if oil demand rises even minimally, and no sizable non-OPEC oil discoveries are made and brought into production quickly, some combination of dramatic price rises, continued economic recession, increased unemployment, and social unrest can be anticipated.

However, if oil demand accelerates in the industrialized or the Third World nations because of a failure to develop alternative energy sources or to find sizable new reserves of oil and gas, the effects may be catastrophic even if the major oil-producing nations experience no major political disruption. To avoid catastrophe, it is urgent that the United States lead a crash effort to encourage diversified energy production all over the world, help make energy use far more efficient, and foster greater international cooperation by helping the oil industry share its technological know-how with nations that could develop their own energy potential. Active energy development should be a cornerstone of the U.S. development assistance program and should receive high-priority attention from the Reagan administration.

Concern over the adequacy of world petroleum supplies was highlighted in an important but little-noted speech by Nordine Ait-Laoussine, a former executive vice president of Sonatrach, the Algerian National Oil Company, at the Second Oxford Energy Seminar on September 3, 1980. Warning that it is dangerous to assume that OPEC will automatically produce enough oil to meet world energy needs, Ait-Laoussine pointed out the inherent conflict between the oil-exporting countries' own long-term interest and their responsibility to help preserve the world economic system. If they continue producing at current rates, the OPEC nations will enter the twenty-first century with "less than one generation's oil reserves left," he stated, and they will have to rely on more expensive energy sources to meet their own rising domestic energy needs. He warned moreover that the huge surplus of funds produced by international sales of oil not only threatens the social fabric of the Arab world but fails also to satisfy their economic self-interest, since interest accrued from investments abroad consistently fails to keep pace with world levels of inflation.[55]

If OPEC were to produce only enough oil for its own domestic needs and financial requirements, production could drop to 15.7 mmbd in 1980 and 18.3 mmbd in 1981, Ait-Laoussine observed. He concluded that if OPEC is to continue being the world's marginal supply source, it is essential that the oil-consuming world recognize OPEC's sacrifice and do the following: support continued oil price increases in real terms; provide technological and financial help to increase the size of OPEC's resource base through exploration, enhanced recovery, and the development of gas reserves; help develop markets for OPEC goods and services; provide greater assistance to the Third World; and support the political aspirations of the oil-exporting countries.

Francisco Parra, former secretary general of OPEC, also addressed the Oxford seminar, arguing that the changing terms of commercial access to oil had transformed the international petroleum market to a degree not yet understood. Parra stated that governments would increasingly allocate oil and that the disposition of crude oil supplies would be "highly charged politically."[56] He expressed concern about the difficulties a de facto allocation system might create in times of oil shortages and the increasing rigidity of contract terms for international oil sales. He was particularly concerned that (1) prices in contracts now change without notice, (2) phase-out provisions (if a price is too high for the buyer) are now irreversible once invoked, (3) the rate at which oil can be produced is either increasingly restrictive or is determined solely by the producing government and not by the company, (4) the destination of oil shipments is almost totally controlled by oil-exporting governments, and (5) whereas in the past only a few international oil companies were in the market, seventy-seven companies had entered the spot market during the Iranian crisis, thus bidding up the price of oil.[57]

No observer of the oil scene in 1980 could fail to realize that access to energy would be increasingly determined by a host of nonmarket factors. The declining power of the international oil companies to allocate supplies, OPEC's growing assertiveness, the lack of effective contingency planning in the major oil-consuming countries, and growing alarm about the stability of the international financial system, made the world ill-prepared to meet the next "supply crisis," which was not long in coming.

THE IRAN-IRAQ WAR

In mid-September 1980, Saudi Arabia raised the price of its crude oil from $30 to $32 a barrel, and for the first time Riyadh announced that its price increase was retroactive to August. This effectively raised the oil bill of the oil-consuming world by $900 million retroactively and $7 billion annually. At the same time, the OPEC oil ministers agreed in Vienna that in the fourth quarter of 1980 they would try to implement a 10 percent production cut (about 2.5 mmbd) to counteract the existing oil glut of about 3 mmbd and announced that they would discuss energy with the industrialized world only in the framework of a global meeting on north-south economic problems, similar to the 1975-1977 negotiations of the Conference on International Economic Cooperation.

Against this backdrop, war between Iran and Iraq erupted on September 21, 1980, removing about 4 mmbd or 10 percent of non-Communist crude oil production from the international market. The breakdown of Iranian and Iraqi oil exports that were curtailed was as shown in Table 1-1.

Table 1-1.   Pre-War Oil Exports from Iran and Iraq, Barrels per Day.

	Iran	*Iraq*	*Total*
Tanker			
Crude	700	2,100	2,800
Products	200		200
	900	2,100	3,000
Pipeline			
Crude		1,000	1,000
Total	900	3,100	4,000

Iraqi Pipeline Exports and Capacity

Destination	Capacity	Exports
Turkey	700	650
Syria	800	350
Lebanon	500	0
	2,000	1,000

Source: *World Oil Supplies and the Iranian-Iraqi War: A Forecast to Mid 1981,* Petroleum Industry Research Foundation, New York, December 4, 1980.

From the table it is apparent that, whereas Iran is totally dependent on the Persian Gulf to export its crude, Iraq has alternative outlets for one-third its crude. The Turkish pipeline was built largely to reduce Iraqi export vulnerability on the Straits of Hormuz. Although the pipeline was put out of operation for a brief period early in the war, the availability of Iraqi pipeline crude softened the price impact of the loss of Iranian and Iraqi crude on the international market.

Despite the withdrawal of 4 mmbd of oil from the world market, the net loss was much less since Saudi Arabia increased its production by 900 mbd to 10.4 mmbd and the other members of OPEC collectively raised their production another 1 mmbd, nevertheless the uncertainty generated by the war sent spot prices as high as $36-$43/barrel.

Concern about the war centers on two questions: Will the hostilities spread to other Gulf nations? Will the vital Straits of Hormuz remain open? The possibility that fighting might close the straits generated fear that 17.5 mmbd of OPEC export supply might be withdrawn from the international market. A catastrophe of that magnitude would eliminate the world inventory "surplus" (the amount of oil available above normal seasonal requirements) within a month and would absorb all available stocks within three months. According to the *Petroleum Intelligence Weekly*, total closure of the straits, by creating a world shortage roughly equivalent to 35-40 percent of present non-Communist world oil demand, would precipitate a crisis of staggering proportions.[58]

Although spot prices rose, the war precipitated no immediate serious oil shortages as a result of the war except for countries that had state-to-state crude oil contracts with Iran and Iraq.[59] Brazil and India, for example, initially lost 40-50 percent of their crude oil supplies as a result of the war. The situation was not so critical for other importers because the world market for crude was very different in Fall 1980 than it had been at the height of the Iranian crisis in 1979. In late 1978 world crude oil inventories had been extremely low, but by Fall 1980 they were at an all-time high. At the height of the OPEC price increases in October 1979 almost 15 percent of all crude oil was being traded on the spot market at premiums of $5 per barrel; on the eve of the war between Iran and Iraq, only about 5 percent of world oil was being traded on the spot market, at premiums of only about 50 cents per barrel.[60]

To offset the shortfall created by the war the other OPEC nations raised production enough to give the rest of the world some breathing room. This, combined with the drawdown of an estimated 400-500 million barrels of surplus stocks, extended from 4 to 7 months the amount of time that Iranian and Iraqi oil production could remain totally closed down without generating major oil shortages.

The shortfall occasioned by the war had no serious repercussions, but there is no reason for complacency. The Iran-Iraq war added a new variable to the world oil supply equation. The consensus among Middle Eastern experts for many years has been that in the event of regional conflict, protagonists in the struggle would refrain from attacking each other's energy facilities. The oil-producing countries all seemed to realize that once conflict escalated to the level of attacks on major oil facilities, the damage done could endanger the region's economy for years to come. Moreover it was feared that escalation of such a conflict could endanger all of the oil-producing fields in the Middle East.

In a short time the Iran-Iraq war had proven this conventional wisdom wrong. For the first time, two Middle Eastern states were bombing and strafing each other's refineries, terminals, pipelines, and oil-producing facilities. Although Iraq appeared to exercise some restraint in its attacks on Iran, the security of the oil fields in the Persian Gulf is for the first time uncertain and it is not clear if they can be made more secure.

The new strategic dimension added to the geopolitics of energy by the destruction of oil facilities in both Iran and Iraq, combined with widespread disagreement among oil experts over how fast oil exports will resume from these nations once the hostilities cease, and whether other oil producers (especially Saudi Arabia and Kuwait), will lower their production levels once large volumes of Iranian and Iraqi oil exports resume, makes the future availability of Middle Eastern oil supplies extremely uncertain for the next several years.

Most energy forecasters optimistically anticipate no major shortfalls in global supplies in the near future. However, we on staff of the Energy and National Security Project of the Center for Strategic and International Studies believe there is a very strong possibility of new "oil shocks" arising from political disturbances in one or more of the major oil-producing nations between now and 1985.

Any appraisal of the oil supply situation in the coming decade must take into account the following questions:

• What are the dangers of a prolonged conflict between Iran and Iraq escalating to include other countries, especially Kuwait and the United Arab Emirates?

- If Iran loses the war, might it strike in desperation at other Persian Gulf oil facilities to teach the West a lesson?
- How soon will the hostilities between the two countries cease, and how long will it be before these countries resume large-scale oil exports?
- With OPEC oil production at the very low levels of 23 to 24 mmbd, how will OPEC make room for sizable volumes of Iranian and Iraqi crude oil exports without creating a new oil glut, thus forcing prices downward? Will Saudi Arabia and Kuwait drastically cut oil production to firm up oil prices once Iranian and Iraqi oil exports accelerate? To what degree will Saudi production decisions be affected by U.S. policy toward the Middle East, especially regarding the Airborne Warning and Control System (AWACS) sale, and the Arab-Israeli conflict?
- What will the impact on global petroleum supplies and prices be if, after the Iran-Iraq war ceases, it becomes apparent that extensive damage to the countries' oil installations presages a prolonged period of reduced exports from these two nations?

In the chapters that follow various energy emergency mechanisms are discussed that could provide the United States with some insulation from oil shocks emanating from abroad. Above all, however, American policymakers must understand not only the realities of domestic politics but also how changes in the structure and logistics of the domestic and international petroleum market and the increased politicization of oil will affect the energy future of this nation and the world. Policymakers must learn to react not to the short-term news of a drop in oil prices or an oil glut but to the long-term reality of energy politics.

NOTES

1. For background see Melvin A. Conant, *Access to Energy 2000 and After* (Lexington: University of Kentucky Press, 1979); John M. Blair, *The Control of Oil* (New York: The Vintage Press, 1978); Neil H. Jacoby, *Multinational Oil* (New York: Macmillan, 1974); Louis Turner, *Oil Companies in the International System* (London: The Royal Institute of International Affairs, 1978).
2. Conant, *Access to Energy 2000 and After*, p. 32.
3. Jacoby, *Multinational Oil*, chap. 4.

4. P. 8 of Report of the President's Task Force on Oil Import Control, 1970, Part 1, Sections 106–113, 117–130; see also Blair, *Control of Oil,* pp. 171–172.

5. Conant, *Access to Energy 2000 and After,* p. 48.

6. Cranford D. Goodwin et al., "Energy: 1945–80," *The Wilson Quarterly* 5 (2) (Spring 1981): 79.

7. For a text of President Nixon's speech, see *Energy Policy, Congressional Quarterly* (March 1981): 237–242.

8. *Project Independence Report,* U.S. Federal Energy Agency, Washington, D.C., 1974.

9. For the text of President Carter's speech, see *Energy Policy,* 2nd ed., *Congressional Quarterly* (1981): 251–253.

10. *The National Energy Plan,* U.S. Federal Energy Administration, Washington, D.C., April 1977.

11. *Powerplant and Industrial Fuel Use Act Annual Report,* U.S. Department of Energy, Washington, D.C., March 1, 1980.

12. Charles K. Ebinger, "U.S. Presidential Election: The Energy Issues," *Defense, Communications and Security Review* 80 (1979): 18–26.

13. Melvin A. Conant and Charles K. Ebinger, "Tremors in World Oil: The Consequences of Iran," *International Security Review* 5 (no. 1, Spring 1980):28.

14. For an analysis of various forecasts and their limitations, see Edwin A. Deagle, Jr., Bijan Mossavar-Rahmani, and Richard Huff, *Energy in the 1980's: An Analysis of Recent Studies,* A Report Prepared for the Group of Thirty, Rockefeller Foundation, New York, June 1980.

15. *Petroleum Intelligence Weekly* November 19, 1979.

16. *World Financial Markets,* Morgan Guaranty Trust Company, New York, November 1979.

17. Deagle et al., *Energy in the 1980's.*

18. U.S. Senate Committee on Energy and Natural Resources, *Energy: An Uncertain Future* (Washington, D.C.: U.S. Government Printing Office, December 1978), pp. 5–15.

19. U.S. Central Intelligence Agency, *Prospects for Soviet Oil Production,* Washington, D.C., April 1977; also by the CIA: *Prospects for Soviet Oil Production: A Supplemental Analysis,* July 1977; *The World Oil Market in the Years Ahead,* August 1977; *The Soviet Economy in 1978–79 and Prospects for 1980,* June 1980.

20. According to the U.S. Central Intelligence Agency Energy Division, Iranian crude accounted for 10 percent of U.S. crude oil imports. Corresponding figures for other countries were: Canada, 15 percent; Japan, 16; France, 9; Germany, 12; Italy, 13; and the United Kingdom, 15.

21. *Report of the President's Commission on the Accident at Three Mile*

Island (Washington, D.C.: U.S. Government Printing Office), October 1979.

22. For a text of President Carter's Energy Message, see *Energy Policy,* 2nd ed., *Congressional Quarterly* (1981): 256–258.

23. Sam H. Schurr et al., *Energy in America's Future* (Baltimore: The Johns Hopkins University Press, 1979); Hans Landsberg et al., *Energy: The Next Twenty Years* (Cambridge, Mass.: Ballinger Publishing Company, 1979); Robert Stobaugh, Daniel Yergin, et al., *Energy Future* (New York: Random House, 1979).

24. Stobaugh, Yergin, et al., *Energy Future.*

25. *The National Energy Plan II,* U.S. Department of Energy, Washington, D.C., 1979.

26. *Major Legislative and Regulatory Impediments to Conventional and Synthetic Fuel Energy Development,* American Petroleum Institute, Washington, D.C., March 1, 1980.

27. Interviews, Conservation Foundation, Natural Resources Defense Council, Resources for the Future, Washington, D.C., June–July 1980.

28. Goodwin et al., *Energy: 1945–80,* p. 90.

29. *The Future of Saudi Arabian Oil Production,* Staff Report to the Subcommittee on International Economic Policy, Committee on Foreign Relations, U.S. Senate, *Petroleum Intelligence Weekly,* Special Supplement, April 23, 1979.

30. *Petroleum Intelligence Weekly,* May 21, 1979.

31. Ibid., July 2, 1979.

32. *Energy Risks and Energy Futures: Some Farewell Observations,* speech by James Schlesinger before the National Press Club, Washington, D.C., August 16, 1979.

33. *Petroleum Intelligence Weekly,* September 10, 1979.

34. *OPEC Oil Capacity, Production and Policies,* U.S. Central Intelligence Agency, September 1979.

35. Ibid. See also *Petroleum Intelligence Weekly,* September 3, 1979.

36. *Petroleum Intelligence Weekly,* Special Supplement, September 17, 1977.

37. *Petroleum Intelligence Weekly,* December 3, 1979.

38. For details of the IEA's contingency plan, see Chapter 5.

39. Ibid.

40. Interviews, World Bank and International Monetary Fund, Washington, D.C., March 1980.

41. Ibid.

42. *Petroleum Intelligence Weekly,* February 25, 1980.

43. Ibid., February 5, 1980.

44. Charles K. Ebinger, *U.S.-Caribbean Energy Relations in a Global*

Strategic Context, Center for Strategic and International Studies, Washington, D.C., November 1980.

45.   *U.S. Energy Outlook,* Exxon Corporation, March 1980.
46.   *World Energy Outlook,* Exxon Corporation, December 1980.
47.   *Petroleum Intelligence Weekly,* April 14, 1980.
48.   For a full text of the OPEC Oil Ministers' "Summary of Recommendations," see *Petroleum Intelligence Weekly,* Special Supplement, May 12, 1980.
49.   For a full text of Admiral Turner's remarks before the U.S. Senate Energy Committee, see *Petroleum Intelligence Weekly,* Special Supplement, May 19, 1980.
50.   *Petroleum Intelligence Weekly,* May 12, 1980.
51.   Ibid., July 14, 1980.
52.   Ibid., September 1, 1980.
53.   Fereidun Fesharaki, "World Oil Availability: The Role of OPEC Policies," *Annual Review of Energy* 6 (1981).
54.   *Domestic Energy Requirements in OPEC Member Countries,* OPEC Secretariat, Vienna, September 1980.
55.   *Petroleum Intelligence Weekly,* Special Supplement, September 22, 1980.
56.   Ibid., Special Supplement, September 15, 1980.
57.   Ibid.
58.   *Petroleum Intelligence Weekly,* September 29, 1980.
59.   Ibid., September 29, 1980.
60.   Ibid., October 13, 1980.

2 THE ROLE OF CONSERVATION IN REDUCING OIL IMPORTS

In 1939 a government energy resource committee argued that the United States was running out of oil and gas and that "we must consider whether to use more wisely our available supply, to manufacture high cost substitutes or to depend on foreign oil for our motor cars and airplanes, our tractors and our battleships."[1] Over forty years later, the United States relies heavily on foreign oil and faces the prospect of manufacturing high-cost oil substitutes (see Chapter 3). However, this country has yet to find a way of using available fuel supplies more wisely—that is, more economically.

A major task for the United States in the 1980s will be to devise conservation policies that not only help to save domestic resources but also reduce our dependence on imported oil. In 1980 the United States imported roughly 6 mmbd of petroleum, amounting to 39 percent of its oil consumption and 18 percent of total U.S energy supply. This dependence exposes the nation to considerable security risks. Sudden changes in the price of availability of fuel can set off shortages in the short term and damage economic growth in the long term. Unpredictable events in the Middle East and other oil-producing areas jeopardize commercial energy operations, complicate diplomatic relations, and raise the possibility of military intervention to secure fuel supplies.

According to recent energy projections the United States will continue to import as much as 5 mmbd of oil through the 1980s. These forecasts assume that many of the political, economic, and regulatory conditions that affect the U.S. energy market will endure. Without some changes in prevailing government policies and patterns of fuel use, therefore, this country cannot expect to reduce the vulnerability it incurs by relying on foreign oil.

The United States could reduce its oil imports below projected levels through greater oil conservation. Although to some, conservation suggests scarcity and the need to ration or not use a limited resource, to economists conservation suggests the most cost-effective use of fuel. Each resource used in the economy—raw material, labor, and capital—has a cost. If the cost of one suddenly increases, more of the others must be used to hold down the overall costs of the activity. When the price of oil suddenly rises, producers and consumers need to use more labor, capital, and other less costly fuels to hold down total costs. Thus oil conservation involves the substitution of alternative energy, labor, and capital for petroleum in order to save money as well as to lower fuel consumption.

It has gradually become apparent that higher oil prices have been the principal means to reducing energy use. When world petroleum prices doubled in 1979–80 the price increase encouraged Americans to cut oil consumption by 8 percent and total energy consumption by 4 percent. Furthermore in the long run (seven to fifteen years), economists now believe that a 10 percent increase in oil prices could cut oil consumption by at least 5 percent in most sectors of the economy.[2] Over this length of time consumers and producers have the opportunity to install more fuel-efficient equipment and replace oil with other fuels that help to lower their costs and their use of oil. Thus as one economist concludes, "to the extent that energy conservation is a goal of energy policy, it is clear that the most effective policy instrument is the price of energy itself."[3]

But even though higher world oil prices stimulate conservation in the long run, they appear to do so only at the cost of recession, inflation, and a massive transfer of wealth to foreign oil producers in the short term. In 1980 the United States spent $78 billion on foreign oil, which equals 3 percent of gross national product (GNP) and 25 percent of business capital investment—dollars that could have been better used at home. The Organization for Economic Cooperation and Development (OECD) estimates that because of the 1979–80 oil price rise, 1981 real economic growth (that adjusted for inflation) in the United States could be 5 percent less than it would have been without the price rise.[4] Furthermore, OECD calculates that the price increase added at least 3 percentage points to inflation in 1981 among its member countries.[5] Thus a conservation policy that relies entirely on international oil market forces runs the risk of winning the battle but losing the war.

Recognizing that higher energy prices will spur conservation, the United States needs to enact policies that will help to protect the economy against the adverse effect of unpredictable jolts in the world price of oil. Certain measures could help to reduce demand for oil imports while accelerating the long-term process of improving fuel efficiency throughout the economy. These measures are fuel economy standards for certain energy-intensive machinery and more liberal tax incentives for investments in fuel-efficient machinery and insulation.

Conservation is not the only means to reduce oil imports. Over the next ten years, the United States must develop its tremendous energy resources in order to have sufficient fuel supplies to replace expensive oil. Federal policies directly influence energy production through environmental regulations, permitting procedures and grants for research and development. To what extent does government policy help stimulate domestic fuel development and to what extent is federal or state intervention in the energy market counterproductive? Chapter 3 assesses the impact of government involvement in fuel production. The present chapter, examines policies that affect oil conservation and the substitution of other fuels, especially gas and coal, for oil in each sector of the economy.

FEDERAL OIL CONSERVATION PROGRAMS

The federal government has tried to encourage conservation by imposing fuel economy standards for machinery and providing tax incentives to invest in alternative energy systems or insulation. The Energy Policy and Conservation Act of 1975 (EPCA) set fuel-efficiency standards for automobiles (passenger vehicles and trucks). The National Energy Conservation Policy Act of 1978 (NECPA) requires the establishment of fuel economy standards for a variety of household appliances and heating/cooling equipment. The Energy Conservation and Production Act of 1978 (ECPA) sets standards for achieving energy conservation in new buildings built or funded by the federal government. Finally, the Energy Tax Act of 1978 provides tax incentives to businesses and householders to invest in insulation and alternative energy systems.

Since their enactment the implementation of these programs has been less than complete, and with the recent change of administration there is considerable debate over whether and how they should be continued. The controversy focuses on the pros and cons of the free market approach to conservation, an approach that depends entirely on the responsiveness of demand to price. The issue is complex because it involves not only the maintenance of fuel economy standards or tax write-offs but of price controls on natural gas. These price regulations influence the degree to which consumers substitute natural gas for oil and the degree to which they invest in conservation.

NATURAL GAS PRICE REGULATIONS

Although President Reagan removed all oil price regulations in February 1981, rate controls still hold down the price of gas. Natural gas prices have been subject to federal regulation since the passage in 1938 of the Natural Gas Act (NGA). The NGA placed the transportation and sale of gas across state lines under the jurisdiction of the Federal Power Commission (FPC), but within their states producers could sell gas to distributors at the going market rate. The difference in pricing practices between the interstate and intrastate markets began to cause supply difficulties in the late 1960s. After shortages developed in the interstate market during the early 1970, the president and Congress decided to control the prices of gas under contract to both the interstate and intrastate markets.

The Natural Gas Policy Act of 1978 (NGPA) sets price controls for some twenty-two categories of natural gas production and a schedule for the gradual deregulation of these categories. By 1985, approximately 35–45 percent of natural gas will remain under price controls[6] and, in 1990 about 14 percent.[7] Nearly all of the regulated supply is under contract to interstate customers. As some of these natural gas wells are exhausted, however, the impact of the controls will disappear, and by 1990 the gas market will be almost entirely free of controls.

The net effect of these price regulations has been to keep gas at roughly half the price of heating oil to most commercial and residential customers. Naturally, the availability of a low-cost alternative to oil has encouraged many homeowners to switch to gas from oil. The American Gas Association (AGA) estimates that some 380,000 households have converted from oil to gas since the passage of the NGPA. This rate of conversion represents an oil savings of at least 25,000 barrels a day if one assumes that each household uses approximately 1,000 gallons of heating oil a year. The AGA asserts that the United States could save roughly 1 million barrels of heating oil per day if all of the 16 million households currently heated by oil switched to natural gas. That oil savings translates into an equivalent reduction in oil imports and an increase in residential gas consumption of at least 2.1 trillion cubic feet (Tcf) per year.[8]

Although these price controls may help to discourage oil consumption in the short term, they could have some damaging consequences in the long run. First of all, no one is sure that the United States can produce enough gas to sustain this rate of conversion in buildings while continuing to supply other gas customers in industry. Although it is beyond the scope of this chapter to examine the prospects for increased natural gas production, it is important to note that geologists and economists differ sharply over the resource potential and the price required to develop and deliver future gas supplies. Most recent forecasts suggest that by 1990, when most natural gas prices are deregulated, U.S. natural gas output will be the same or slightly less than the current level of 20 million cubic feet per year.[9] If residential, commercial, and industrial users continue to switch from oil to gas, they could put considerable pressure on available natural gas supply. In some parts of the country, demand for gas could drive the price beyond that of oil, and in others consumers could experience shortages.

A second disadvantage of price controls is that such rules in the short term encourage waste and the use of less efficient equipment because they insulate customers from paying the full price of energy. Furthermore, they reduce the incentive to design highly efficient machinery. For example the fuel economy of most gas boilers used in space heating is only 50–60 percent, so half the energy is wasted in transmission. As long as price controls artificially lower the cost of using gas, these inefficiencies will persist.

In an entirely free market for energy, realistic prices would create incentives for manufacturers to design the most fuel-efficient equipment and for consumers to shop around for the heating system that uses the least fuel. The accelerated or immediate decontrol of natural gas prices would certainly enhance conservation. However, this market solution also has important economic and political drawbacks. First, immediate decontrol could suddenly double natural gas prices to homeowners, many of whom may not yet have had the opportunity or finances to insulate houses or install the most efficient gas heating system. Thus, the economic impact could be so severe that it could create a political outcry for the reimposition of controls, if not at a federal level, then at the state level. Second, in some areas, natural gas prices could suddenly rise to a level greater than oil prices. As a result, many consumers that have the flexibility to use both gas and oil—especially manufacturers and businesses—could switch back from gas to oil. This unpredictable shift in pricing would run counter to the goal of most U.S. energy legislation, which has sought to reduce not increase oil consumption.

To the extent that oil import reduction is a major goal of U.S. energy policy, a case can be made for maintaining current regulation of natural gas prices. But without federal government enforcement of fuel economy standards for gas-consuming equipment and provision of additional tax incentives to consumers for insulation and the installation of very efficient gas boilers and furnaces, consumers will not be adequately prepared to face total deregulation of natural gas prices. However, as we argue in Chapter 4, it is important to overall U.S. energy policy that natural gas price deregulation occur as soon as possible. Thus consumers must be assisted now.

OIL AND GAS CONSERVATION IN HOUSEHOLDS AND BUSINESSES

The United States has three major programs to encourage conservation in households and businesses: appliance performance standards and conservation services required by NECPA; tax credits for conservation and solar energy use set by the Energy Tax Act of 1978; and the loan program for solar energy and energy conservation established by the Energy Security Act of 1980. The U.S. Department of Energy (DOE) has begun to set minimum energy efficiency levels for heating/cooling equipment (the law required action by December 1980) and standards for other machinery are to be set by November 1981.

After the tax credits have been in effect for a reasonably long time, it will be possible to judge whether or not they have had an impact on fuel use.

Households and businesses currently burn roughly 2 mmbd of oil and roughly 7.6 Tcf of gas, equivalent to 3.7 mmbd of oil. Together oil and gas account for just under one-half the total energy consumption in this sector. The rest is electricity sales and energy used in generating electricity. About one-half the oil that households and businesses consume is heating oil; the rest is liquified petroleum gas (LPG) used for cooking and residual oil used by businesses to generate power or heat. Thus the main target for conservation in this sector should be heating oil.

A 1980 survey by the U.S. Department of Commerce revealed that about 14 million households use oil as their main heating fuel, over 60 percent of them in the Northeast and North Central United States.[10] According to a survey of existing furnaces and boilers, most of these units have an efficiency of only 50 percent—that is, half the heat content of the oil is lost in transmitting warmth to the building.[11] Thus households in the eastern half of the United States have tended to waste half of the fuel that they buy because of the inefficiency of their heating systems.

Three factors make it difficult for households and businesses to lower oil consumption: first, heating/cooling equipment with 80–90 percent efficiency is not readily available; second, replacing old systems entirely is expensive; and third, it is contractors, not homeowners, who are responsible for choosing heating systems for new houses and often for oil-to-gas conversions. They often pick the least expensive and least efficient gas furance or boiler.

Under the authority of NECPA, DOE has proposed minimum efficiency standards for gas- and oil-burning furnaces and boilers. This program would require manufacturers to produce oil furnaces and boilers with an efficiency of at least 75 percent commencing in 1981 and no less than 80 percent in 1986; the standard for gas boilers and furnaces would be 65 percent in 1981 but roughly 80 percent by 1986. Although manufacturers already produce a variety of high-efficiency furnaces and boilers ranging 75 percent to 90 percent efficiency, they continue to make a relatively inexpensive, low-efficiency model, the "builder-model" lines that contractors typically install in new houses. If the federal government required that all furnaces and boilers meet a relatively high standard for fuel economy, contractors no longer would have access to the cheap builder-model lines. Thus DOE's program addresses a significant quirk in the current housing construction system that tends to counteract efforts at fuel conservation in buildings.

The NECPA program also requires the manufacturer and salesmen to provide consumers with information on the fuel efficiency of each heater. DOE has devised a generic test that the manufacturer uses to assess the efficiency of each model, the results of which are published in a consumer guide. This has proved to be no small feat since there are about 4,300 models of gas-fired furnaces and 1,700 models of gas-fired boilers that the program covers.

Even though new high-efficiency gas and oil boilers are becoming available, householders often do not have the financing to replace their old oil-fired heaters. Consumers are often unwilling to switch from oil to gas because the money that they have today is worth more to them than the money they could save tomorrow. Those who do consider such investment often expect to see the new system pay for itself in fuel costs saved within a few years, whereas with a piece of equipment that should last at least twenty years, a short payback period probably represents a higher rate of return than is fair to expect. Finally, current tax credits for conservation do not apply to the installation of new highly efficient gas heating systems.

At present government policy encourages insulation, a limited range of conservation devices for existing heating systems and installation of solar heating equipment. The Energy Tax Act provides a credit of 40 percent on the first $10,000 for a wind or solar system; a tax credit of 15 percent for the first $2,000 spent on weather stripping, storm doors, and storm windows; and a similar credit for investments in mechanical furnace ignition systems that replace gas pilot lights, as well as other mechanical features that help to save fuel.

Although these tax credits are a step in the right direction, they do not go far enough. The list should be broadened to include credits for installing a new gas heating system with at least 75 percent efficiency, and for other alternatives to oil heat, such as wood stoves, heat pumps, and electric furnaces (which are 100 percent efficient). The problem is that the conservation measures and solar systems that existing legislation encourages do not apply to the long-range problem that the East Coast faces: continued dependence on insecure and increasingly expensive supplies of heating oil. The key to reducing homeowners' vulnerability is complete replacement of the oil-fired heating systems. Energy tax legislation should reflect that goal with credits that give homeowners in the oil-dependent Northeast an incentive to invest in alternative systems suited to their climate, such as gas-fired heaters and those that burn wood and other biomass fuels.

Similarly businesses should be able to accelerate depreciation of investments in high-efficiency heating or power equipment. The best systems proposed thus far would allow businesses 100 percent depreciation in a single year. Indeed many industrialized countries have similar rapid depreciation clauses for most capital investments. This one-time write-off would not only help to improve fuel efficiency in the industrial and commercial sectors but would benefit companies economically as well. As several economists have noted, companies must depreciate assets at the original rather than replacement cost. When inflation is high, the relative value of depreciation deductions decreases, eroding the benefit of the tax write-off. If companies could deduct a depreciation expense in one year, they would not pay this "inflation penalty." [12] An accelerated depreciation program for businesses, combined with more liberal energy tax credits for replacement of oil heaters in households, would go far toward decreasing petroleum consumption outside of transportation.

OIL CONSERVATION IN INDUSTRY

The main thrust of government policy to encourage oil conservation in industry has been to force manufacturers to replace both oil and gas with coal. The Powerplant and Industrial Fuel Use Act of 1978 (FUA) has aimed to reduce oil and natural gas use by the oil equivalent of about 1.0 mmbd by 1990. FUA immediately barred companies from building new oil-fired or gas-fired generators, and large boilers capable of burning 16.5 barrels of oil equivalent an hour. Furthermore, FUA orders companies not to increase their use of natural gas above the level consumed in a specified base period. Finally, the law prohibits gas consumption by all electric utilities and large industrial boilers beginning in 1990. Total industrial consumption of oil and gas currently amounts to the oil equivalent of 8.8 mmbd, roughly half of which is natural gas.

The implementation of the FUA has aroused tremendous controversy. On the one hand, economists state that the low price of coal, which is roughly one-third the price of oil and two-thirds the price of natural gas for utilities and manufacturers, is incentive enough for industry to switch from oil and gas to coal, so the legislation is unnecessary. On the other hand, some industrial users contend that the extra costs of using coal—pollution-control costs, transport and handling costs—make coal less economical than gas or oil, so the legislation would force them into a less cost-effective use of resources. However, in favor of FUA, some would argue that industry has the time and financial resources to invest in conversion to coal. Furthermore, national security requires the switch from limited supplies of oil and gas to abundant and cheap supplies of coal as quickly as possible.

The problem with FUA and other legislation that would enforce coal conversion by industry is that such laws assume that manufacturers have fixed fuel requirements for running machinery. Thus manufacturers should replace more expensive oil and gas with cheaper coal. However, energy use in any industry is part of an evolving manufacturing process that is ever adjusting to new economic conditions—not only fuel costs, but capital, labor, and raw material costs. A law like FUA largely addresses the use of fuel to raise steam, but such a law simply becomes irrelevant as processes that require steam are either phased out or modified to require considerably less energy. In short, it is impossible to legislate energy use for a host of manufacturers since no one can predict what products or processes will characterize the U.S. economy in the future.

THE PATTERN OF INDUSTRIAL FUEL USE

Manufacturers were the largest energy consumers in the United States in 1980, using the oil equivalent of 15.4 mmbd: 40 percent of total energy use in this country. Industry uses more natural gas than any other sector—the oil equivalent of 4.2 mmbd, or 41 percent of total gas supply—and 4.5 mmbd of oil. By contrast, industrial use of coal accounts for only 10 percent of that sector's energy consumption—the oil equivalent of 1.69 mmbd. Electricity provides the remainder of energy supply for industry.

Manufacturers use fuel in boilers to raise steam or heat water in order to generate power, provide warmth for buildings, and certain processes. They also use fuel to fire such equipment as kilns and furnaces. Finally fuel such as oil, gas, and coal is a raw material required for processing certain products, especially chemicals and steel.

Although recent statistics are lacking, a survey in 1974 indicated that boiler fuel consumption accounted for about one-quarter of industrial energy use. Natural gas provided one-half the boiler fuel, oil one-sixth, and coal another sixth.[13] If a similar pattern of fuel consumption still holds, then the total amount of oil and gas currently burned by boilers in 1980 would be the oil equivalent of 2.7 mmbd— 2.1 mmbdoe gas, 0.6 mmbd oil.

The greater part of industrial energy use is for a variety of miscellaneous uses (30 percent), process heat (22 percent), and raw materials and feedstocks (22 percent). A study for the President's Commission on Coal in 1980 revealed that replacing oil and gas with coal in most of these applications would be infeasible not only technically but economically. "Direct use of coal," noted the report, "is a proven technology for only a small portion of the gas and oil currently consumed in process heat equipment" and "the potential for converting existing process heat equipment to coal is limited."[14] Coal could not be substituted for oil and gas as a feedstock in producing most chemical substances. Since legislation could not possibly cover the other miscellaneous uses of energy in industry, government could attempt to regulate the use of oil and gas only as boiler fuel. The question is whether or not the government, through FUA, can bring about a massive switch from oil and gas to coal or other sources of energy (possibly electricity) as a boiler fuel in the 1980s.

The answer to that question is no, because the main influence over fuel conversions is the price of fuel, not the mandate to cease gas consumption by 1990. The government policy that most affects the decision to replace oil and gas with coal or other fuels is the deregulation of oil prices, which is already in effect, and the gradual decontrol of gas prices. Furthermore, under the current NGPA rules and FUA, the price of natural gas already is priced at the same level as residual fuel, the heavy refined fuel used in boilers. Thus the market signals already are in place to manufacturers to replace oil and gas either with other fuels or to convert equipment and processes in order to use oil and gas more efficiently.

With the additional burden of a ban on gas use in large boilers during 1990, the government would force manufacturers to make the choice between investing in more efficient oil-using equipment or investing in a boiler that burns coal, biomass, or a synthetic fuel. Under the FUA rules, manufacturers can receive a permanent exemption that allows them to switch from gas to oil if they can show that coal supply is not available, site limitations prohibit conversion to coal, and, most important, coal or a nonpetroleum fuel "will not be available at a cost (taking into account associated facilities for the transportation and use of such fuel) which, based upon the best practical estimates, does not substantially exceed the cost, as determined by rule by the Secretary [of Energy], of using imported petroleum as a primary energy source during the useful life of the plant or installation involved."[15] In short FUA permits the manufacturers to make precisely the economic decision they would make in the absence of FUA.

With a schedule for natural gas deregulation in place and the effects of higher oil prices, manufacturers already have sufficient incentive to switch from these fuels to coal, electricity, or alternative fuels for use in boilers. FUA as written appears to be irrelevant to the task of lowering oil and gas consumption in industry. The president and Congress therefore should consider repeal of the FUA instead of devoting federal funds to enforcing a program whose effects would be minimal.

The other major reason for implementing FUA has been to reallocate gas supplies from industries and utilities to households and businesses. However, in designing FUA, legislators ignored the important part that large industrial gas users play in the logistics and economics of gas distribution to all sectors of the economy.

At present several areas of the country, especially in the oil-dependent eastern United States, are not hooked up to the natural gas distribution system. Vermont, for example, does not receive any gas from the interstate pipeline network. In order to expand lines into certain regions, distributors need some guarantee that the market in a particular area will be large and steady enough to compensate for the costs of installing a new service. For example if a large industrial user in the area were to decide to switch from oil to gas, then in the course of installing a line to the manufacturer (or utility), the distributor could also start to hook up residences and businesses along the route. If legislation discourages large companies from switching to gas, however, then distributors may not receive the signals from the local market encouraging expansion of service. Distributors would naturally be wary of installing new lines while facing the prospect that the major gas customer in the area might be forced to switch to other fuels after the line was built.

To sum up, U.S. conservation policy should encourage industry to use oil and gas more efficiently as a response to realistic fuel prices, but the federal government should not impose a ban on oil or gas use by industry in any of its processes. More than any other sector of the economy, manufacturers already have increased the overall efficiency of energy use. A recent government report has noted that the energy efficiency of manufacturers—that is, the amount of energy used to produce a dollar of GNP—improved by 15.4 percent between 1972 and 1979.[16] Indeed, as the report notes, "the absolute level of energy consumption as measured in Btu's, for the ten most energy-intensive reporting industries has fallen by 2.25 percent since 1972, during a period when the output in manufacturing has risen over 17 percent."[17] Thus industry has demonstrated its ability to adjust to higher fuel prices without any loss in productivity. It is questionable that any government mandates to industry on fuel use could have achieved these results.

OIL CONSERVATION IN TRANSPORTATION

Because transportation accounts for roughly one-half the total oil consumption in the United States, more efficient use of gasoline and other motor fuels could have the most significant effect on oil imports. In 1980 total oil consumption in transportation came to 9.1 mmbd, of which gasoline use was 6.5 mmbd. Recent experience has shown that higher gasoline prices have the most direct impact on motor fuel consumption. The steady rise in oil prices since January 1979 helped to cut gasoline consumption by 12 percent between 1978 and 1981, a savings of 1 mmbd of motor fuel—and total oil imports were reduced by 2.6 mmbd (30 percent) in the same period. In short, market forces, not government policies have proved to be the most effective means of reducing oil imports.

If price is the principal instrument for reducing gasoline consumption, then the critical question for government is whether or not to impose a hefty tax on motor fuel sales. Many state and local governments already have raised the tax on motor fuel or imposed a tax on refiners that they pass through in the form of higher fuel prices to consumers. However, federal efforts to enact a national gasoline sales tax have met tremendous political opposition. Bound up with this policy debate is an academic dispute over the long-term responsiveness of gasoline demand to price increases. In order to assess whether or not a gasoline tax is necessary to lower gasoline consumption over the long term it would be useful to examine the relation between price and demand in the long run.

The effect of a change in price on the consumption of any commodity is known as the price elasticity of demand. This figure measures the percentage change in demand over different periods of time induced by a 1 percent change in price. For example, if the price of oil rises by 1 percent, in the short term, within one to three years, demand for oil may drop by about 0.2 percent, an elasticity of −0.2. When the response to price is so low, the demand for that commodity is considered to be relatively inelastic. In this short period of time consumers simply do not change their pattern of oil use regardless of the rise in price. However, over a longer period of time—five years or more—consumers have time to change their habits. In order to save money on fuel they may replace an older gas guzzler with a smaller car that gets better mileage or organize car pools, or decide to use public transportation some of the time. Thus the price increase, which may change travel habits very little within a year or two, could stimulate a considerable drop in oil consumption over a longer period of time.

In projecting oil consumption for the 1980s the federal government has tended to treat petroleum demand as relatively inelastic. Policymakers assume that a rise in price one year will reduce oil consumption in following years by only a small amount. Thus, in the *Annual Report to Congress of 1980, Volume III, Forecasts,* DOE states: "insufficient data are available with which to calculate the price elasticity of oil. An elasticity of 0.1 has been used for 1985 in all scenarios and 0.2 for 1990 for 1995."[18] If DOE is correct, a 10 percent rise in price during one year would reduce demand in that year and over the following years by roughly 1–2 percent. Thus in order to have a steady reduction in oil consumption of 1–2 percent annually, oil prices would need to rise by 10 percent per year. Evidence suggests that even in the short term, however, DOE has underestimated the responsiveness of demand to price while in the long run, the price elasticity of gasoline demand could be roughly five times greater than DOE suggests. If price alone can stimulate significant reductions in oil use, then a federal gasoline conservation policy may become unnecessary.

In the course of 1979 the price of gasoline rose by 60 percent from 69.5¢ to $1.11 per gallon in January 1980. In the same period gasoline consumption fell from the average 1978 rate of 7.4 mmbd to an average rate for 1979 of 7.0, a decline of 5 percent. This relation between price and demand can be expressed as a ratio of 0.08. If the price rise between January 1979 and January 1981 is related instead to the drop in consumption for the same period, the ratio appears to increase. Thus an 82 percent price increase in this two-year period coincides with a 14 percent drop in consumption, from 7.4 mmbd to 6.4 mmbd in 1981. This relation translates into a ratio of 0.17, or twice the ratio attained in the first year. These empirical data show how even within a short period of time a large price increase can gradually act to reduce consumption.

Several economists have argued that the price elasticity of demand for gasoline over the long run, seven to fifteen years, could be in the range of -1.0.[19] If that is the case then the 60 percent price increase of 1979 could set in motion a sharp reduction in gasoline use over the next 10 years. Some economists estimate that by 1985 the demand for gasoline could fall to 5.8 mmbd and total oil consumption in the United States to 16.5 mmbd from the current level of 17 mmbd.[20]

If the United States lowers gasoline consumption to 5.8 mmbd by 1985, the level of oil imports could also decline significantly. Since gasoline is the principal product of crude oil processing, refiners tend to calculate their total crude oil needs by the demand for motor fuel. Under present economic and operating conditions, roughly one barrel of crude oil yields just under one-half barrel of gasoline (48 percent). The other half of the barrel becomes distillate fuel (heating oil and diesel fuel are both middle distillates), residual oil, and several special by-products.

In 1980 refiners used 13.5 mmbd of crude oil to produce about 6.5 mmbd of gasoline. Since domestic petroleum output was 8.6 mmbd, 5 mmbd of crude oil was imported to make up the difference. The balance of oil imports, roughly 1.68 mmbd, were oil products such as residual oil, gasoline, and distillate.

The United States could lower crude oil imports to about 4 mmbd in 1985 if gasoline consumption declines to 5.8 mmbd and domestic oil production stays at the current level of 8.6 mmbd or does not drop below 8.0 mmbd. Refiners would need approximately 12.0 mmbd of crude oil to process 5.8 mmbd of gasoline. This same amount of crude oil under current operations would yield just under 3 mmbd of distillate, which would be enough to meet transportation fuel needs as well as heating oil requirements, particularly as more households switch from oil to gas and other fuels for heating. Thus it is likely that the level of crude oil imports will be 4.0 mmbd or less in 1985.

That is roughly the level attained in 1975, when domestic oil production was 8.3 mmbd compared to 8.6 in 1980 and gasoline consumption 6.7 mmbd compared to 6.6 in 1980.

CONCLUSIONS

By using energy—especially oil—more efficiently, the United States can expect to see significant reductions in its oil imports. The key to lowering oil consumption in the next five to ten years is to encourage consumers to switch to machinery that uses oil and gas more efficiently or that runs on other forms of energy. To achieve this goal government should maintain fuel-efficiency standards for nontransport energy-intensive equipment, expand present tax incentives for replacing inefficient oil-fired heating and power systems, and, finally, repeal legislation that restricts gas use when that restriction encourages switching to oil.

Left to themselves market forces are likely to effect considerable fuel switching and conservation, but consumers might speed up the shift away from oil if they could take advantage of tax credits or rapid depreciation policies that give an equal advantage to all technologies designed to increase energy efficiency. With tax credits in place for insulation and the installation of highly efficient non-oil-powered equipment, the U.S. government could be assured that the deregulation of natural gas prices by the late 1980 will not catch households and businesses unprepared. These tax measures in conjunction with the prospect of rising gas prices can ensure that all sectors of the economy use fuel as efficiently as possible. By conserving heating oil in the residential and commercial sector and gasoline in the transport sector, the United States can be assured of lowering its petroleum imports to roughly 4 mmbd by the middle of the 1980s.

NOTES

1. Quoted in *Energy Policy in Perspective: Today's Problems, Yesterday's Solutions,* ed. Craufurd D. Goodwin (Washington, D.C.: The Brookings Institution, 1981), p. 7.
2. See Robert S. Pindyck, "The Characteristics of Energy Demand," in *Energy Conservation and Public Policy,* ed. John C. Sawhill (Englewood Cliffs, N.J.: Prentice-Hall, 1979), p. 42.

3. Ibid., p. 44.
4. OECD, *Economic Outlook,* December 1980, p. 13.
5. Ibid., July 1980, pp. 122–123.
6. ICF Inc., "A Preliminary Analysis of the Gas Cushion," a study prepared for the U.S. Federal Energy Regulatory Commission, November 1979.
7. U.S. Department of Energy, *Energy Programs/Energy Markets, Technical Papers,* July 1980, p. 28.
8. The American Gas Association, "An Analysis of Oil-to-Gas Conversion Trends in the Residential Gas Spaceheating Market," September 18, 1980, p. 2.
9. See U.S. Department of Energy, *Annual Report to Congress, Volume III: Forecasts,* March 1981, p. 112.
10. U.S. Department of Energy, *Residential Energy Consumption Survey, Consumption and Expenditures, April 1978 through March 1979,* July 1980, p. 120.
11. Office of Technology Assessment, *Residential Energy Conservation,* vol. 1, Washington, D.C., p. 39.
12. Dale W. Jorgenson and Peter Navarro, "10-5-3: 'Deeply Flawed'," *The New York Times,* May 5, 1981.
13. Energy and Environmental Analysis, Inc., "Energy Consumption Data Base, Volume I, Summary Document," prepared for the U.S. Federal Energy Administration, 1977.
14. Energy and Environmental Analysis, Inc, "An Analysis of the Potential for Coal Use in the Industrial Sector," prepared for the President's Commission on Coal, March 15, 1980, Section 3.3.2.1.
15. The Powerplant and Industrial Fuel Use Act of 1978, Title II, Section 212(a).
16. "Annual Report to the Congress and the President on the Industrial Energy Efficiency Improvement Program in 1979," December 1, 1980, p. i.
17. Ibid.
18. Pindyck, "Energy Demand."
19. Sawhill, ed., *Energy Conservation and Public Policy.*
20. Petroleum Industry Research Foundation, Inc., "U.S. Petroleum Product Demand Trends and Refinery Operations to 1985," a paper presented by John H. Lichtblau, February 24, 1981.

3 GOVERNMENT INVOLVEMENT IN ENERGY PRODUCTION

The United States faces two major challenges in the 1980s: To maintain current levels of gas and oil production and to develop new forms of energy that can replace petroleum in the established pattern of fuel use. As was concluded in Chapter 2, the United States could lower oil use in the next ten years if consumers switch to other fuels and more efficient cars and heating equipment. To convert those savings into a comparable reduction in oil imports, however, the United States must have adequate energy supplies to replace foreign fuel. Without greater energy production, conservation alone may only temporarily reduce reliance on imported oil.

The federal government has long been engaged in research and development of alternatives to oil and gas. After the development of atomic weapons during World War II, the federal government heavily subsidized the development of technology for generating electricity from nuclear reactors. The Atomic Energy Commission was formed in 1946, and through the Atomic Energy Act as amended in 1954 Congress established a program of financial assistance to utilities for developing large-scale light water reactors in order to bring nuclear power to commercialization. Through the Tennessee Valley Authority and other organizations, the federal government subsidizes hydropower plants. Research on solar electric power began in the late 1960s as an outgrowth of the space program. Finally, the U.S. government has conducted research into synthetic fuels from coal and shale oil production since World War I, when concern over a shortage of oil for military transport fuels created an interest in oil substitutes.

The Iranian oil shortage of 1979–80 reawakened government interest in synthetic fuels as a means of reducing dependence on oil imports. The synthetic fuels program established by the Energy Security Act of 1980 is the most ambitious federal energy project since the development of atomic power. The legislation calls for $200 million in feasibility studies, $300 million for cooperative agreements between government and companies, and $20 billion for a Synthetic Fuels Corporation (SFC), of which the corporation will dispense roughly $17 billion in loans.

The U.S. government takes considerable risks in choosing synthetic fuels as a major instrument for achieving greater energy security. First, economic and regulatory obstacles could block the commercialization of experimental synfuel technologies, so synfuels may do little to reduce oil imports before the advent of the 1990s. Second, synthetic fuels may be entirely the wrong solution to the oil import problem. The United States could best take advantage of the resources that it has in abundance—coal, uranium, and renewable energy such as geothermal and solar power—by using them to generate electricity. In the long term, the key to achieving energy independence could be the substitution of electricity and electric appliances for oil and gas.

As the United States embarks on a synthetic fuels program it would be useful to distinguish between the long-term and short-term options the country has for achieving greater self-reliance in energy. The synthetic fuels program should be treated as one of several tactics for improving the leverage the United States and all other oil-importing countries have over the petroleum exporting nations in matters of price and supply contracts. Since the goal of the Energy Security Act is to reduce oil imports, the federal government through the SFC should also provide some financial assistance for other projects that could quickly reduce oil imports, notably improvements in refinery technology and accelerated conservation.

In the long term the United States needs to develop a comprehensive policy on electric power. Before the country can undertake massive electrification, many regulatory, financial, and technical obstacles will need to be overcome. Under current market conditions, it is difficult to gauge how great the demand for electricity may be in the next ten to twenty years and thus how large a share coal, nuclear power, and renewable energy may have in the nation's fuel mix. From the standpoint of environmental quality and safety, considerable trade-offs exist among the major sources of electric power. Whereas coal combustion pollutes, the use or abuse of nuclear power poses the risk of radiation. Thus, even though electric power has the greatest potential for providing energy security, it also presents some of the greatest difficulties for the president and Congress to resolve.

THE SHORT-TERM OPTIONS FOR ENERGY SECURITY

In the Energy Security Act, Congress declares that it will use its full constitutional powers through the synfuels program, "to improve the Nation's balance of payments, reduce the threat of economic disruption from oil supply interruptions and increase the Nation's security by reducing its dependence upon imported oil."[1] The major goal of the legislation is "the production from domestic resources of the equivalent of at least 500,000 barrels of crude oil per day of synthetic fuel by 1987 and of at least 2,000,000 barrels of crude oil per day of synthetic fuel by 1992."[2] Synthetic fuel is defined as:

> any solid, liquid, or gas, or combination thereof, which can be used as a substitute for petroleum or natural gas (or any derivatives thereof, including chemical feedstocks) and which is produced by chemical or physical transformation (other than washing, cooking or desulfurizing) of domestic sources of —
> (i)   coal, including lignite and peat
> (ii)   shale;
> (iii)   tarsands . . . heavy oil . . . and . . . mixtures of coal and combustible liquids, including petroleum.[3]

In establishing the Synthetic Fuels Corporation (SFC), Congress recognized that synfuel production would "require financial commitments beyond those expected from nongovernmental capital sources and existing government incentives."[4] Although market forces eventually will determine the commercial viability of individual technologies, the SFC through loans and government purchase guarantees provides the initial financial boost for building large-scale demonstration plants. These could go into commercial operation on their own if and when the price of oil or gas rose to a level sufficiently high to allow the new fuels to compete, a situation that has been adversely affected by the current slide in oil prices.

From the standpoint of national security, the synthetic fuels program offers two major benefits. First, if the United States demonstrates that it can produce as much as 500,000 barrels a day of synthetic fuel, it will hold in hand one more card that could help moderate price increases. This is especially true in the event that oil demand rises again in response to temporarily stagnating oil prices. The oil-exporting countries could be reluctant suddenly to push prices too high, because the higher the price of oil goes, the more rapidly synthetic fuels would become competitive with oil and the more quickly synfuels capacity could be expanded. Ironically a successful synthetic fuels program, one that could moderate price increases, could slow down the commercialization of synthetic fuels.

The second benefit of the synthetic fuels program would accrue if oil prices were suddenly to accelerate because of some unpredictable political disruption of oil production or exports, for the United States would have in place considerable productive capacity. Under such circumstances a sudden price increase in the world oil market would act as a tripwire accelerating the commercialization of synfuels plants previously subsidized by the U.S. government. Thus, the synthetic fuels program could provide significant economic benefits under both turbulent and relatively calm market conditions.

While considering the merits of synthetic fuels development, the federal government should recognize that other energy security measures the nation can undertake could be as effective as synthetic fuels without posing the same level of financial risk. For example a crash program to upgrade refineries by means of known technologies and reliable cost estimates could help to cut oil imports sharply and also increase the flexibility of companies to compensate for shortages of certain types of crude oil. Similarly a crash program to develop an electric automobile within the next ten years could sharply cut motor fuel use and thus lower oil imports. Synfuels development is only one among several viable strategies for increasing the security of the fuel supply available to the United States and influencing the world oil market.

The federal government should use the SFC to help fund a broader range of projects that could help to lower American oil or gas imports. The legislation calls for new fuel production by means of "chemical or physical transformation" of coal, shale, and petroleum, but it specifically excludes coking and desulfurization. Yet these conventional refining techniques can help refiners get the most from each barrel of oil. If each refinery were equipped to upgrade heavy oil or high-sulfur residual oil, refiners could do without much of the oil they currently import from Africa and the Middle East. By providing loans for refinery upgrading, the SFC would not only help to reduce oil imports but would see a guaranteed return on its investment.

A second important reason for broadening the scope of the SFC is that the private sector can bring certain synfuels technologies to commercialization without government subsidies. Before passage of the Energy Security Act, several industry estimates suggested that the United States could produce 100–300 mbdoe of liquids from coal, 300–800 mbdoe of gas from coal, and 400–600 mbdoe of oil from shale by 1990.[5] These forecasts assumed that techniques currently under development could comply with present environmental regulations and compete with conventional fuels with or without government financial support. Most analysts suggested that liquid fuel from coal or oil shale would become commercially viable when oil prices reach $30–50 a barrel and gas from coal when oil prices reach $30–40 a barrel (1980 dollars).[6] Thus under current market conditions, when oil is roughly $32–41 a barrel, gas from coal is close to commercialization whereas shale oil and some coal liquefaction processes appear to be just out of reach.

Even if a project receives federal funding, there is no guarantee that these new technologies will succeed in the demonstration phase of development. The success of every new technology depends on circumstances largely beyond the control of lending institutions: construction costs, the availability and price of other resources needed for synfuel processes, technological innovations, and the ability to operate within the limits posed by environmental, safety, or zoning regulations. Thus to maximize the effectiveness of the SFC Congress should liberalize the terms of the legislation to allow funding of some refining projects.

THE SECURITY BENEFITS OF IMPROVED REFINING TECHNOLOGY

To cope with the risk of sudden shortages and the long-term depletion of desirable types of crude oil, refiners need to upgrade their facilities to handle a wide variety of heavy, sulfurous oils. Many refineries currently lack desulfurization equipment or sophisticated catalytic cracking units that could help convert heavy oil into useful light fuels. Certain coking processes can also upgrade approximately 85 percent of a barrel of residual oil into light products.

The use of refinery technology provides a partial solution to the problem of vulnerability to oil supply disruptions. Currently the United States produces about 1.4 mmbd of residual oil and imports 750,000 barrels per day of fuel oil from Caribbean refineries or Venezuela. As noted in Chapter 2, utilities and industries use this heavy oil as boiler fuel, but as they shift to other forms of energy, this heavy fuel oil could become a feedstock for processing the light oil products that are most in demand: motor fuels, heating oil, and chemical feedstocks. With this capability the United States could substitute at least 1.5 mmbd of domestic residual fuel for an equivalent amount of oil imported from unstable countries in the Middle East or Africa. Furthermore the same processes could be used to improve the quality of heavy high-sulfur petroleum from Venezuela and other western hemisphere sources. Thus the United States could shift its reliance on oil imports away from the eastern hemisphere to more reliable exporters closer to home.

According to the *Oil and Gas Journal* oil companies are already planning to install 650,000 barrels per day of capacity for upgrading heavy oils by means of coking or new catalytic conversion methods.[7] Most of these projects are being undertaken by major oil companies with refineries in the Texas Gulf Coast. Smaller, independent companies across the country also need to upgrade facilities. Considerable financial difficulties could keep these refiners from making the substantial capital investment in new upgrading equipment.

Three major issues need to be addressed in developing a loan policy for refineries: the problem of excess capacity, the effect of foreign refining competition, and the effect of regulatory constraints. American oil companies already have installed distillation capacity of 17.79 mmbd in the United States but in 1980 processed on average only 13.5 mmbd of crude oil. Thus roughly 24 percent of total capacity is idle. The task that faces oil companies is not to build new, highly sophisticated refineries but to improve the flexibility of existing refineries.

To some extent small, relatively primitive teakettle refineries account for the idle excess distillation capacity. Such plants consist of a distillation tower that turns out a considerable amount of heavy oil and coke but very little useful light fuel. Most came into existence to take advantage of the financial benefits accorded the small refiner under the old crude oil entitlement system; with full decontrol many will go out of business. Large independent refineries, however, would be economically viable after decontrol but may lack the necessary resources to upgrade their equipment. These are the companies that should be able to apply to the SFC for loans to enhance their processing flexibility.

Local zoning, environmental, and building permit regulations could deter many refiners from installing sophisticated new equipment that might bring increased pollution and pollution control costs. Indeed similar dilemmas face nearly all energy projects in the United States. The burgeoning expense of installing appropriate controls and of legal fees to obtain construction permits and other forms of regulatory compliance could deter many companies from attempting to enhance refinery operations in certain parts of the country. The impact of these domestic constraints could be that domestic refiners will be unable to compete with refineries in the Caribbean that already have considerable desulfurization and catalytic cracking capacity as well as less stringent environmental controls. Under such circumstances light product imports from the Caribbean could increase because of a decline in domestic refining capability and despite a slight drop in overall petroleum demand.

U.S. policy needs to recognize the advantages of upgrading refineries and incorporating their improvement into an overall short-term strategy for energy security. With these considerations in mind, Congress should revise the Energy Security Act so that the SFC can fund suitable refinery projects. Refined oil is after all a synthetic fuel, a chemical transformation of hydrocarbons. By providing loans for upgrading the bottom of the barrel, the SFC could go far to reducing dependence on foreign oil.

THE ELECTRIC OPTION

Electricity should play a major part in reducing U.S. oil imports over the next decade or two. First, other sources of power must gradually replace the 1.3 mmbd of residual oil that utilities currently burn to generate electricity. Second, electrical power and heating equipment as well as motor vehicles could replace conventional oil- or gas-powered machinery in most sectors of the economy. Thus in the long range electricity could hold the key to U.S. energy independence.

Forecasts of future growth in electricity demand and the types of electric generating capacity needed to meet it vary substantially not only because of uncertainty over potential economic growth but also because of specific financial and regulatory difficulties that affect the use of certain sources of power—atomic energy, coal, and renewable resources. Currently coal is used to generate roughly one-half of U.S. electricity; nuclear power provides roughly 10 percent. Oil and natural gas together provide 30 percent and renewable resources—hydropower and geothermal energy—account for roughly 13 percent. Various forecasts of electricity demand by fuel type for 1990 are given in Table 3-1. As the table shows, several analysts project an increase rather than a decrease in utility oil consumption over the next eight to ten years. Furthermore estimates on the growth of nuclear power vary widely, anywhere from a threefold to fivefold increase in power generation. The consensus on increased use of coal for electric power suggests that the obstacles to increasing coal-fired electric capacity may be considerably less than for other sources of power; however, this will not necessarily be the case given the very real environmental problems surrounding enhanced coal utilization.

Although electricity cannot currently replace oil in the transportation sector or in many industrial applications, the construction and use of new electric power plants is crucial to the task of preventing an increase in oil consumption and ensuring adequate power supply over the next decade. The National Electric Reliability Council (NERC) estimates that by 1985 utilities could burn an additional 697,400 barrels of oil per day compensating for delays in the start-up of nuclear power plants that are already completed.[8] DOE estimates that a moratorium on the use of all nuclear power plants would double oil consumption by utilities.[9] At least 30,000 barrels of oil per day would be needed to replace a 1,000-megawatt nuclear power plant. Furthermore the price of electricity would increase 25 percent if electric companies that had planned to use nuclear power were forced instead to use oil.[10] Finally, the Electric Power Research Institute (EPRI) estimates that the cost of short-term electricity outages could be $2-3 per kilowatt hour (kWh) contrasted to the market rate of $0.05 per kWh.[11]

Because of these significant economic consequences, the federal government while moving vigorously forward with a long-term nuclear waste program must act to preserve the viability of nuclear power and

Table 3-1. Forecasts of Electricity Generation by Type of Fuel for 1990, Billion Kilowatt-Hours.

Fuel Type	1978 Actual	Projections					
		1978 Annual Report C-High[a]	1979 Annual Report Middle[a]	1980 Annual Report Middle[a]	EPRI[b]	DRI[c]	EEI/NERC[d]
Fossil fuels							
Oil	365	43	122	152	300[e]	198	447
Natural gas	305	54	247	33		203	120
Coal	976	2,407	1,786	1,822[f]	1,900	1,742	1,727
Subtotal	1,646	2,504	2,155	2,007	2,200	2,143	2,294
Nuclear	276	829	709	705	1,240	684	959
Hydroelectric	280	314	325	302	450	310	265
New technologies	3	34	41	100	NA	13	25
Total generation	2,206	3,681	3,233	3,118[g]	3,890[g]	3,150	3,543

Sources:

[a]U.S. Department of Energy, Annual Report of the Energy Information Administration, 1980, Volume III: Forecasts (Washington, D.C.: Government Printing Office, 1981), p. 110

[b]Electric Power Research Institute. Overview and Strategy. July 1979. pp. 11-32.

[c]Data Resources Inc., Energy Review, Autumn 1980.

[d]National Electric Reliability Council, 1979 Summary of Projected Peak Load, Generating Capability, and Fossil Fuel Requirements for the Regional Reliability Councils of NERC, July 1979, pp. 28-31, projections for 1988.

[e]Includes oil and natural gas generation.

[f]Includes generation from coal and oil mixtures.

[g]Includes interregional transmission losses and Canadian imports not allocated by fuel.

ease the constraints on installing all new electric generating capacity. The top priority should be to shorten the regulatory process by which utilities win approval to build and operate a plant.

In formulating a long-range policy on electric power, the United States government must recognize the considerable trade-offs that exist among the various electric power resources. Although nuclear power does not pollute the air with sulfur, dust, or nitrogen oxides, spent fuel poses the potential risk of radiation contamination. Although coal combustion creates major environmental problems— sulfur pollution, acid rain, and other forms of air or water pollution— in many parts of the country coal is also the least expensive and most secure source of fuel. Renewable resources are environmentally the most acceptable but because of institutional, legal, and technological constraints are still in the experimental stage of development and may not prove economical for years to come. Finally, natural gas is the cleanest and for some utilities the most economical fuel at this time. As the price of gas rises to a level equal to or perhaps greater than oil, however, most electric utilities may use more natural gas if allowed but will be unable to afford an entirely gas-fired system. Hence at this time coal and nuclear power seem the most likely future sources of electricity, and the U.S. government must do what it can to ensure that new coal and nuclear power plants are constructed in time to meet future demands. In making its assessment, the government should also assess the role that accelerated conservation may play in reducing the demand for these new facilities.

THE LICENSING PROCESS FOR NUCLEAR POWER PLANTS

Permission to construct a nuclear power plant must be obtained from some twelve agencies, but it is the Nuclear Regulatory Commission (NRC) that plays the dominant role in licensing. An applicant must obtain a construction permit to start work on a power plant and, about two to three years before the plant is to be completed, must apply for an operating license.

To receive a construction permit the company goes first to the NRC. Then the Atomic Safety and Licensing Board (ASLB) receives any appeals or petitions concerning the application. The NRC next reviews the safety aspects of the proposed power plant and examines the suitability of the site on which the plant is to be built. In the course of this evaluation NRC must also assess the overall environmental effects of the plant and determine the need for electric power and generating alternatives in the area. All of these criteria affect the decision to grant a construction license.

Once the plant is close to completion, from five to six years later, the company and government agencies must repeat the process in order to issue an operating permit. Frequently this process takes as long as seven months while the NRC prepares another environmental impact statement and another safety evaluation report and receives further petitions or appeals at public hearings upon request. If and when the firm finally receives permission to operate, it loads the fuel core into the reactor and is ready to start up commercial service.

During the course of the plant's life the NRC issues amendments to the operating license when the company must make routine changes in the plant's functions such as refueling. Until 1980 the NRC was not required to hold hearings or issue prior notice to issue an amendment as long as it had "no significant hazards consideration." However, the court decision in the case *Sholly vs. The U.S. Nuclear Regulatory Commission* (November 19, 1980) would require the NRC to hold a hearing prior to issuing a license amendment whenever an interested party asks for one, whether or not the NRC determines that the amendment involves significant hazards considerations.

If this decision became a permanent part of the permit process, it could complicate an already lengthy and cumbersome regulatory review of nuclear power operations. The change in legal procedure would allow legal obstruction of nuclear power generation by people opposed to nuclear power since anyone could request a hearing even though it had little or nothing to do with the safety aspects of the plant. As one authority notes, the decision could result in:

> lengthy and costly hearings precipitated by a simple request and having the potential for shutting down many of the nuclear power reactors now operating in this country. These shutdowns could easily last for nine months or more. The economic impact of these shutdowns on utilities and their customers would be dramatic—typical costs for replacing the power generated by a nuclear plant range between $250,000 and $500,000 a day. Over nine months, this would amount to $67.5 to $135 million.[12]

The Supreme Court will decide whether to uphold or overrule decision, but in any event the *Sholly* case demonstrates the degree to lack of political consensus in the United States about the degree to which this energy source should be utilized.

The *Sholly* arose in the wake of the accident at Three Mile Island (TMI) near Harrisburg, Pennsylvania, when General Public Utilities (GPU) needed to release krypton gas pent up inside the reactor. GPU had to apply to the NRC for a licensing amendment to do this. Before the NRC allowed GPU to vent the gas, which is not considered a hazardous substance but requires considerable examination, it held numerous public meetings, consulted six federal agencies on the health hazards of the action, received some 800 written comments and released for public record an environmental assessment. In short, there was extensive public participation in the decision without an actual hearing before the NRC. Furthermore, the amendment could have been reversed by a court injunction, which in the case of TMI was not granted. As the legal system itself creates more opportunities for intervention in the routine operation of plants, nuclear power generation will be interrupted more frequently, regardless of the plant's efficiency or safety.

If the Supreme Court upholds the *Sholly* decision, further legislation will be necessary to counteract the effects of the ruling. The NRC has already prepared a proposal to tighten the language contained in laws governing its activities to ensure that it can issue license amendments regardless of a pending request for a hearing. Such a change would allow hearings after issuance of an amendment but would not allow a pending request to hold up the procedure.

The *Sholly* decision is one example of the vast legal and regulatory constraints that are likely to hamper the future development of nuclear power. Although minor legislation may be able to straighten one kink in the network of rules, it will do little to streamline the extensive procedures involved in building and operating these plants. A far more extensive congressional review of the procedures is required if nuclear power generation is to be accelerated in the United States.

Federal regulatory reform should aim to lessen the opportunities for interference in the construction and operation of nuclear power plants once utilities have received permission to break ground for a new facility. The strategy should be to encourage public participation in the preconstruction phase through hearings, appeals, and petitions. If the NRC and the community rule that a nuclear power plant should not be built, then in the long run all parties concerned would have saved time and money. However, once the community and the

NRC decide in favor of a nuclear power plant, the procedure for obtaining an operating license as well as amendments to that license should be streamlined to reduce the opportunities for further regulatory intervention. Although the NRC should invite public comments on the environmental or economic impacts of the plant, it should not be required to hold public hearings on request before issuing an operating license. Once the license is issued, any party can bring actions against the project through conventional legal channels.

The NRC is a technical reviewing body, not a court. It does not need to duplicate legal services offered to plaintiffs by the legal system. The executive branch cannot and should not seek to obstruct the judicial channels through which complaints against the nuclear industry flow, but it does not need to create extra instruments for those actions. Above all, the NRC and the courts need to declare clear winners and clear losers in the political debate over the establishment of nuclear power plants. It would be far more economical for all parties if a project were entirely overruled before it breaks ground than halted because of public objections once substantial investment has been made in it.

SPENT NUCLEAR FUEL

The problem of accumulation of spent nuclear fuel demands urgent attention because space in present spent-fuel storage pools at reactor sites is inadequate for long-term needs. If methods for disposal are not tested and implemented immediately, storage facilities are likely to reach maximum capacity after 1983 (at present rates of production) and reactors will have to be shut down.

Because of President Carter's concern that nuclear waste might be diverted clandestinely and the plutonium extracted and made into nuclear weapons, the Carter administration ceased the Waste Isolation Pilot Plant project whereby waste would be packaged and then placed in salt caverns beneath the ground surface in New Mexico. President Carter's action stirred a great deal of controversy because $90 million had already been invested in the project. In its place the administration substituted an alternative plan to evaluate the long-term storage possibilities of salt domes in Mississippi, Louisiana, and Texas as well as basalt and granite formations in Texas, New Mexico, Nevada, Utah, and Washington.[13] These locations are to be identified and tested by 1985 for use in 1995. Since there are no central repositories for storage of used fuel rods from commercial reactors before that time, the administration also planned to have at least one central "away from the reactor" (AFR) site prepared by 1983. To date, the Reagan administration has not yet put forward a plan for nuclear waste storage.

In contrast to congressional desires for an immediate or permanent storage site, the Carter administration opted for time to collaborate with state government and experiment. With these purposes in mind, President Carter appointed a state planning council to advise him on matters of nuclear waste transportation and disposal. So far, however, no state has expressed willingness to serve as a major repository for nuclear wastes. Without an acceptable solution to this problem, Congress could muster enough strength to impose a ban on construction if storage measures are not enacted by 1985. It would not be in the security interest of the United States to allow this to happen. The Reagan administration must resolve this delicate technical and political problem. It may become necessary to exercise federal preemptive rights against the states if state governments continue policies that could hinder the future use of nuclear electricity.

Some of the difficulties of spent fuel disposal could be mitigated by reversing the Carter administration's decision to prohibit commercial reprocessing of spent fuel that arose as a result of fears of global nuclear weapons proliferation. However, as long as there is slackening demand for electric power in general and nuclear power in particular, there is no urgency to develop a capacity to reprocess spent fuel. It is unlikely that a shortage of uranium could develop in the short term under such circumstances. Nevertheless, in the long term as both Europe and other oil import dependent nations shift from oil to nuclear power, demand for uranium could increase. Therefore the United States should be developing a capacity to reprocess nuclear fuel. Foreclosing this option would be impolitic especially if the United States develops a firm commitment to fostering the use of electric power worldwide.

ENVIRONMENTAL REGULATION

The production and consumption of energy in all its forms affects the environment. Coal mining disturbs land formations and can contaminate local streams with trace metals and acids. Coal combustion releases sulfur dioxide (SO_2), nitrogen oxide (NO_x), and grit (particulates into the atmosphere in quantities large enough to impair the health of the community. Nuclear power emits radiation and creates radioactive waste in the form of spent fuel. Finally, the use of oil and natural gas can pollute the air with carbon monoxide, sulfur oxides, particulates, and other chemicals. Table 3–2 summarizes the environmental impact of these fuels.

Over the past twenty years, the United States has enacted a series of laws to prevent or eliminate damage to the environment. For nearly every major pollutant (SO_2, NO_x, CO, and particulates) there is an emissions standard and regulations to ensure compliance. These rules have had a considerable economic and legal impact on the energy market. Large energy projects involve lengthy procedures for obtaining construction permits as well as continuous monitoring during operations. An electric utility must allow twelve to fourteen years from start to finish for a new nuclear power plant and at least seven years for a coal-fire generator. Companies can spend three to five years obtaining various permits for synfuels projects or oil shale plants. Examples abound of delayed or denied energy projects.

Compliance with environmental rules imposes considerable costs on both government and industry. In a recent report DOE notes that "pollution control has increased energy prices and restricted the production and use of some fuels (e.g., high sulfur coals) and that the fuels with the greatest environmental problems associated with their production and use (coal and oil) bear the major brunt of the restrictions."[14] Government could spend as much as 71.7 billion dollars annually (in 1977 dollars) administering pollution control standards 1977–1986.[15] The National Commission on Air Quality (NCAQ) notes that pollution controls could cost companies as much as $37 billion in 1987 (in 1978 dollars) compared to $11–17 billion in 1978, which represented approximately 2.4 percent of total capital expenditures for all industries.[16] Specifically, NCAQ estimates that a new coal-fired industrial boiler "could require as much as six times the pollution control capital costs as those necessary to control a comparable oil-fired boiler to similar control levels."[17] However, the annualized total costs of burning coal are bound to be less than half those of burning oil twenty years from now if oil prices prove to be three times greater than those for coal measured in terms of heat content.[18] Thus even though coal proves to be the least expensive fossil

Table 3-2.   Principal Pollutants from the Various Fuels.

Fuel	Air	Water	Land
Natural Gas	Sulfur oxides Particulates Nitrogen oxides Carbon monoxide Hydrocarbons Flared gases	Production liquids	Drilling muds
Nuclear	Radiation	Radiation Suspended solids Iron Manganese Acidity Nickel Zinc	Mining slag Milling slag
Hydroelectric		Silt	Inundation of pond area

Oil	Particulates
	Sulfur oxides
	Nitrogen oxides
	Carbon monoxide
	Hydrocarbons
	Flared gases
		Production liquids
		Refinery waste
		Water
		Refinery-generated toxic
		  and hazardous
		  substances
			Drilling muds
			Refinery-generated toxic
			  and hazardous
			  substances

Coal	Particulates Sulfur oxides Nitrogen oxides Carbon monoxide Organics	Waste waters Suspended solids Iron Maganese Nickel Zinc	Mining slag Cleaning and preparation plant slag Fly and bottom ash Scrubber sludge

Source: DOE/EPA *Energy/Environment Fact Book.*

fuel, it will still require considerable expenditures on pollution controls to use coal in the future.

The United States has made a major commitment to preserving the quality of the environment, which it need not abandon in order to develop its enormous coal and shale resources. However, the experience has shown that the United States cannot expect to have adequate industrial or energy development without some discharges of pollutants into the atmosphere. While applying the best available technology for controlling effluents the United States must also adopt a new approach to both environmental and financial regulation of energy intensive industries such as electric utilities. On the one hand, environmental regulations must reflect recognition of the economic costs of controls; on the other, government regulation of electric utility rate structures and tax policies should seek to alleviate the financial burdens borne by power companies for installing pollution control equipment and constructing new plants.

ENVIRONMENTAL REFORMS

The policy recommendations of the National Commission on Air Quality published in March 1981 should be followed. Although economic considerations should not overrule the enforcement of pollution standards, the approach to air pollution control should be based on economic incentives, not direct regulation and monitoring of each pollution source. For example, it may be possible to devise a tax or fee commensurate with different levels of pollution. It is already possible for companies to strike deals among themselves whereby one receives some credit or direct payment for reducing emissions to allow another company to increase temporarily its emissions of a certain chemical. Through this "bubble policy" single large industries or groups of several small companies have been able to develop their own plans for controlling pollution collectively by offsetting emissions in one area or taking turns reducing emissions of each major pollutant (sulfur compounds, nitrogen compounds, ash, and particulates). One hundred bubbles nationwide are in the process of being approved by the Environmental Protection Agency (EPA); ten have already been approved. By the end of 1981 $200 million is expected to be saved through this innovative approach initiated by the EPA during the Carter administration.

In line with this economic approach to environmental regulation NCAQ also recommends reform of rules on the prevention of significant deterioration (PSD) in areas whose air quality already exceeds national standards for common air pollutants. NCAQ states that these PSD standards should apply to wilderness areas and national parks but should be reformed to allow some level of industrial and energy development in other areas. Similarly regulation of increased air pollution in nonattainment areas (those whose air quality is worse than national averages) would also require modification. In these areas, notably regions in which heavy industrialization has already occurred, it would be useful to allow companies to come up with their own offset strategies and apply the bubble policy approach so that new companies have a chance to locate in these areas. Such regulatory changes could facilitate the greater use of coal as well as synthetic fuel processing in parts of the country that were previously off-limits because of complex and conflicting pollution control rules.

FINANCIAL REGULATIONS

Utilities currently face formidable financial difficulties not only because of the costs of environmental compliance but also because of mounting construction and operating costs. This is especially true of utilities that are shifting to coal. Handling, transportation, and additional manpower costs can complicate the operation of electric power plants that run on coal. Frequently, however, state public utility commissions (PUCs) do not recognize the short-term economic difficulties of power companies when they calculate the consumer rates. Most PUCs allow companies to factor in the costs of pollution controls, but many do not allow the utility to pass on to the consumer full construction costs. Nor do they provide an inflation factor in calculating the rate of return allowable to a utility. For example the average rate of return allowed to utilities is 14.3 percent, but the actual return has been closer to 11 percent because of inflation.

The Federal Energy Regulatory Commission (FERC) should take the lead in providing standard guidelines for establishing rates of return and calculating the rate base to be adopted by state public utility commissions. FERC should first require state commissions to allow companies to pass on the full costs of current construction to the consumer. Rapid depreciation of these capital expenditures should also be considered. To ensure timely alterations in the rate base (individual rate case reviews can drag on for years) FERC should propose some time limit for rate reviews by the PUC. If the PUC does not act within a year the rate change applied for should automatically go into effect without any penalty to the utility. Finally research and development costs should be allowed in the rate base to help companies shoulder the costs of research that may not have an immediate pay-off. This is particularly important in an era when federal funding for research and development is being cut back.

CONCLUSIONS

The federal government has an important role to play in enhancing the security of the nation's fuel supply. Through a successful demonstration of synthetic fuel production, the United States could help to stabilize oil prices in the world market. Although the Synthetic Fuels Corporation will help to establish synfuel capability, economic forces will also bring these fuels to market. Thus some SFC loans should be made to certain refineries for installing the sophisticated equipment required for processing heavy or high-sulfur petroleum, including residual oil. These proven techniques could be used to replace 1.5 mmbd of imported fuel with domestically produced fuel oil or heavy oil that has been upgraded into light products.

In the long term, the United States must move toward greater use of electricity to replace oil and gas in every sector of the economy. The role of government is particularly important in cutting through much of the red tape that currently weakens the ability of electric utilities to construct and operate power plants. The licensing process for nuclear power must be reformed to reduce opportunities for obstruction of operations and to ensure that once a plant is constructed it can be operated. To facilitate the greater use of coal, the federal government should move toward a cost-effective approach to environmental regulation. Through offsets and more widely applied bubble policies, the EPA and private companies could work out new strategies for preserving air quality in the general region without excessive monitoring of each and every pollution source.

Finally the federal government may need to intervene in state and local regulation of utilities to ensure that the rate base reflects current economic conditions. FERC needs to provide guidelines on costs that can be included in the rate base—such as current construction costs, research and development expenditures, and pollution controls—and guidelines for setting a fair rate of return. Presently, rate structures vary considerably from state to state, leaving some utilities in worse financial straits than others. To ensure that the entire nation has adequate power supplies in the future, federal and state agencies must cooperate now to improve the economic stability of the electric power industry.

NOTES

1. Public Law 96-294, June 30, 1980, 96th Congress, 94 Stat. 616.
2. Ibid.
3. Ibid., 94 Stat. 631.
4. Ibid., 94 Stat. 616.
5. The American Petroleum Institute, *Two Energy Futures* Washington, D.C., 1980, p. 96-98.
6. Ibid., p. 105.
7. *The Oil and Gas Journal* 79 no. 7 (January 5, 1981): 44.
8. U.S. Department of Energy (DOE)/The Economic Regulatory Administration (ERA), *Electric Power Supply and Demand for the Contiguous United States 1980-1989,* DOE/RG-0036, June 1980, p. VII.23.
9. DOE/ERA, *Energy Programs/Energy Markets, Technical Papers,* July 1980, p. 142.
10. Ibid.
11. "Synthetic Fuels: Meeting the Costs of Environmental Protection," *EPRI Journal* (April 1981): 21.
12. Jay E. Silberg, *Testimony before the Subcommittee on Nuclear Regulation of the Senate Committee on Environment and Public Works,* March 25, 1981, p. 3.
13. David Burham, "Carter Urges Drive to Perfect Storage of Nuclear Wastes," *The New York Times,* February 13, 1980.
14. DOE/ERA, *Government Actions Affecting the Environment and Their Effects on Energy Markets,* August 1980, p. 43.
15. Ibid., p. 40.
16. *To Breathe Clean Air, Report of the National Commission on Air Quality* Washington, D.C., March 1981, p. 4.1-4.
17. Ibid., p. 2.1-89.
18. Ibid.

4 PLANNING FOR AN ENERGY EMERGENCY: LONG-TERM MEASURES

Contingency planning to date has taken a backseat to other issues in the development of national energy policy, even after the 1973-74 oil embargo. This should not be. In large measure, current economic difficulties are the result of higher oil prices caused by only moderate shortfalls in oil supplies. A large disruption would cause almost incalculable problems, but the likelihood of such a disruption is real. At the start of the 1970s energy analysts looking into the future predicted an excellent outlook for oil supplies. No one foresaw the 1973 embargo or the 1979 collapse of Iran or the 1980 war between Iran and Iraq. In 1981 people are predicting that the next four years will see excellent supplies of energy *if no unforeseen events occur.* If the past is any guide to the future, "unforeseen" events will occur, and the United States is ill-prepared to deal with them.

The United States has experienced seven energy emergencies in recent years: the 1965 New England power outage, fuel and propane shortages in 1972, the 1973-74 oil embargo, national coal strikes in 1974 and 1977-78, the natural gas shortage in the winter of 1976-77, the Iranian production curtailment in 1978-79, and the war between Iran and Iraq in 1980-81. In addition, world oil supplies have been affected by two blockades of the Suez Canal, the bombing of an Iraqi pipeline, a fire in a Saudi oil field, and the destruction (by a plow) of part of the Trans-Arabian pipeline. Despite these events the federal government under both Republican and Democratic administrations, has yet to develop an effective policy for coping with a sudden energy cutoff. Programs that have been implemented more often than not have worsened crises.

The gasoline rationing plan used during World War II is often cited as a possible response to any future energy emergency. One U.S. contingency plan—now shelved—included a coupon-based rationing system inspired by the World War II experience. But government officials planning energy policy today operate in a totally different atmosphere from their World War II counterparts: They do not have the same clear-cut support of the public or top administrators, they are not free to operate in secrecy, they face a more diffuse threat than the Nazi war machine, and they have to work out energy problems in the context of international obligations and a complex set of environmental and other regulations that did not exist during the Second World War. They do not agree about how serious a disruption might be, let alone how to respond to it, and how much to spend gambling on a crisis, or how to coordinate domestic and international planning.

And they work with the knowledge that inappropriate policy responses may worsen the effects of a disruption. The 1974 oil embargo, for example, may have affected the New England and Mid-Atlantic states more than others because of the logistical snafus caused by the Federal Energy Office's crude allocation plan.

On the other hand, the energy disruptions experienced in the last few years have taught the United States some valuable lessons. For example Iranian oil production dropped from 5.5 mmbd in October 1978 to 3.5 mmbd in November. By January 1979 Iran was producing only 445,000 bd, and all exports had been suspended. Panic was almost instant despite the fact that total non-Communist production fell by only 2.2 mmbd between December 1978 and January 1979 (it was actually increased at the peak of the crisis).[1] Iran provided only 9 percent of total U.S. oil imports in 1978, but the disruption still had a major impact on the U.S. economy. By May the supply shortage produced queues at gasoline stations and panic buying in California, a state particularly dependent on cars for transportation. Yet the gasoline shortage from May to July in 1979 has been estimated at only 7 to 10 percent of actual supply.[2]

Assessing the relative importance of any of the factors that contributed to the 1979 oil shortage is difficult, but their cumulative impact was apparent. Uncertainty and panic were augmented, not reduced, by government intervention. Measures to ensure equitable distribution of oil supplies failed miserably because the government failed to predict how consumers in different parts of the country would behave during a shortfall. Government efforts to dampen price increases also failed; at best, government action only delayed the inevitable. And finally, the shortfall was caused mainly by events in the international oil market over which the government had little influence. The margin for government response was minimal.

The shortage of 1979 and the 1973–74 oil embargo taught the United States several other things as well. Those crises showed that if the market system is allowed to react freely, the economic effects of a shortage will tend to be felt sooner rather than later (until the market corrects itself). Meanwhile, attempts to regulate supply and demand early in a crisis are apt to aggravate economic dislocation, not mitigate it. Moreover, a disruption may be caused by something as definite as political turmoil in a producer country or a political decision to reduce exports, but it may also be caused by international panic in anticipation of something happening. Whatever causes the disruption, normally there would be several months' delay before a disruption of energy supplies caused a substantial imbalance in the economy. This period could be shortened considerably if panic occurred, whether because of real, immediate shortages or because of scare headlines or reports. No government policy is effective in a panic situation, so the first step in meeting a crisis must be to reduce both domestic and international panic. When panic has been allayed, policies aimed at reducing energy use or encouraging fuel switching seem to be the most effective way of meeting a shortage. Attempts to allocate supplies seem to worsen the situation, and increasing domestic production takes too long to be effective in an emergency. Finally, disruptions are open-ended. It is not always clear when they begin, and it is certainly not clear when they end: the world is still reverberating from the 1973–74 oil embargo.

The lessons learned from the energy disruptions of the 1970s helped the United States keep problems in the world oil market to a minimum when the war between Iran and Iraq broke out in 1980. Despite the substantial decrease in oil exports from Iran and Iraq and the real possibility that the war might overflow into other major oil-producing countries, panic and supply shortages were avoided. Governments of the industrial countries, backed by the knowledge that oil inventories were at an all-time high, moved quickly to assure their citizens that a problem did not exist (even though it did). It helped that energy consumption had significantly decreased because of a recession and continued energy conservation efforts, but the West did seem to be learning how to respond to an oil crisis.

Even so the world has yet to face a cutoff of 20 percent or more in oil supplies. The United States does not have a clear idea how it would respond to such a situation; energy planners are not even sure what constitutes a threat to oil security. President Reagan's program to achieve economic stability involves emasculating the U.S. Department of Energy (DOE), the most logical base for developing a response to threats to national energy security. Yet several independent studies have concluded that failure to develop an energy emergency planning program could ultimately lower the gross national product by billions of dollars and cause large increases in unemployment and inflation.

The dependence of the United States on oil imports has long been considered the cause of its energy dilemma. The Joint Economic Committee of Congress concluded in a 1980 study that until 1990 and probably until 2000 the United States will be "too reliant upon insecure foreign energy sources." And energy independence is impossible. The committee believes that even if U.S. domestic energy production increases 24 percent by 1990 and oil imports remain at the 1979 level, there will still be a national security problem.[3] The issue is not whether the United States can reduce its level of imports per se but how it can reduce its vulnerability to the *effects* of a disruption. Our dilemma is not our dependence on imports but our failure to develop a coherent energy policy, especially for energy emergency planning.

In a sense contingency planning is a hedge against disaster, a form of national insurance on the energy future, but emergency planning need not preclude prudent domestic energy policy. It is useful to distinguish between short-term and long-term plans, but contingency planning, which assumes the possibility if not the likelihood of a major disruption in the next ten years, requires a long-term outlook and willingness to commit funds—just as long-term planning, which can be viewed as the nation's contingency plan for five, ten, or fifteen years from now, should be flexible enough to accommodate any short-term crises.

By its nature contingency planning must be flexible and open-ended. No one can be sure if one or more or no disruptions will occur, how long they will last, or how severe they will be. Nor can anyone be sure if a particular contingency plan will work. On the other hand, a credible emergency plan may actually deter a disruption by convincing energy producers that nothing can be gained by provoking a disruption.

Various long-term strategies for avoiding the economic effects of a major oil disruption have advantages. Although decontrol of oil and natural gas prices is probably the most important step the government can take toward reducing energy demand, the pros and cons of oil import fees can also be discussed. But oil imports can probably never be eliminated, and import reduction policies alone will not remove the danger of a major disruption of supplies. Other measures include supply diversification, development of surge capacity, and strategic stockpiling, as well as more immediate measures for meeting a serious shortfall (see next chapter).

POLICIES TO REDUCE OIL IMPORTS

Measures to reduce oil imports generally either restrict imports directly through a pricing mechanism or affect price indirectly by restricting supplies. Available measures include taxes on domestic or foreign oil and oil import quotas. Two of the most widely discussed policy options for reducing oil imports are the decontrol of oil and natural gas prices, and oil import fees, both of which are discussed below. The President already has wide legal authority to control oil imports.[4] Yet it has often been difficult to exercise this authority because of widespread public opposition to the higher energy prices that would ensue.

DECONTROL OF OIL AND NATURAL GAS PRICES

President Reagan took a major step toward reducing U.S. dependence on foreign oil imports on January 28, 1981, when he signed Executive Order 12287, removing all remaining controls on the price of crude oil (although controls would have ended anyway on September 30, 1981, as a result of the phased-in decontrol of domestic oil prices approved by President Carter on April 5, 1979). Meanwhile, the

Natural Gas Policy Act (NGPA) of 1979 provides for a phased, but partial, deregulation of natural gas prices by 1985, and there is a good possibility President Reagan will accelerate that process. Decontrol of oil and even partial decontrol of natural gas will provide significant incentives to reduce oil-import demand and increase domestic production.

Decontrol of oil prices will probably not substantially increase domestic oil production. In fact, DOE in a recent "best estimate" foresees U.S. oil production decreasing from 8.5 mmbd in 1979 to 7 mmbd by 1990.[5] Most industry analysts agree that domestic production will continue to decline or will stabilize at present levels. According to one congressional estimate, decontrol may cause a short-term increase in production, providing an additional 200,000 to 405,000 bd between 1982 and 1985,[6] but few oil industry executives are so optimistic. Still, even a small increase in domestic supplies would be important in a disruption.

More important, higher oil prices will provide a powerful incentive to reduce oil consumption. One extremely optimistic analyst goes so far as to suggest that U.S. oil imports could be reduced to zero by the year 2000 if energy were priced at world levels and conservation pursued aggressively.[7] However, higher oil prices carry a cost for the economy as a whole. Price decontrol will increase the share of income spent on oil, reducing expenditure on other goods and increasing inflation. The present costs must be compared to the future costs incurred if the United States does not adjust its economy to the real price of energy. By continuing to disguise this cost by subsidizing energy prices, the government will only encourage inefficient energy use.

One DOE study concluded that failure to implement decontrol for *all* gas sources rather than just *new* gas will result in slower development of U.S. natural gas resources. Partial or full decontrol of all natural gas prices in 1982 could reduce oil imports by 300,000–600,000 bd by 1985. Without full decontrol, only 11,000 bd of oil could be displaced by gas in 1985.[8]

These figures are optimistic. Efforts to accelerate gas production might deplete the reservoirs and concentrate development in easy-access areas, drawing attention away from unconventional gas sources which, in the long run, may provide the most supplies.

However, it is now apparent that in the medium to long term, U.S. gas supplies from both conventional and unconventional sources are more substantial than originally thought. The United States must therefore begin to bring these supplies onstream as soon as possible.

Under decontrol the wellhead price a pipeline company pays to a gas producer will be allowed to rise. The current system of gas pricing permits lower prices for old gas, which is "rolled in" to the overall price of gas. The cheaper gas lowers the average price of gas so more expensive sources, for example imported gas from Canada and Mexico, can be priced competitively with oil. Producers want gas prices to rise to the energy equivalency of oil prices. But at higher prices residual fuel oil may become even more attractive than it already is for industrial and utility boilers. Should the "cheaper" gas be eliminated, little incentive would remain to switch to gas from oil, particularly as the new market for gas is now soft because of significant gas discoveries, relatively higher gas prices, lower residual fuel prices, and economic recession.

Full decontrol of natural gas prices may produce an increase in oil imports of 730,000 bd if the gas market goes slack.[9] In this market, full decontrol could lead U.S. gas consumers to switch to foreign oil, thereby increasing U.S. dependnecy on foreign energy. But this is only a temporary increase. If the domestic natural gas supplies from both conventional and unconventional sources (including coal gasification and biogas) are as plentiful as the American Gas Association and Potential Gas Committee claim, then the development of these supplies will be promoted by a higher price for gas. In the long run immediate decontrol of natural gas prices can only improve the market for gas. Thus, decontrol for natural gas prices should be the policy pursued.

Higher prices will result in some production increases and encourage reduced and more efficient consumption. The economy will pay a price for these benefits, but the benefits outweigh the costs. By disguising the true cost of energy, price controls encourage the use of oil and natural gas and discourage alternatives. Decontrol will increase inflation and transfer substantial wealth from consumers to producers, but under present policy, the government will capture some of this transfer through a crude oil excise tax. Proceeds from this tax, which is to be phased out in 1988 or after $227.7 billion is raised (whichever is later), should be used to encourage domestic energy production, including renewable energy resources, and conservation.

How will higher oil and gas prices now help the nation adjust to an energy disruption later? Apart from encouraging increased domestic production and more efficient use of energy, decontrol will force the economy to begin adjusting to higher prices immediately rather than months or years hence, when those prices are sure to be even higher. Decontrol, although it will not solve the nation's energy problems, is the cornerstone for developing a better response to the cost of oil imports. Without decontrol, many other programs—especially conservation—are weakened.

OIL IMPORT FEES

One way to encourage more efficient use of the country's energy resources while weaning it from energy imports is to make imports more expensive than domestic supplies. Typical of this approach are policies advocating oil import fees, quotas, or security premiums. Such policies have never been warmly greeted by the public. In March 1980 President Carter proposed a $4.62 per barrel fee on imported crude oil and a tariff of $0.10 per gallon or $4.20 per barrel on imported gasoline. The gasoline consumer would have paid the full burden of the increases. The public balked at higher prices, and Carter's effort to impose an oil import fee failed.

The oil industry opposed the import fee as a revenue measure to balance the federal budget rather than as an energy measure to reduce demand. The oil companies believed that the fee would distort the gasoline market, squeezing the profit margins of small refiners, enhancing the power of major oil companies, and encouraging some refiners to reduce their gasoline production. Also, restricting price increases to gasoline seemed difficult; some thought the price of oil, especially, would also increase. Congress finally voted down the fee. The wide opposition to the president's authority to restrict oil imports indicates the difficulty in implementing other such measures.

The oil import fee has not died, however. Many energy analysts have discussed the idea of imposing a "security premium" on imported oil.[10] Advocates of the premium believe that decontrol alone will not reduce imports enough. A security premium could be imposed through several devices—among them, quotas, tariffs, and import licenses. In effect it increases the cost of imported oil over domestic, in principle reflecting the higher "security" cost of being dependent on imports. Wealth transferred from consumers to producers or the government could be returned to the consumer through the tax system or as direct rebates.

The idea behind a security premium is to include in the price of oil the additional (and hidden) costs to society of continued dependence on imports. But coming on top of decontrol the security premium presents problems. With decontrol domestic energy prices should rise to the level of world prices; a tariff or quota would bring import prices above world prices, and domestic prices would arise accordingly unless controls were imposed.

A substantial increase in domestic oil prices on top of the rise following decontrol would exacerbate inflation, and the monetary transfer from consumers, even if partially mitigated by tax policy, could contribute to a recession. There is no doubt that our society could benefit from a policy that made imports more costly than domestic supplies, providing an implicit subsidy to the development of both conventional and unconventional resources (including renewables). But such a policy should await more stable economic conditions than those currently prevailing.

More important, import reduction, while helpful, should not be perceived as the main objective of energy planning.[11] Rather than embark on a crash program to reduce oil use as much as possible, the United States should consider a multipronged approach, using diplomatic initiatives to moderate price increases while at the same time pursuing a gradual transition to a different energy mix. Part of that approach should be full decontrol of all oil and natural gas resources.

SUPPLY RESPONSES

Increased energy supplies do not, ipso facto, reduce dependence on oil imports but they may lessen the vulnerability of the United States to the effects of an oil supply disruption. One response to the threat of supply shortages is to diversify *supplies* (a policy discussed in Chapter 2). Other possibilities include diversifying *suppliers,* developing surge capacity, and building up an emergency reserve of stocks—either through a national strategic petroleum reserve or through private reserves.

DIVERSIFYING OIL SUPPLIERS

A major increase in oil production outside the Middle East has occurred since the late 1970s. OPEC's share in free-world output fell from 63.4 percent in 1979 to 59.4 percent in 1980, when output for every OPEC nation but Saudi Arabia declined. In 1980 OPEC produced 26.8 mmbd, an eight-year low, while the rest of the world produced 32.6 mmbd.

The United States should encourage this trend. By diversifying suppliers, the West lessens the potential for any one country or region to jeopardize the world's energy supplies. Production increases should be encouraged not only in the Middle East but in other parts of the developing world. Proven oil and gas reserves in the Middle East and North Africa stand at 552,202 million barrels of oil equivalent. Outside this region, in the rest of the Third World, proven oil and gas reserves are at 146,365 million barrels of oil equivalent.[12] And ultimate recoverable resources will be substantially greater than known reserves. For example Mexico's proven hydrocarbon reserves are placed at 72 billion barrels, but according to some estimates there is at least a possibility that the Mexican resource base is as great as 250 billion barrels.

The Middle Eastern members of OPEC have a current installed capacity of 34 mmbd, well below the 40 mmbd experts predicted for the area by 1985.[13] In Chapter 9 are discussed approaches the U.S. government can take to encourage development of Middle Eastern resources. To diversify sources, however, the United States should probably look toward other parts of the developing world. This would require a change of U.S. policy toward the Third World, including an end to woefully inadequate levels of bilateral and multilateral development assistance. The Europeans have long recognized that there is a quid pro quo for gaining access to raw materials in developing countries, and that is opening up their markets to goods from less-developed countries (LDCs), assisting them with technology transfer and offering other assistance, and helping to stabilize market prices for fluctuating primary product exports. Other countries have taken the lead in energy diversification. The United States has done very little.

What can it do? First, Washington can encourage multilateral development efforts such as the World Bank proposal for an affiliate lending agency for energy development. Not only would such an agency help to develop energy resources all over the world (Gulf Oil has a project in Pakistan established with World Bank aid), but the bank could act as an honest broker between the companies and the consumers, alleviating the developing countries' fears of multinational corporations and alleviating the oil companies' fears of nationalization.

The United States could also provide more bilateral assistance for the development of oil, gas, and other energy resources in developing countries. Through the Arms Control and Disarmament Agency and DOE the United States is already working to provide alternatives to expanding nuclear power as a way of meeting the electrical power needs of developing countries. The Agency for International Development (AID), through its Institute for Scientific and Technological Cooperation, has provided development aid and research assistance for energy projects around the world. All too often bilateral aid is viewed in this country either as a giveaway program or as a tool for bribing Third World states into supporting U.S. foreign policy interests. In fact, technical assistance for energy development provides a market for U.S. goods and services, while aid helps maintain the economic and social stability of states important to U.S. national security. Without energy development, the economic systems of many of these states would collapse, posing potentially catastrophic problems for the international banking system to which they are heavily indebted (as indicated in Chapter 7). Military assistance is not enough: Military assistance can not be eaten.

The U.S. government can also encourage investment in foreign energy development through the Export-Import Bank, which provides loans in support of U.S. exports, and the Overseas Private Investment Corporation, which insures U.S. investments against risk, including the risk of expropriation. The largest loan the Export-Import Bank ever granted was in support of Westinghouse Corporation's sale of a nuclear power plant to the Philippines. In the future, developing countries may become sizable markets for U.S. coal exports and energy technologies, especially technologies to harness renewable energy sources (the sun, wind, and ocean). The federal government needs to aid such ventures rather than drastically reduce foreign assistance.

DEVELOPING SURGE CAPACITY

Just as a policy of world energy development is in the U.S. interest, so is development of a worldwide surge capacity for oil and gas production. A built-in surge capacity permits a nation to increase oil and gas production rapidly from existing or capped wells in the event of a sudden disruption. Since the middle of 1972 nearly all of the U.S. oil-producing fields have been producing at their optimal marginal efficiency rate (MER), the point at which all of the production curves from all of a field's reserves, when aggregated, peak. Some high-quality fields can exceed their MER for up to six months with minimal risk of damaging the reservoirs and thereby reducing ultimate recovery rates. But associated gas flaring would result, and that gas would of course be lost forever.[14] As for gas, DOE estimates that production could increase by over 1 mmbd of oil equivalent and that there is spare capacity of more than 1 mmbd of oil equivalent in existing pipelines. If the United States is to rely on rapidly increasing production from existing wells, however, it has to look beyond the United States to the North Sea, Canada, and the Third World.

Convincing other countries to build in excess capacity will require convincing them to forgo an economic return today so they can capture it tomorrow. Encouraging excess capacity will require long-term initiatives in the diplomatic arena and in some cases direct aid. Above all, it will require an understanding that mutual interests exist. Conceivably, long-term supply contracts, now anathema to most producing countries, could be negotiated, providing supply guarantees above prevailing market prices. Or excess capacity could be developed in return for concessions in other areas, such as markets for LDC goods at lower tariffs, or none. Current capacity is not great and has been decreasing steadily. Although spare capacity in the industrialized nations was 6.2 mmbd in 1960, it has now practically disappeared.

Spare capacity can prevent an oil crisis from occurring. Saudi excess capacity and willingness to use it prevented disaster in the world oil market when Iran and Iraq destroyed each other's export capability. But what if the disaster were in Saudi Arabia? What other country could quickly increase production to cover a Saudi shortfall? The answer is none.

The spare capacity of all current OPEC members is not sufficient to replace a Saudi disruption. It is imperative that such capacity be developed elsewhere in the world. Unfortunately it is unlikely that another Saudi Arabia will be discovered. Hence exploration and development must be encouraged wherever in the world energy resources are indicated. Too long America's energy policy has focused on domestic supplies and the strategic petroleum reserve (SPR) (examined in the next section). The energy crisis is international; our approach to solving it should be international.

STRATEGIC STOCKPILING

The major focus of emergency supply planning in the United States has been the development of a strategic oil reserve program. Strategic stockpiling has long been part of U.S. defense policy; as early as 1912 President William Taft set aside petroleum fields to ensure strategic stocks for the naval fleet (whence the name *naval petroleum reserves*). With the passage in 1975 of the Energy Policy and Conservation Act, Congress authorized the strategic petroleum reserve (pronounced "SPRO," for Strategic Petroleum Reserve Office), establishing for the first time the concept of a petroleum reserve for the civilian economy.

To some extent, the stockpiling of emergency reserves is meant to deter the intentional cutoff for oil supplies to the United States; more important, its purpose is to lessen the shock of a disruption, to maintain the viability of the national economy in the absence of critical oil imports. Unfortunately SPR has run into more than its share of problems, chief among them a recurrent tendency to stop filling it or to fill it at a slower rate. The underlying problem is partly a failure to understand the nation's defense needs: we will spend billions of dollars to develop new weapons systems to protect our interests in the Persian Gulf and Indian Ocean regions, but we hesitate to spend the $3.8 billion required in 1982 to bring SPR up to a capacity that will ensure the continued viability of the civilian and defense sectors in the event of a disruption.

SPR's failure to date cannot be explained away easily. Early problems of mismanagement did not help, but SPR has been handicapped by constraints of many kinds: world oil shortages in 1978, political pressures from Saudi Arabia not to proceed with the fill, and now, at a time when President Reagan is trying to cut the federal budget, an increase in the price of oil because of decontrol. And some problems are intrinsic to the concept of the program. Essentially SPR is the nation's insurance policy against energy insufficiency. As with any major insurance policy, the cost is high, it takes considerable time to build up equity, and you get the best return only in the event of disaster.

This section suggests solutions to some of the problems that have plagued SPR. Problems of cost and control, the two factors most difficult to come to grips with in any discussion of SPR's future, underlie many of the questions that shape the debate about our national energy reserve system: How large should we make the reserve? How fast should we fill it? Where should be put it? Where should we purchase it? How do we finance it? And finally, how do we use it? Before considering each of these questions in turn, it may help to have a little background.

In 1975 Congress directed President Ford to create a reserve "for the storage of up to 1 billion barrels of petroleum products, but not less than 150 million barrels of petroleum products" by the end of 1978. One year later, DOE submitted a plan to Congress for storing 150 million barrels by December 1978 and 500 million barrels by December 1982. In April 1977 President Carter announced a new target of 1 billion barrels by 1985, but less than two years later all SPR procurements were suspended to free supplies for domestic use during world oil shortages. Partly because of political pressure from Saudi Arabia and partly because of import limits agreed to at the Tokyo economic summit meeting in 1979, supply procurement did not resume until 1980, when Congress mandated an average annual fill rate or at least 100,000 bd for fiscal year 1981, with a target of 750 million barrels total. In December 1980 Congress called on the president to "seek to undertake" to fill the SPR at 300,000 bd. In the years 1976–1980, Congress appropriated $6.9 billion for SPR; only one-third of that amount, a little over $2 billion, was spent. By the end of 1981 SPR should contain about 230 million barrels of crude oil, enough to supply U.S. 1980 import needs for about thirty-seven days.

From the start SPR fill targets have been determined more by domestic political considerations than by firm assessments of need and cost. One study concluded that a six-month oil supply would be enough to deter an embargo because producers could not afford to go beyond that period without revenue.[15] Another analyst considers the equivalent of eight to ten months' imports from OPEC to be an optimal target (roughly 750 million to 1.5 billion barrels).[16] With a very large stockpile the United States would come under considerable pressure from its allies to use more of its reserve stocks, thus freeing more oil from the international market for them. And although the key to stockpiling may be "the more the better," sometimes it is impossible to obtain more. The federal government should set a realistic target for SPR—probably 500 million barrels—and try to reach it.

Setting a target is one thing; determining how fast to fill it is another. A high fill rate would send world oil prices skyrocketing in a tight market. Congress has mandated an average annual rate of at least 100,000 bd and would like 300,000 bd. Senator Bill Bradley, a leading proponent of SPR, has advocated a rate of 400,000 to 500,000 bd. DOE's Office of Policy and Evaluation has called for 550,000–600,000 bd. It is technically feasible to fill SPR at a rate of 500,000 bd, but existing storage would be quickly filled and lead times for construction of new storage capacity prevent significant increases in capacity above the 500 million barrel level before 1986 unless storage facilities other than salt caverns are used. Yet these are much more costly than caverns. In the context of current construction plans, a fill rate of 200,000 bd, matching oil to capacity, is optimal. A higher level might be warranted but would require a change in construction plans.

Where are reserves stored? What is commonly known as SPR is actually the early storage reserve (ESR), which consists of several salt caverns located along the Gulf of Mexico in Texas and Louisiana, near three pipeline systems, the Seaway, Texoma, and Capline (see the map, Figure 4-1). Current capacity in the salt caverns is 248 million barrels, slightly less than one-third the 750 million barrel capacity that has been authorized for construction by 1989. (An additional 290 million barrels of capacity is to be built by 1986, the final 212 million barrels by 1989.) The original enabling legislation also called for the development (by no specific date) of a regional storage program of 24 million barrels, to be located in New England, Hawaii, and Puerto Rico. Despite political pressure in favor of these areas, the regional program has not yet been established.

As currently conceived, SPR feeds into the U.S. pipeline system, the hub of America's emergency spare wheel. Can it do the job? One analyst believes that it is inadequate to the task, that if we lose imports faster than we can draw down supplies from SPR, shortages will appear throughout the system. If storage is regionalized, he argues, SPR would appear less like a wheel and more like a spider's web, linking regional refineries and pipelines.[17] However, a regional approach might incur higher cost. The best solution would be to combine the two approaches to provide a rapid-response capability.

Although the present system encountered severe start-up problems, the costs for salt cavern storage are considerably lower than such

Figure 4-1. Location of Strategic Petroleum Reserve Facilities (Salt Cavern Storage)

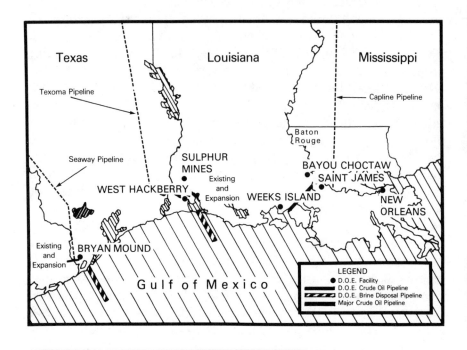

Source: U.S. D.O.E., *Strategic Petroleum Reserve*, Annual Report, February 16, 1980.

readily available alternatives as tankers, mines, and steel tanks, all of which will face some of the same problems. For example, it took the government two years to negotiate with Louisiana the environmental and other permits needed to begin construction. Abandoned underground mines might be an acceptable alternative if they are located near pipelines and refineries, but they often are not. Steel tank storage allows greater geographical flexibility but also costs more; storage capacity for 1 million barrels of oil requires about 3,400 tons of steel and now costs about $14 per barrel. (To give some idea of the magnitude of storage problems: A reserve of 1 million barrels would fill a ten-story office building with sides the length of a city block.[18] Multiplied by 250, this represents a considerable investment.) A small refinery might need several small tanks to separate grades of crude oil, adding an effciency cost not found in salt caverns. The caverns contain about half and half sweet (low-sulfur) and sour (high-sulfur) crude, separated within those types by grade. All in all, salt domes offer both the cheapest and most secure storage currently available.

More than half of U.S. oil imports now flow through terminals located in the Gulf of Mexico. However, U.S. reserve supplies are not limited to those in the salt caverns. In addition to oil in SPR the United States has significant undeveloped oil reserves in its naval petroleum reserves (located in California and Wyoming), its naval oil shale reserves (located in Colorado and Utah), and the national petroleum reserve (NPR), located in Alaska. (Table 4-1 shows estimated reserves in these areas.) Proved reserves from these three sources stand at 993.6 million barrels, and the naval petroleum reserve's maximum efficient rate of production is about 180,000 bd, so these reserves could bring some relief in the event of a disruption, although the ones in California are already producing at their maximum production rate.

A more limited quantity of stock can be found in ships at sea (about thirty days' worth of supplies), oil industry inventories (about 1.1 billion barrels of crude and products, of which about 75 million barrels would be available in an emergency), and end-user inventories, particularly those of utilities, which hold nearly 87 million barrels of petroleum, of which about 23 million barrels might be available in a disruption. Other industrial end-users could supply an estimated 3 million barrels.[19] Thus about 101 million barrels is currently available from domestic inventories in the event of a major emergency, the equivalent of about forty-five days' worth of imports. Although these stocks would be helpful, they do not provide the country with enough emergency insurance. Clearly if the concept of a strategic petroleum reserve has any merit, which it certainly does, stockpiling needs to be more aggressive.

Determining how to fill the SPR has been even more difficult, particularly since the June 1979 Tokyo economic summit (at which the United States agreed to set import ceilings), and because of the country's interest in maintaining good relations with the Saudis, who have applied pressure to slow down the SPR fill if not stop it.

Before 1979 nearly all of the oil for SPR was purchased by the Defense Department through short-term supply contracts and spot purchases abroad. The oil came principally from Mexico, the United Kingdom, Iran, and Libya (not from Saudi Arabia, curiously). After 1979, when Congress mandated a fill rate of 100,000 bd, policy changed and domestic oil was used to fill the reserves. As owner of

Table 4-1. Undeveloped U.S. Government Petroleum Reserves.

| | Million Barrels of Oil | Million Cubic Feet of Gas | Estimated New Reserves | | Area, Acres | Maximum Production Rates, Thousands of Barrels per Day | Maximum Efficient Rate of Production, Thousands of Barrels per Day |
			Million Barrels of Oil	Million Cubic Feet of Gas			
Naval Petroleum Reserves (NPR)							
1. Elk Hills, California	970	1,162.9	250	250	46,095[a]	176 (197 by 1982)	300
2. Buena Vista Hills, California	4.0	NA	0	0	30,181[b]	8.3	8.3
3. Teapot Dome, Wyoming	26.0	8.0	0	0	9,481	3.3	8-10
Naval Oil Shale Reserves (NOSR)							
1. Rifle, Colorado			22,000		40,760		
2. Vernal, Utah			4,000		90,440		
3. Rifle, Colorado			[c]		10,333		
National Petroleum Reserve							
Alaska			550-15,800	2,500-27,400	37,000 (sq. mi.)		
Totals	1,000.0	1,170.9	26,800-42,050	2,750-27,650		187.6	316.3-318.3

Source: Conversations with U.S. Department of Energy officials, 1981; Hearings before the Subcommittee On Energy Resources and Materials Production, Senate Committee of Energy and National Resources, April 18, 1980; Hearings before the Subcommittee on Military Construction and Stockpiles, Senate Armed Services Committee, November 18, 1977; Hearings before Subcommittee on Military Construction and Stockpiles, Senate Armed Services Committee, July 19, 1979

[a]Both government and privately-owned land.

[b]Most of NPR 2 is leased to private interests.

[c]NOSR 3 was purchased to provide additional working space for NOSR 1.

the naval petroleum reserve (NPR) but not the producer (a private company) the federal government receives a share in the production of oil. This share was exchanged for crude oil to be delivered to SPR. The decision to use NPR oil for SPR, in a sense robbing Peter to pay Paul, reflects the view that SPR oil is more accessible than NPR oil; it can be pumped out faster and is more readily moved into the national pipeline system. Moreover, some of the NPR oil was price-controlled, lower tier oil, and therefore cheaper than foreign oil. With oil prices decontrolled the price differential no longer holds, however, and of course filling SPR with domestic oil did not lessen our import dependence, because refineries that previously had depended on the domestic oil now had to buy it on the world market. With NPR oil now selling at world prices, it is extremely questionable whether the government should continue to maintain the facade of not buying reserve stock on the world market.

On the other hand, the government must deal with the enormous question of cost. To date, except for the now defunct entitlements payments from the NPR, SPR has been financed out of the general budget. The fixed cost of operating SPR are relatively low: about 80 percent of SPR cost is in acquiring oil. The cost of filling SPR has increased dramatically, however. For example the first 91 million barrels purchased cost $1.3 billion; 43 million barrels purchased since September 1980 cost $1.7 billion.

Nevertheless, with oil now at the world price, the current cost of filling SPR is almost certainly well below the price oil will probably be if the reserves should have to be drawn down. If a disruption occurs the difference between the present cost of the oil and the prevailing prices at the time will probably represent a net savings, even taking into account the changing value of money. In addition the drawdown of SPR will help to reduce general economic costs incurred during an emergency.

Because developing a billion barrel reserve could easily cost more than $50 billion, a variety of proposals have been made for lowering the costs, some of which would involve the private sector. One proposal is to have the government sell materials currently stockpiled by the Federal Emergency Management Agency.[20] Another is to have the government take its royalty share of oil production on federally leased lands in kind rather than in cash.[21] One suggestion is to use NPR oil exclusively for SPR. Another proposal, hardly designed to endear politicians to their constituencies, calls for an oil import fee, the revenue from which would be used to purchase more oil imports.[22] David Stockman, then a congressman from Michigan, now director of the Office of Management and Budget, once argued forcefully for the use of "oil bonds" to finance a reserve.[23] Private investors would purchase shares, or oil bonds, in the SPR, which could be traded with a return based on the anticipated (high) price of oil during a disruption. This program would minimize government funding—a prospect that delights budgetmakers—but the Reagan administration has recently rejected the concept in the belief that the return on investment would be too low to attract investors.[24] All of these policies in one way or another result in a cost to the U.S. taxpayer, in the sense that money put into oil in the ground is money that could otherwise have been invested in a productive enterprise. Investing in gold or silver shares is not the same as investing in SPR shares, because the SPR remains an instrument of national security. No matter who is perceived as paying the initial costs, it is the American taxpayer who bears the ultimate burden, and no matter who appears to control the stocks, it will be the federal government who decides how they will be used. The only relevant questions are those of cost (which kind of program is cheapest?) and time (which can be developed the most quickly?).

Central to the problem of cost is how to use the reserves: A 248 million barrel reserve is engineered to be drawn down at the rate of 1.7 mmbd. At the 538 million barrel level, the rate is 3.5 mmbd. How does the government, or private investors for that matter, determine under what conditions and at what price SPR will be used? Assuming that there is a crisis in the Middle East and for one reason or another all oil exports are cut off for an uncertain period of time, what should the president do—order SPR to be drawn down immediately or wait until conditions become more serious? And how serious do they have to become? DOE is now trying to develop a "utilization plan" that would detail how, when, and at what price oil would be withdrawn from SPR.

However, in a crisis the government may not know the optimal drawdown schedule for SPR. It will not know how long the crisis will last. Moreover, in a directed embargo, Washington will have less desire than usual to draw on reserves, as every drop released will place the nation more at the mercy of the embargoing states. The country will be under considerable pressure from its allies to coordinate its stockpile strategy with theirs, a policy that may well be disadvantageous from a strictly U.S. perspective. Finally it will no doubt be extremely difficult for any president to justify a drawdown policy that is perceived as emerging from Washington's sterile bureaucratic laboratories. As soon as a policy is announced it is sure to be attacked.

The legislation that established SPR called for the establishment of an industrial petroleum reserve (IPR) and studies on additional reserve possibilities. To date, nothing has been done to involve the private sector in the emergency reserve program, although many major allies support private stockpiling practices. In Japan, for example, some reserves are maintained by the government and some are held commercially. Germany and the Netherlands permit special corporations to control reserves. In France and Italy the oil companies manage the entire strategic reserve program. Only in the United States is the reserve solely under federal control.[25]

There are many arguments for diversifying our reserve system either by providing financial support for commercial stockpiles or by mandating certain reserve inventory levels in the private sector. Apart from the obvious advantage that a private reserve program would provide additional insurance against a shortage, it can also be argued that the private sector might operate a reserve program more efficiently and at less expense than the federal government. Additional storage capacity could be built more quickly and in some cases existing surplus storage capacity could be used, thereby reducing cost. Since private reserves would be scattered, there would be less need for a federal regional petroleum reserve; with stocks localized, logistical problems would be reduced. Moreover private firms could stockpile both crude stock and refined products. The higher costs of storage would be passed on to the consumer, thereby promoting conservation, rather than being passed to the taxpayer through the federal budget. And reporting requirements would provide the government with more specific information than it now has on private stocks.[26]

The chief disadvantage of an IPR would be the impact of the large capital expense involved on the structure of the industry. Money spent on the industrial reserve would be diverted from investment elsewhere, and the industry would have trouble recovering its costs in a competitive marketplace. Introducing this new factor would affect industry competitiveness because each firm would have a different marginal cost curve. Indeed, one problem would be figuring out how to handle requests for exemptions from firms for which the added expense would make it difficult to compete. Moreover the government would have to create another regulatory administration to monitor the creation of new stocks, prevent seasonal and working inventories from being included, check to see that offshore stocks are not just moved to onshore facilities, and determine that supplies are the appropriate grade.

For all the difficulties an IPR would introduce, it remains an attractive option. And except for the requirement that industry own oil and products in the IPR, in amounts not to exceed a fixed percentage, there are at least three different ways to approach an IPR program. One possibility is a mandatory federal program requiring the oil industry to hold and maintain reserve stocks at a certain level; another is a quasi-public oil storage corporation, modeled on the German Erdölbevorratungsverband (EBV) corporation; and the third is to encourage but not require private-sector reserve inventories.[27] Devices to encourage industry participation include a tax incentive or subsidy program, a selectively rebated import fee, and an oil import quota plan with bonus quotas for additions to the reserve. In other words the reserve could be owned and operated by the government, with access leased to industry; it could be wholly owned by industry; or a mixed approach, such as the Germans use, could be adopted. If our allies have successfully developed private industry stockpiles, why not the United States?

There are good reasons for legislating an IPR rather than relying on voluntary development of private reserves. First, the oil industry cannot be expected of its own volition to accumulate and maintain enough stocks for a meaningful strategic reserve. Shareholders expect oil companies to keep inventories at a level that strictly maximizes short- to medium-term profits. If they maintain extra inventories in the national interest, they will have to be compensated somehow. Second, inventories the oil industry holds at any point are a function of many factors, among them oil prices, the cost of money, market perceptions, storage capability, and security of supply. There is no clear norm against which to measure the quantity of added stocks that would be needed in an IPR.

All of these programs come to grief on the questions of cost and control. Ideally, the government wants a program that minimizes the effect on the budget while maximizing its control over energy resources. Unfortunately industry wants the same conditions. On the one hand, private inventories may not be released in a disruption because their owners might reasonably assume that prices will go higher.

On the other hand, inventories may never be built up to sufficient levels because private investors cannot be assured that the government will not impose price controls or tell them when to draw down their stocks. It's a "no-win" situation for both government and the private investor because no one can be certain what conditions or policies will prevail in a national emergency. For this reason private stockpile systems have not had much support.

Moreover serious questions have been raised about the value of a stockpile program altogether. Critics of SPR and the concept of IPR feel that the reserve programs attack the symptoms, not the basic problem, of oil vulnerability. Oil stockpiles cannot change the way society consumes energy, and during the period when the reserves are being filled, American dependency on oil imports is actually increased. At best, reserves might delay the upward movement of prices in the event of a disruption. In an embargo extra supplies might be of little value because OPEC could simply regulate its production according to our drawdown schedule. The threat of OPEC retaliation might even keep us from using SPR; this country certainly obliged when Saudi Arabia discouraged us from filling it in 1979.

Basically SPR is useful only in the event of a surprise cutoff—a surprise both to us and to the producing countries. The storage program is worth pursuing but only if its value is understood clearly. The purpose of the strategic reserve program is to lessen the shock of a disruption and to serve as a deterrent. Stockpiling strategies operate on a different level altogether from import reduction strategies.[28] Stockpiling can help alleviate some of the social and economic stress of a disruption, but it cannot prevent energy from becoming more expensive. And there is some question about how quickly it could be brought to the level where it would ease the effects of a crisis. According to a Congressional Budget Office study, a billion barrel reserve would almost completely negate the effects of a 3 mmbd shortfall in 1984,[29] but it would be practically impossible to establish by that date. To proceed on a business-as-usual approach to SPR and related programs—selling oil, for example, from NPR 1 to small California refineries or reducing the SPR fill for budgetary reasons—is inviting disaster.

The high cost of the stockpile program must be recognized and borne, if the United States is going to be able to respond adequately to an oil emergency. SPR and other programs affecting supply and demand must be in place now—not tomorrow or the day after tomorrow—and they are the federal government's responsibility.

CREATING AN EFFECTIVE
RESPONSE NETWORK

No policy response will be effective without an appropriate setup for taking action. As the U.S. Department of Transportation has pointed out, the issue in an energy emergency will not be how to save petroleum ("The petroleum is 'saved' by definition") but how to make the best use of what petroleum is available.[30] Any effort to hand emergency plans down from the top without developing a base of local support will aggravate rather than alleviate the effects of a disruption.

Although state and local energy offices should be the critical links in contingency planning, they are traditionally underfunded, understaffed, poorly directed, and given very low priority.[31] A network of effective state and local offices for dealing with energy problems is as vital to the nation's security as a new missile system, but these agencies can be brought to an effective level only if they are given considerably greater financial and technical assistance from the federal government.

First, however, the federal government will have to get its own house in order. At present, authority for energy planning is scattered. Overall responsibility during a crisis resides with the secretary of energy, who chairs a cabinet-level, interagency task force (the Energy Coordinating Committee),[32] which has no role to play except during an emergency. The Federal Emergency Management Agency (FEMA) is responsible for all disaster planning, whether the disaster is natural or man-made. Although most energy-related preemergency planning is done by DOE, and although DOE and FEMA have established a working relationship, it is not clear what role either FEMA or DOE would play in an energy disruption. Within DOE, the responsibilities of various offices overlap. The Office of Energy Contingency Planning (part of the Economic Regulatory Administration—ERA) plans for possible energy interruptions, but its focus is strictly domestic. ERA's Energy Liaison Center provides a point of contact between DOE and the state energy offices, but it is separate from the Energy Information Administration (EIA), which is responsible for gathering energy data from all over, including the states. Within DOE, offices in charge of oil supply security, emergency conservation programs, utility systems, and the strategic petroleum reserve, among others, share often overlapping responsibilities for developing energy emergency policies. On February 24, 1981, DOE announced a reorganization of it contingency planning offices and programs under an assistant secretary for environmental protection, safety and emergency preparedness. But it is not clear how much responsibility this office will have, and international aspects of emergency planning are outside its purview. Meanwhile budget cuts by the Reagan administration have emasculated the Economic Regulatory Administration and EIA, all but eliminated the emergency gasoline-rationing programs, and gutted funding for state planning.

Under existing federal legislation the president has almost complete freedom to act as he sees fit when he decides an energy emergency exists. Under Title II of the Emergency Energy Conservation Act (1979), if he decides that an actual or potential energy shortage exists, the states must submit emergency energy conservation plans to DOE within forty-five days of the president's findings. However, it is physically and financially impossible for most states to carry out the level of sophisticated planning required without considerable federal assistance.[33] For every emergency measure a state considers, it must determine a vast array of facts—a determination even the federal government has been unable to accomplish in its contingency planning.

Few states have developed their own energy offices because it would cost too much or because they perceive energy as a national problem. Yet the energy system in each state or region is different. Some regions are net energy exporters, some are more dependent on one form of energy than another, and the geographical locations of some make it difficult to export energy to them during a shortage.

Local administrations are even less well-equipped to deal with energy problems than the states, but countless activities can be handled best at the local level. Local governments can identify where the elderly and the poor live (two groups that will be seriously affected by energy costs) and decide which areas of the economy need energy most. They can deal with such practical problems as finding people who might lend space heaters to the needy. They can develop temporary mass transit plans—modifying school hours, for example, so that school buses can be used by the general public as well as school children. They can inform citizens about local emergency efforts and can participate in the national planning process. Citizens should be telling the federal government what they can do to prepare for an energy interruption and what assistance they require to do it. Ironically Reagan's philosophy of returning power to the states, power that is essential to effective emergency planning, is less likely than ever to be realized, because of his austerity program. The "New Federalism" cannot be realized without federal funding.

What can be done?

First, an office for energy contingency planning (ECP) should be established in DOE with responsibility for all aspects of emergency planning, both domestic and international. The assistant secretary for ECP would be responsible for integrating FEMA's crisis management efforts, developing an improved information gathering and dissemination system and chairing an interdepartmental task force drawn from other sectors of the government critical to managing an oil crisis, including personnel from the Departments of Treasury, Commerce, and Transportation. The secretary's work would be supplemented by a permanent private-sector task force representing segments of the energy industry as well as other major industrial and commercial energy users. This group would work regularly with government planners. It might be necessary to first review and possibly revise antitrust laws, but an approach like this is probably essential to rational planning.

The Reagan administration plans to return to the old system of relying on industry for its energy statistics. This would be disastrous both politically and practically. In an emergency the public will find the information suspect and will conjure up visions of an oil industry cartel manipulating supplies. The present system, with its ninety-day time lag, is inadequate. Unless an information system can be developed that provides accurate, up-to-the-minute information on petroleum stocks and their location, efforts at contingency planning are doomed.

Finally contingency planning must occur at every level of government—federal, state, and local—both to promote a wider understanding of what the energy problem really is and to develop the national consensus needed for an effective crisis response. It is time to decentralize decisionmaking, but this cannot be done without federal aid. The federal government should continue to provide financial and technical assistance to state and local governments for energy emergency planning at the same time that it brings order to the national planning effort.

NOTES

1. See Richard B. Mancke, "The American Response: On the Job Training?" in *Oil Diplomacy, the Atlantic Nations in the Oil Crisis of 1978–1979,* Foreign Policy Research Institute, Philadelphia, c. 1980, p. 30.
2. See U.S. Department of Energy (DOE), *Final Report to the President on Oil Supply Shortages During 1979,* DOE/S-0011, Washington, D.C., July 1980, p. 12.
3. Joint Economic Committee, U.S. Congress, *Energy and Materials: A Shortage of Resources or Commitment?* a staff study, Washington, D.C., August 1980, p. 1.
4. The president's legal authority over imports is contained in the International Emergency Economic Powers Act of 1977 (IEEPA), Section 122 of the Trade Act of 1974, Section 251 of the EPCA, Section 4(a) and 13 of the EPAA, and Section 1013(a) of the Defense Production Act.
5. DOE, *Reducing U.S. Oil Vulnerability, Energy Policy for the 1980's* (sic), Washington, D.C., November 10, 1980, DOE/PE-0021, p. II–A–2.
6. U.S. Congressional Budget Office (CBO), *The Decontrol of Domestic Oil Prices: An Overview,* Washington, D.C., May 1979, p. xiii.
7. *The New York Times,* "Gains in Saving Oil Change U.S. Outlook," January 4, 1981, p. 1. Roger Sant, director of the Carnegie-Mellon Energy Productivity Center, claims that oil imports could be cut to 2 mmbd in 1990 and to nearly zero by 2000 if energy were priced at world levels and conservation measures vigorously pursued.
8. DOE, *Reducing U.S. Oil Vulnerability,* p. II–B–8 and p. II–B–1.
9. Ibid., p. II–B–33, Table 14.
10. See DOE, Policy and Evaluation, Office of Gas and Integrated Analysis, Staff Working Paper, Tom Neville, Jerry Blankenship, Mike Baccon, and William Lane.
11. See William W. Hogan, "Import Management and Oil Emergencies," in *Energy and Security,* ed. Joseph S. Nye and David A. Deese (Cambridge, Mass.: Ballinger Publishing Company, 1981), pp. 261–302. Also see Henry A. Nau, "Securing Energy" *The Washington Quarterly* 4, no. 3 (Summer 1981).
12. Calculated from Table II.1, Annex II, pp. 80–81 of the World Bank, *Energy in the Developing Countries,* Washington, D.C., August 1980.
13. *Petroleum Intelligence Weekly,* January 5, 1981, p. 5.
14. National Petroleum Council, *Emergency Preparedness for Interruption of Petroleum Imports into the United States,* Washington, D.C., 1974, p. 83.

15. Robert Stobaugh and Daniel Yergin, eds., *Energy Future* (New York: Random House, 1979), p. 46.

16. Egon Balas, *The Strategic Petroleum Reserve: How Large Should It Be?*, DOE, Contract no. EL-78-X-01-5221, Washington, D.C., June 1979, p. 5.

17. See Edward N. Kraples, *Oil Crisis Management, Strategic Stockpiling for International Security* (Baltimore: The Johns Hopkins University Press, 1980), p. 92.

18. JRB Associates, Inc., *Final Report, Feasibility Study for Requiring Storage of Crude Oil, Residual Fuel Oil and/or Refined Petroleum Products by Industry*, Contract no. C0-05-60477-00, submitted to the U.S. Federal Energy Administration, Mclean, Virginia, December 2, 1976, pp. 2–10.

19. U.S. Government Accounting Office (GAO), *Factors Influencing the Size of the U.S. Strategic Petroleum Reserve*, ID-79-8, June 15, 1979, pp. 18–20. The oil industry retains a margin of stocks as protection in the event of late resupply, demand surges, requests for stock exchanges, and seasonal changes. Their minimum operating level is about 720 million barrels.

20. See Richard D. Lyons, "The Nation's Strategic Oil Reserves Are Thirsting Anew," *The New York Times*, June 22, 1980, p. E-9.

21. See GAO, *Issues Needing Attention in Developing the Strategic Petroleum Reserve*, EMD-77-20, Washington, D.C. February 16, 1977, p. 7. In the past, FEA rejected acquiring royalty oil because (1) it would adversely affect small refiners now dependent on access to royalty oil; (2) it would require termination of existing government contracts; (3) supply of royalty oil is not sufficient for the SPR; and (4) the transportation costs for moving dispersed oil will be greater than the cost of unloading ocean tankers. See ibid., p. 8. Other problems raised were that the purchase of royalty oil would place an administrative burden on the government, some of the oil was not suitable for storage, and the purchase of royalty oil would pass the cost of the reserve to oil users rather than taxpayers. See GAO, *Letter to the Secretary of Energy*, EMD-79-1, October 6, 1978, p. 3.

22. See GAO, *Issues in Developing the Strategic Petroleum Reserve*, February 16, 1977, p. 15. GAO advocates a tariff on imported oil or an excise tax on gasoline. The principle of such a user fee is to make those who benefit from imported oil also those who pay for the oil "insurance."

23. U.S. House of Representatives, Committee on Interstate and Foreign Commerce, Subcommittee on Energy and Power, House hearings, *Filling the Strategic Petroleum Reserve: Oversight*, April 25, 1980, Washington, D.C., p. 20.

24. See Robert D. Hershey, Jr., "Shift in Fuel Plans Hinted," *The New York Times,* February 11, 1981, p. D-5, and Clyde H. Farnsworth, "A New Plan to Finance Oil Reserve," *The New York Times,* January 15, 1981, p. D-3.
25. Kraples, *Oil Crisis Management,* pp. 58–59.
26. See GAO, *Size of the U.S. Strategic Petroleum Reserve,* p. 21.
27. See Glen Sweetnam, "Stockpile Policies for Coping with Oil Supply Disruptions," paper presented at the Conference on Policies for Coping with Oil Supply Disruptions, American Enterprise Institute for Public Policy Research, Washington, D.C., September 8–9, 1980, p. 16.
28. See William W. Hogan, "Import Management and Oil Emergencies," in Nye and Deese, eds., *Energy and Security,* p. 263.
29. U.S. Congressional Budget Office (CBO), *An Evaluation of the Strategic Petroleum Reserve,* Washington, D.C., June 1980.
30. U.S. Department of Transportation, *Transportation Energy Contingency Strategies, Part One, The Planning Process: Roles and Responsibilities,* Washington, D.C., March 1980, p. 8.
31. National Conference of State Legislatures, *Energy and the States: What Future Directions?,* conference held December 15–17, 1980, Washington, D.C.
32. The Energy Coordinating Committee was established by Executive Order 12083 (September 27, 1978). The committee meets at the chairman's discretion. When it is not meeting, its functions are delegated to an executive council. The executive council is chaired by the secretary of energy; its members are the director of the Office of Management and Budget, the chairman of the Council of Economic Advisers, the National Security Affairs adviser, and the Domestic Affairs and Policy adviser.
33. U.S. House of Representatives, Committee on Government Operations, *Emergency Energy Conservation Programs: Department of Energy Oversight,* Washington, D.C., September 26, 1980, p. 5.

5 PREPARING FOR AN ENERGY EMERGENCY: SHORT-TERM RESPONSES

Should another major oil disruption occur, which is all too likely, the president of the United States will have to take immediate action on a wide range of international and domestic problems. Should Saudi Arabia's oil exports be cut off, for example, 18 percent of the non-Communist world's oil would disappear; that is 25 percent of the world's crude oil reserves and almost 30 percent of OPEC oil production. Prices for oil would rise probably to over $100 per barrel.

The United States, Japan, and Western Europe could respond by launching aggressive unilateral campaigns to ensure access to oil supplies. The Third World countries, unable to pay for the high cost of oil imports, would be plunged into social and economic chaos. The poorer members of these populations would begin hoarding all available fuel sources: Trees would be cut and scrub brush gathered, accelerating deforestation and guaranteeing long-term famine. The OPEC countries would invalidate their contract sales and place all their oil in the spot market, causing chaos on the world oil market.

In the United States cities would darken. Businesses and shopping malls would close down as mobility and disposable income decreased. In colder states the poor would have to choose between food and fuel; food supplies to urban areas would be disrupted. The strongest effects of the crisis would be felt among the poor and elderly and in the rural areas, where mass transit is not available. Colder climates such as the Northeast would become gloomy as industry moved to warmer climates, but the sunbelt states would also be gravely affected, primarily because of their lack of public transit, their urban sprawl, and their energy needs for air conditioning. As unemployment increased, more crime would be committed on bleak city streets.

Politicians would insist that if they had been in control OPEC would not have "gotten away with it." With the public clamoring for greater government intervention, industry-government relations would be polarized. The oil and gas industry, as scapegoats for the energy crisis, would probably be nationalized in response to public demand. Air quality would worsen with increased coal use. Decades of effort to improve the environment would be lost as policymakers concentrated on increasing energy sources rapidly.[1]

Such a situation can be avoided if action is taken now. Some of the more immediate emergency measures that can be undertaken are allocation and rationing plans, use of surge capacity and emergency fuel switching, and various energy conservation measures. And because energy disruptions occur and must be planned for in an international context, we also analyze the impact on U.S. domestic planning of its responsibilities under the International Energy Agency Agreement.

PROPOSALS TO ALLOCATE SCARCE SUPPLIES: RATIONING VS. FREE MARKET

The purpose of any contingency effort should be to control the price effects of a supply disruption. A disruption almost instantly raises the price of oil. The higher price transfers income from consumers to oil producers (both nations and the industry). Because the income cannot be immediately recycled into the economy, even with a windfall profits tax, to purchase U.S. goods and services, total demand for those goods and services falls, causing GNP to decline. This delay, known as the "oil price drag," can theoretically be countered by fiscal and monetary policies. Still, it is unclear what policies should be used, how to use them, and what their effects will be. And no matter what policy is used, it is impossible to eliminate totally the oil price drag. While the transfer of money from one group to another reduces aggregate demand, the higher cost of oil (an input of most production processes) increases costs for goods and services, so that aggregate supply declines and prices rise. Contributing further to inflation, labor demands higher wages to offset the income loss incurred.[2] Government policy, therefore, needs to address issues of both demand and supply.

Although economists generally agree that the free market is the most efficient allocator of scarce resources, a free-market approach to oil supplies has been opposed in the past for a variety of reasons. First, the level to which oil prices would have to rise to clear the market would be politically and socially unacceptable. So price controls help reduce the sudden rise in production costs. Second, because of oil price drag, funds are pulled from all sectors of the economy and relocated in the petroleum sector, an income transfer that contributes both to inflation and recession. Finally, the transfer of income to oil producers is considered inequitable.[3] For these reasons various policymakers have advocated price controls, petroleum allocation plans, coupon rationing, and gasoline tax and rebate schemes that increase the price of gasoline through taxes, which are rebated to the consumers.

Allocation and rationing schemes have been notoriously difficult to implement. The problem of being equitable has increased exponentially since World War II, when rationing was last tried because of more people, more cars, more highways, and more businesses. The allocation program the nation tried at the time of the 1979 oil crisis failed miserably.

One of the programs advocated most widely by energy security analysts is some type of tax and rebate scheme. With this approach, prices would be allowed to rise to the market-clearing level and a percentage would be taxed away from the industry through the current windfall profits system by the government and rebated to consumers. The program can be extended to taxing all petroleum products and issuing a general rebate or limited to taxing just one product, such as gasoline.

The main arguments for this scheme are that it would use the existing administrative system and would not require a new currency, like gasoline coupons (for which a black market existed in World War II).

However, the economy would still feel some of the effect of the oil price drag because of the inherently uneven nature of the rebate: It is impossible to put money back in one pocket right away after taking it from the other pocket. Inflation would probably climb because there would be no control on prices. And an element of inequity could not be avoided; the problem would remain who should receive what rebate and when.[4] A tax and rebate plan would have much the same economic effect as gas rationing.

Government policy under the Reagan administration is to allocate oil supplies or control gasoline prices only in the event of a "severe, critical shortage . . . [such as] a warlike situation."[5] To do so without an established program will be difficult, however. It is important that policy planners know what the problems have been with previous petroleum allocation and rationing policies and what the alternatives are, because if a disruption occurs, the government will be under extreme political pressure to react despite all earlier enthusiasm for letting the market work.

Until President Reagan decontrolled oil prices and eliminated funding for the nation's gasoline rationing program, the federal government's program for responding to a near-term energy emergency consisted primarily of the allocation and price control system provided for in the Emergency Petroleum Allocation Act of 1973 (EPAA) and a gasoline rationing program mandated by the Emergency Energy Conservation Act of 1979 (EECA). Now there is no emergency program at all. Allocation controls formally ended September 31, 1981, when the EPAA expired. Under the Reagan budget no funding is now provided for the gasoline rationing program.

The EPAA guaranteed that during a petroleum shortage customers would be allocated a share of supplies proportionate to their share before the shortage and that prices would be frozen at a level that allowed oil companies to maintain preshortage profit margins. The EECA required the president to devise "one or more energy conservation contingency plans and a rationing contingency plan." As part of the conservation contingency plans, President Carter proposed measures to lower the speed limit, introduce building temperature restrictions, and increase public awareness of the energy problem and ways to meet it. Despite considerable opposition, the Carter plan, which allotted gasoline on the basis of the total number of state vehicle registrations and historical use rates, was approved on July 30, 1980, and went on standby status. Businesses were to receive special coupons based on their previous use rates, and a system of priority use was established that gave the agricultural sector top consideration. None of the allocation and rationing programs achieved public acceptance; they were all challenged before and after they were developed, and all of them, including the energy conservation measures, were rejected by Reagan.

Part of the problem is that no one really knows how the market is going to react to a crisis before the crisis occurs. No one can be sure how well our economy would adjust to a drop in supplies, particularly a severe shortage.

One can argue that the world is always subject to unforeseen catastrophes, but an energy crisis can to some degree be foreseen and prepared for. Within the next 50 years, the world will have developed energy alternatives to petroleum, but while the energy crisis lasts the United States should not give up on developing appropriate allocation and rationing plans to get through severe crises.

In a major emergency the United States may well have to use military force to secure foreign oil-producing areas. If so, the Department of Defense will most certainly require priority fuel allocations, but DOD will have to be backed up by the 20,000 defense industrial contractors that support its efforts. In fiscal 1978 these contractors consumed an estimated 450,000 bd of oil, almost the same as DOD. Should the Reagan administration's proposed defense spending increases be approved, both the military and its industrial contractors will increase their oil consumption.[6] In addition, if foreign oil field facilities are damaged, as they are likely to be, the military will need support from the civilian economy in the form of technicians, equipment, and supplies to restore the fields to operation. Meanwhile to avoid economic collapse in the civilian sector, there will have to be an emergency program for energy conservation and fuel allotment. There is absolutely no way the government can avoid some form of rationing and allocation, no matter how those devices aggravate economic dislocations. But the machinery of government must be in place before such a crisis occurs. An allocation program requires an extremely sophisticated, accurate oil stock information system and a regulatory structure that ensures the public's welfare. It would be folly for the government to be unprepared for a major energy crisis even if general policy is to rely on market forces. Even the National Petroleum Council (NPC), a major oil industry group, advocated a standby emergency allocation program after the 1973–74 embargo, stating the need for an effective data-gathering system and a standby organization that could allocate and possibly ration crude oil and refined products in an emergency.[7]

In a 1981 study the NPC called for a free market but advocated mandating a crude oil distribution program in a major crisis.[8] The organization is obviously concerned about the financial viability of its member companies if a supply disruption occurs. Without guaranteed access to crude supplies some of the smaller refineries might be forced to close. The NPC basically wants an allocation program for producers, not consumers, but any allocation program requires careful organization.

With decontrol and budget cuts the main instruments for administering fuel allocation and rationing are being disbanded. The current administration believes, correctly, that in minor crises market forces should be allowed to operate without government regulation. However, a system should be in place for managing a severe disruption of 25 percent or more. Effective preemergency planning requires a sophisticated ongoing information network and a planning team that not only researches allocation and rationing strategies but is available to implement those strategies if the need arises. An ad hoc response is likely to worsen the effects of the disruption. It is thus important as part of the government's military planning that it continue to develop an allocation program that can be implemented in a very severe oil crisis.

SURGE CAPACITY AND FUEL SWITCHING

In an emergency the United States would have two main policy options. One is to curtail demand for energy. The other is to increase the supply of energy by producing more energy or by switching from one energy source to another, or both.

The nation's surge capacity (the potential for bursts of increased production) is limited. Most domestic oil fields are now producing at their marginal efficient rates (MER). A few could produce more, but only for short periods of time. The National Petroleum Council estimates that an additional 320,000 bd can be supplied, mainly from fields in Prudhoe Bay, East Texas, and the naval petroleum reserve. It would require four to six months to reach this level and shortly afterward a decline in production would set in. By 1985 surge capacity will be limited to 140,000 bd if additional pumping capability is not built on the Trans-Alaskan Pipeline System. To increase production state and federal regulations that now limit production levels would have to be changed.[9]

DOE estimates place additional surge supplies of natural gas at 2.5 to 3.1 quads per year; 2.12 quadrillion Btu (10^{15}) per year, or quads, equals 1 mmbd, so this is slightly more than 1 million barrels a day of oil equivalent (mmbdoe).[10] The NPC's estimates are less optimistic: 600,000 bdoe in summer months and 300,000–350,000 bdoe in the winter when demand increases.[11] Whether we can actually use these extra gas supplies depends on several factors. For one thing it is not certain how long maximum production can be sustained without damaging long-term production rates. Further, production increases may require higher prices and other incentives as well as compensation for changing prevailing contracts.[12]

Coal production in the United States could be increased fairly immediately by 140 million tons, from the 760 million tons of coal produced in 1980 (of which about 80 million tons were exported) to a total production and transportation capacity of 900 million tons annually. This increase would be the equivalent of nearly 14 million barrels of oil. The problem is that there is no one new to use this resource. The electric utilities are the main coal consumers but most of the burners and boilers that can use coal are already doing so. If coal is going to occupy a larger role in America's energy mix, it will not happen soon, even if an energy crisis does occur.

We could achieve a fairly rapid increase in energy supplies by hastening the licensing and construction of the fourteen nuclear power plants now under planning and construction. These plants have a total planned output of 14,582 megawatts (Mw), which would displace almost 200 million barrels of oil a year. In addition, already existing nuclear power plants could be authorized to operate at above normal levels. By current estimates nuclear power plants could run safely an average 4 percent over their licensed maximum capacity.[13] Nuclear power is one of America's most easily available short-term supply alternatives in a disruption, but with a decrease in economic growth, electricity demand will also fall.

Optimistically, increased short-term production from all of America's energy resources could displace almost 2 mmbd of oil, assuming three things: that no legal barriers are placed in the way of production, that demand and fuel-switching capability exist, and that current projections are accurate. Under any sustained disruption, this figure will decline after a certain point as the faster rate of drawdown damages petroleum and gas fields. It would be wrong therefore to base emergency planning on the perception that a significant surge capacity exists.

The second principal approach to increasing energy supplies is to substitute another energy resource for oil, shifting the displaced oil to fill demand in a sector where it is needed more. Energy demand is derived demand, valued not in itself but for how it can be used, whether to heat homes or as plastic for grocery bags. And energy is highly substitutable. Houses can be heated by oil, gas, coal, or electricity.

Of all the fuels we use, gasoline—from which most of our petroleum products are made—is the most difficult to obtain a substitute for but it is also the one most subject to discretionary and more efficient use. Supplies of distillate and jet fuel could not be curtailed sharply without affecting productivity. Consumption of residual fuel oil can be reduced somewhat among utilities that can switch to alternative fuels such as coal and natural gas.

The NPC believes that 640,000 bd of oil could be made available by fuel switching, mainly in the electric utility sector. Fuel-switching potential in the residential and commercial sectors is less easily accomplished in the short run, not only because these sectors depend less heavily on oil to meet their energy needs than do the other sectors but also because it is not as easy for them to switch to other fuel sources in a hurry. In particular, residential demand for home heating oil is not likely to change quickly.

Over a longer period oil consumption in the commercial sector would decrease if the economy slowed down. Changes in the residential sector will vary according to oil's share in a market; in parts of the country where oil is important for home heating little can be done to provide alternative fuel sources in the short term. It takes time and money to retrofit home boilers. New England, New York, New Jersey, and the Mid-Atlantic states alone consume 70 percent of all household fuel oil used.

The impact of an oil shortage would be felt first in the transportation sector, where almost no fuel substitutes are available. Petroleum provided 97 percent of the energy used by this sector in 1980, and few believe that the use of electric vehicles or other transportation alternatives will increase greatly by 1985. Transportation accounted for over one-fourth of the petroleum consumed in the United States in 1980, over 75 percent of it used by cars and trucks. In the long run, it will be important to develop more fuel-efficient vehicles and mass transit systems; in an emergency commuter pooling is one of the few measures that will reduce energy use without reducing economic output. Of the nearly 9 mmbd of oil used in transportation, 1.8 mmbd is used in daily commutes to work. The fuel savings available from commuter car pooling are limited, perhaps only a few hundred thousand barrels a day, but in an energy-intensive sector that does not lend itself to quick technological fixes, any savings is important.

The industrial sector may have a fuel-switching potential of 260,000 bd, but it would take about six months to accomplish this switch.[14] Some firms may switch from oil to gas, but potential for conversion to gas is limited. If demand for industry's goods falls, there may be no need to worry about finding alternative energy resources.

Fuel substitution in electric utilities has been the focus of much attention. In 1980 when oil produced about 13 percent of America's electricity, utilities purchased almost 44 percent of the nation's residual fuel oil. Of the 1.25 mmbd electric utilities consumed, 1.1 mmbd was residual and 150 mmbd was distillate oil. Even in this sector, however, the possibility for conversion from oil use is limited. Electric utilities used 75 percent of the coal produced in 1979; coal already meets almost 50 percent of utilities' energy demand. And 80 percent of the oil used by utilities is consumed in regions of the country that cannot readily shift to alternative fuels: California, New Jersey, the southeastern part of New York, and, most dependent of all, Florida and New England.

The short-term potential to power-wheel (shift electricity from one utility to another through a third) or to import more electricity from Canada is limited. As one industry observer notes, in an oil disruption, the electric utility industry cannot "respond quickly with some substitute fuel or electricity source to replace the lost oil."[15] The system is virtually unable to power-wheel because of the diversity of utility capabilities and transmission capacities. At best something like 30,000 bd could be displaced through power-wheeling.[16] In the short run not much can be done to increase transmission capacities.

DOE estimates total fuel-switching capacity among electric and industrial utility units with a dual fuel capability to be 1.4 mmbd of oil equivalent. However, this capability is limited by three factors. Some of the plants are "peaking units" used only to meet high seasonal demand. Economic problems caused by an energy crisis will limit energy demand. And although residual fuel oil is the principal fuel consumed in these facilities, it is the lighter product that will be in demand during a crisis.

EMERGENCY ENERGY CURTAILMENT MEASURES

In the short term, the United States can do little in a fuel crisis but conserve energy. Emergency energy curtailment can accomplish a great deal with little harm to the economy. Changes in transportation habits, especially—driving at reduced speed limits, purchasing gasoline only on odd- or even-numbered days, and car pooling, for example—could reduce U.S. energy use by 615 million barrels a day, according to one study.[17] Programs to reduce energy use in the residential and commercial sectors could save another 150,000 barrels a day, not a large amount but still a contribution. The potential to save energy will gradually dwindle as inefficient equipment is replaced and as the "easy" conservation efforts, such as lowering thermostats and insulating homes, are accomplished.

As required by the Energy Policy and Conservation Act of 1975, DOE developed three standby conservation plans that it estimated could save 610,400 barrels of oil a day: emergency building temperature restrictions (which it estimated would save 360,000 bd); emergency weekend gasoline sales restrictions (246,000 bd); and emergency advertising lighting restrictions (4,400 bd). Congress passed only the first of these plans as bills, giving DOE standby authority to implement the building temperature restrictions. The Reagan administration has rejected all of the Carter administration plans but two: a public relations program and a minimum requirement for gasoline purchases. Although these programs can accomplish much good, they are not a sufficient response to the problem.

The Reagan administration believes that "an unregulated market may now provide sufficient assurance of an orderly adjustment to any future energy supply interruptions" and that the Carter plans were opposed by individuals and businesses because "several of the emergency energy conservation measures . . . would impose costs far in excess of their benefits."[18]

It is dangerous not to have a backup plan should the "market" not work, however, because the initial reaction to a severe disruption of energy supplies will be panic. Policymakers should take steps now to educate consumers on the nature of the energy problems and the programs available to cope with a major disruption and should see that those programs are available. It is foolish to think that individuals and businesses who want to let the market operate freely in the normal course of events will not want government intervention when they begin to suffer the effects of a major disruption.

Moreover the government can develop low-cost programs with a high return, particularly in the transportation sector. Increasing the use of mass transit systems—including school buses, jitneys, and taxis—could free oil for use in other parts of the economy. A shortened workweek, according to one DOE study, could save from 190,000 to 280,000 barrels a day of oil equivalent, assuming even as few as 42 percent of all employees participated.[19] Substantial savings can be achieved with only minor changes in lifestyle.

Each community can tailor conservation measures to its own needs, but for maximum effect these programs should be developed today—not when an energy crisis comes along. Transit is the weak link in America's energy system, a primary cause of the nation's oil vulnerability that cries out for thoughtful planning, not a wait-and-see policy.

THE INTERNATIONAL ENERGY AGENCY

Domestic efforts to deal with an energy crisis will not take place in a vacuum. As a member of the International Energy Agency (IEA), the United States is required to reduce its energy use if an oil disruption occurs. As a major oil producer, the United States is in a better position than many of its allies; conceivably we might reduce our oil use only to see that oil sent abroad for use by our allies. But because America's energy security depends on closer cooperation with its allies on energy problems, the United States should take the leadership in strengthening the IEA, an organization it has never fully understood or supported.

In February 1974 at U.S. insistence thirteen industrial states met to coordinate a response to the energy crisis brought on by the 1973–74 OAPEC oil embargo. Following that meeting sixteen countries[20] signed an agreement establishing the IEA, based in Paris, as an autonomous body within the Organization for Economic Cooperation and Development (OECD). The IEA was to be the basis for a consumer cartel that, over time, would counterbalance producer power, placing downward pressure on oil prices.

To reduce dependence on oil imports, the member states were to cooperate in three areas: energy conservation, energy research and development, and the development of alternative energy sources. Not much has been accomplished in terms of conservation and the development of new energy sources, partly because IEA's charter is large and unfocused and partly because projects are inadequately financed. Technical cooperation among states for rapid development of new energy sources (including energy sources in the Third World) needs to be encouraged.

At the heart of the IEA program was its emphasis on short-term responses to energy crises. Thus it was to develop an emergency stockpile program, a demand-restraint (conservation) plan, an international allocation system, and an information system about the international oil market. On the whole IEA's information system has been more successful than the other programs, but problems have plagued every area of activity.

One of the first things the member states agreed to develop was an emergency reserve stockpile program to establish self-sufficiency in oil supplies in the event of a crisis. Reserves were to be large enough that by 1980 there would be enough oil to last ninety days with no net oil imports. This has been accomplished but only by loosely defining what constitutes reserves. For example, the emergency reserve commitment is satisfied by oil stocks, fuel-switching capacity, and standby oil production, not just by a large strategic petroleum reserve. The chief problem has been strictly defining what emergency stocks are and determining how to use them.

Participating countries have developed different approaches to a strategic stockpile program. Some, like the United States, segregate their emergency reserves from their commercial inventories; others, like Italy, combine official emergency reserves with commercial stocks; and states such as Germany and Japan use a dual approach, with some reserves held privately and some officially. IEA member states need to redefine the emergency reserve stock system and agree on how to treat commercial and state reserves.

They need to coordinate drawdown strategies for different types of reserves, to work out a formula by which member states can draw oil from the reserve both in an emergency and to counteract the inflationary effect of mini-shortfalls. They also must agree on the issue of states taking over privately owned stocks in an emergency. Priority consideration should be given to coordinating use of inventories to dampen oil market demand, as such a policy could reduce the danger of an oil disruption.

In an emergency the IEA program calls for a two-step response, with a program of demand restraint followed if necessary by allocation of the IEA stockpile to member states as needed. Demand restraint has been so liberally interpreted that no real program has developed. The success of a demand restraint program depends on the disposition of each member state to restrain domestic demand, and there is little the IEA can do to see that these programs are carried out. Even current U.S. measures are woefully inadequate, and those that have been considered would save little energy in the short run when the need for such programs may be the greatest. More research is needed in this area.

Demand restraint and allocation procedures come into effect when the secretariat and the governing board of the IEA agree that one of the participating countries or more has experienced a shortfall of at least 7 percent or more. With a shortfall of 7 percent each state requesting emergency stock must first reduce demand by 7 percent; with a shortfall of 12 percent, demand restraint must be at least 10 percent. The IEA must review demand restraint (energy conservation) programs but has no authority to change them. It may be that setting stricter oil import ceilings makes more sense than the current emphasis on national energy conservation programs. By setting overall targets the IEA can avoid the politically contentious issue of trying to achieve uniform demand-restraint policies. As it is, the system is forced to move directly to the stage of oil allocation, whereas a common, vigorous approach to reducing demand could possibly obviate the need for allocation of emergency stock.

In any case, the allocation system, which is extremely complex and awkwardly described, has never been used. Member states have hesitated to implement the system for fear that it would not work—and it might not, without some form of international price controls. The few times a country has appeared close to activating the allocation system, the IEA or the oil companies have found cargoes to divert to the needy state. When Turkey lost almost 60 percent of its oil supply at the height of the Iran-Iraq war of 1980–81, the IEA did nothing because the crisis was "unofficial"; Turkey finally found its own oil with little IEA assistance.[21]

While IEA's allocation and stockpile programs have received the most public attention, IEA's information system has probably been the agency's most constructive development. IEA's information-gathering activities have helped to standardize and improve international energy statistics. A fundamental problem of energy planning has been the lack of accurate information on energy consumption and supply; the IEA has provided both a forum for discussion and an instrument for energy data collection on the operations of oil companies (from corporate and financial structure to production rates and costs), demand-restraint plans, levels of emergency reserves, availability and use of transportation facilities, and current and projected levels of international supply and demand. In the long run IEA's information system may be more important to a coordinated international response to the world's energy problem than any of its other programs.

Major oil companies cooperate voluntarily with the system, which guarantees confidentiality of corporate information, but U.S. antitrust law has inhibited cooperation between the oil companies and the IEA. The United States has feared that too detailed a reporting system would facilitate collusion among the oil companies, permitting them to act as a cartel. The oil companies, of course, have feared that disclosure of their financial situation would make them vulnerable to competition. Now companies report complete details to their home states, which aggregate the data before transmitting it to the IEA secretariat. If a company were to refuse to cooperate with the IEA, perhaps out of fear of reprisals from an oil-producing state, the IEA would have to depend on the home government's sanctions to assure cooperation; it is uncertain what the home governments would do.

Every effort should be made to improve the quality and quantity of information flowing to the IEA. The U.S. government should re-evaluate its policy of monitoring oil company participation in the IEA and analyze how much government antitrust policy inhibits the free flow of information to the secretariat and hence IEA's ability to monitor and allocate oil supplies in a crisis. The number of oil companies reporting should be expanded, and all oil flows should be reported, including oil in transit. Also, spot-market transactions should be reported and the IEA should consider licensing spot-market dealers. Currently, the IEA lacks control over, or information about, the spot market, which could channel oil from long-term arrangements to short-term sales.

The IEA is at a crossroads. If it continues to develop on the path it is now following it could become a major force in the international oil market. Of course as IEA's power increases, the individual sovereignty of each state will decrease accordingly. But unless this happens the IEA will remain a loose organization of states, consulting on energy issues without agreeing on a common approach. OPEC too is a loose grouping of states but with the power to influence others. As a reactive, indeed essentially defensive, organization, the IEA must exhibit greater internal cohesion than does OPEC if it is going to respond adequately to the world energy market. Should oil supplies be severely disrupted, the agency will disintegrate, each state will search for supplies on its own, and the impact on other alliances, such as NATO, will be considerable.

NOTES

1. See Richard J. Kessler and Charles K. Ebinger, "Scenario for a World Nightmare," *The Washington Star,* April 27, 1980, p. A17.
2. See U.S. Department of Energy (DOE), Policy and Evaluation, Office of Oil Supply Security, *Allocating Petroleum Products during Oil Supply Disruptions: A Comparison of Four Alternative Plans,* preliminary staff analysis, September 1980, p. 6.
3. These points are taken from an extremely insightful paper by George Horwich, "Government Contingency Planning for Petroleum Supply Interruptions: A Macro Perspective," presented at the Conference on Policies for Coping with Oil Supply Disruptions, American Enterprise Institute, Washington, D.C., September 8–9, 1980, p. 2.
4. DOE, *Allocating Petroleum Products,* p. 19.
5. "Edwards Wants Free-Market Approach to Price, Allocation of Gasoline Supplies," *The Washington Post,* March 12, 1981, p. D–1.
6. Richard J. Kessler, "Defense Department Moves to Reduce Its Import Needs," *The Oil Daily,* November 10, 1980, p. 10.
7. National Petroleum Council (NPC), *Emergency Preparedness for Interruption of Petroleum Imports into the United States,* draft report, Washington, D.C., 1974, p. 43.
8. NPC's Committee on Emergency Preparedness, *Emergency Preparedness for Interruption of Petroleum Imports into the United States,* draft report, Washington, D.C., February 18, 1981, p. 20.
9. NPC, *Emergency Preparedness,* 1981, p. 7.
10. Assistant Secretary for Policy and Evaluation, U.S. Department of Energy, *Reducing U.S. Oil Vulnerability, Energy Policy for the 1980's,* DOE/PE-0021, Washington, D.C., November 10, 1980, p. II–B–35.

11. NPC, *Emergency Preparedness,* 1981, p. 8.
12. DOE, *Reducing U.S. Oil Vulnerability,* p. II–B–35 and II–B–38.
13. Ibid., p. II–D–8–9.
14. NPC, *Emergency Preparedness,* 1981, chap. 5, p. 8.
15. Michehl Gent, "Meeting Electricity Demand without Oil," paper presented at Stanford University Conference on Contingency Planning for an Energy Emergency, June 16–18, 1980, p. 1.
16. NPC, *Emergency Preparedness,* 1981, chap. 2, p. 34.
17. Ibid., April 1981, p. 28.
18. *The Washington Post,* March 9, 1981, p. A3.
19. DOE, *Reducing U.S. Oil Vulnerability,* p. II–I–10–13.
20. Participants were Belgium, Canada, Denmark, France, Federal Republic of Germany, Ireland, Italy, Japan, Luxembourg, Netherlands, Norway, United Kingdom, and the United States. The IEA now has twenty-one members. Initial signatories included all of the earlier Washington meeting participants except Norway and France, and additionally Austria, Spain, Sweden, Switzerland, and Turkey. Later Greece, Australia, and New Zealand joined. Norway was given associate status in 1975. Iceland and Finland did not become members. Portugal is the latest member.
21. *Petroleum Intelligence Weekly,* January 26, 1981, pp. 6–7. Other cases have involved Sweden and Italy.

6 THE CHANGING TERMS OF COMMERCIAL ACCESS TO OIL

Over the past ten years, the international petroleum market has undergone fundamental changes. In 1970 a handful of large, vertically integrated companies dominated the world oil industry. These private companies owned 94 percent of oil production in the non-Communist countries and sold 91 percent of all refined products. By 1981, however, nationalization of oil reserves and production in most African and Middle East countries had reduced the private companies' share of crude oil ownership to only 40 percent. By contrast national oil companies—in both oil-exporting and oil-importing countries—had expanded their ownership of crude oil from 6 to 55 percent while raising their share of refined fuel sales from 9 to 18 percent. In short, while the governments of the producing nations mostly control the "upstream" phase of the industry, crude oil production and pricing, the private companies of the consuming countries largely continue to regulate "downstream" activities, refining, transportation, and marketing. Figure 6-1 describes these structural changes.

The growth of state ownership of petroleum production came largely at the expense of the seven major multinational oil corporations: Royal Dutch/Shell Group, Exxon Corporation, Gulf Oil Corporation, Texaco, Inc., the British Petroleum Company Ltd. (BP), Mobil Corporation, and the Standard Oil Company of California (Socal). In 1970 the Seven Sisters had exclusive rights to 61 percent

Figure 6-1. *Changing Structure of the Oil Industry, 1970 and 1979*, Non Communist World.

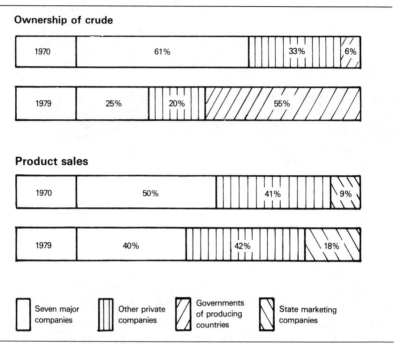

Ownership of crude

1970	61% ... 33% ... 6%
1979	25% ... 20% ... 55%

Product sales

1970	50% ... 41% ... 9%
1979	40% ... 42% ... 18%

Seven major companies   Other private companies   Governments of producing countries   State marketing companies

Source: Shell Briefing Service.

of oil production in the non-Communist world. Since they had more crude oil than they could refine, they sold considerable quantities of crude to other refiners worldwide through third-party contracts. By 1979, however, the Seven Sisters had direct access to only 25 percent of non-Communist world production. Their loss of secure crude oil had two major consequences. First, the volume of oil available for third-party contracts was cut in half and, second, some of the Seven Sisters must now compete with other firms on the open market to obtain part of the supplies needed to satisfy their basic demand (see Table 6-1). Thus over the past ten years the major oil companies have not only ceased to be the principal crude oil salesmen but also in some cases have become as vulnerable to the vicissitudes of the open market as smaller independent companies.

Just as the Seven Sisters lost control over world oil production in the 1970s, so in the 1980s the multinational companies could lose their hold over the extraordinary refining and marketing network

Table 6-1. Open Market Dependence of the Seven Sisters, Thousand Barrels of Oil Daily.

	BP	Gulf	Shell	Exxon	Mobil	Socal	Texaco	Total
Spot purchases	600	175	400	330	30	0	0	1,535
Basic demand	3,100	1,500	4,600	4,800	2,300	3,100	3,300	22,700
Percentage dependence on spot market	19	12	9	7	1	0	0	7

Source: *Petroleum Intelligence Weekly*, April 14, 1980, p. 2.

that they built up in the preceding thirty years. The oil-producing nations are determined to create their own vertically integrated oil companies so that they can control the flow of oil—and oil revenues—in all phases of the industry. With exclusive access to crude oil the producer nations are in a strong position to expand downstream. But they are still in the learning phase and depend strongly on private companies as the ultimate outlet for their oil.

Under these circumstances three fundamental questions arise for the major oil companies and the consuming nations that they serve: If the producer nations controlled the flow of oil products as well as crude oil, could the consuming nations respond effectively to a major oil import disruption? Is it in the best interest of the industrialized oil-importing countries to cooperate with the oil-producing nations in the development of their downstream operations? And have changes in the commercial terms of access already undermined the ability of major oil companies to manage an oil shortage whether or not the IEA supply-sharing agreement (discussed in Chapter 5) is implemented? To answer these questions this chapter first reviews how the producing countries acquired control over their oil production and how they have begun to move into the "downstream" development projects.

NATIONALIZATION OF PRODUCTION

Up to 1970 the Seven Sisters dominated world petroleum trade. They produced the oil, shipped it to major markets in Europe and Japan, refined it and sold the products to the final user. Vertical integration gave the companies extraordinary logistical flexibility. As the main suppliers of crude oil to most refiners worldwide and as distributors of refined products, they could readily adjust supply and demand in most markets. Furthermore, even when a few countries nationalized production—notably Mexico and Iran in the 1930s and 1950s—power over the downstream end of the industry allowed the companies to maintain considerable control over the market for those nations' crude oil. As one historian of the oil industry has noted,

> However successful host governments were in finding technicians to help keep the oil flowing, they were lost without customers on world markets. These were difficult to find as long as the bulk of the world's refineries

have either been owned by the majors or tied to them by long-term supply contracts, and this difficulty was exacerbated by the general world glut of oil in the 1960s.[1]

Thus, with the ability to restrict markets for the producing nations for their crude oil, the major companies could preserve their preeminence in both the upstream and downstream aspects of the industry.

Originally the major oil companies received concessions from the oil-bearing countries of Latin America and the Persian Gulf, under which the companies developed oil fields in certain areas for a given length of time (fifty years, for example). In return the companies paid royalties or excise taxes to their "host" governments. This system gave the companies complete control over the rate of oil production, pricing, and exports. In short, the companies took all the risks of failure and all the financial rewards of success. The countries by contrast received an income from production with little investment of capital or labor.

"The concession system," as one expert has noted, "by its very nature could not satisfy the desire of producing-country governments for more influence on the rate at which their oil was produced or on other decisions concerning the exploitation of their resources."[2] Any reduction in prices for crude oil because of market conditions automatically cut revenues to the producing government. Moreover, the gradual depletion of reserves eroded the base for future revenues, especially for the Persian Gulf states, since oil is virtually their sole source of income.

Concerned about the exploitation of their resources, some of the Middle Eastern oil producers—Saudi Arabia, Iran, Iraq, and Kuwait—joined Venezuela in forming the Organization of Petroleum Exporting Countries (OPEC) in 1960.[a] OPEC set out to coordinate long-term policies on production rates, pricing, and taxation of the companies. During the 1960s OPEC wielded little power, largely because of a world oil glut and constant price-cutting as older companies battled with newer companies to preserve or increase markets. The price wars eventually led to a confrontation between the oil companies and the producing countries that would mark the end of oil company control over world oil production.

---

[a]OPEC now represents Algeria, Indonesia, Iran, Libya, Nigeria, Saudi Arabia, United Arab Emigrates (UAE), Venezuela, Ecuador, Gabon, Iraq, Kuwait, and Qatar. The Organization of Arab Petroleum Exporting Countries (OAPEC) represents Algeria, Libya, Saudi Arabia, UAE, Iraq, Kuwait, and Qatar.

In 1969 Muamar Qaddafi overthrew King Idris and established a revolutionary government in Libya. That year Libyan oil production had peaked at 3.1 mmbd, nearly displacing Iranian output (3.3 mmbd) and surpassing that of Saudi Arabia (2.9 mmbd). To compete with the Persian Gulf states the independent oil companies had rapidly developed the oil fields and cut prices. Qaddafi was determined to increase the nation's income from oil production in order to finance development projects. Since the government's taxes and royalties were based on the price of crude oil, it became imperative to raise the price of oil substantially. In 1970 Qaddafi ordered a cut in production and a price increase, threatening to expropriate companies that did not comply. Once Qaddafi had succeeded in extracting a considerable price increase, other OPEC countries negotiated similar price and tax rises.

With power over pricing the OPEC nations gained confidence in their ability to take over the petroleum industry. The concession system rapidly gave way to outright nationalization or "participation." Under participation, the countries increased their ownership of existing concessions to at least 51 percent. Algeria nationalized production in 1971–73, Iraq in 1972–75, Kuwait in 1976, Qatar in 1977, and Saudi Arabia in 1976 (formalized in 1980). Libya nationalized some interests but has 51 percent participation in other concessions. Nigeria and Abu Dhabi also have participation agreements with major oil firms.

Nationalization and participation have given OPEC producers the chance to compete directly with the major oil companies in all aspects of crude oil marketing. Although at first, private companies received the right under participation to buy back oil that they produced, the state oil companies or agencies increasingly sold crude oil directly to independent refiners or new state companies in the consuming nations. In 1981, Petromin, the state oil company of Saudi Arabia, sold 1.7 mmbd of crude oil while the ARAMCO partners (Exxon, Mobil, Socal, and Texaco) sold the remainder (some 6.8 mmbd of oil). Even when the producer governments supply the companies with crude oil under "buy-back" agreements, however, they do not give the companies absolute freedom to market the crude oil as they see fit. Unpredictable breaches of contract by the producer states can suddenly increase prices or reduce the volume of oil available to the companies. In addition, the producer states increasingly add restrictive clauses to supply contracts that limit the resale of oil or the shipment of crude oil to certain countries. These practices further jeopardize the security of world oil supplies in a market already complicated by political interference.

PRICING

After the oil embargo of 1973–74, OPEC began to set a uniform price for crude oil. As the largest producer, Saudi Arabia was usually able to provide the "benchmark" price of crude oil for OPEC, because in effect it could raise or lower prices by raising or lowering its production. Although this pricing formula worked from 1974 to 1978, during the Iranian oil shortage of 1978–79 the OPEC nations ceased to agree on a single price. In a sellers' market characterized by panic buying, the OPEC producers went their separate ways, getting whatever they could for crude oil in the open market. At the height of the Iranian revolution, for example, Libyan crude oil was roughly $9 per barrel more than Saudi crude oil even though the difference in quality and location would justify only a $3–4 premium per barrel. After the Iranian oil shortage, most of the OPEC producers affixed premiums several dollars above the "official" price of OPEC oil set by the Saudi Arabians until the price erosion during the so-called oil glut in 1981.

Fixed contract prices have also become irrelevant, because producer governments simply decree increases whether or not the contract provides for readjustment. Countries impose price increases on existing contracts and impose retroactive increases on oil long after it has been produced and sold. Furthermore, the OPEC producers have attempted to sustain surcharges even when the open market prices have been considerably lower. In an extreme move to force companies to accept surcharges, Kuwait in April 1981 suspended major oil contracts because companies would not accept surcharges in renewed contracts. Since the companies affected could pick up an equivalent amount of crude oil at much lower spot prices, the move did not affect supply. Although later rescinded in response to market conditions, Kuwait's action demonstrates the lengths to which the producer states may attempt to impose their will regardless of market conditions.

THE SPOT MARKET

During the Iranian-induced oil shortage, the OPEC producers broke contracts with the major companies so that they could sell single cargoes for much higher prices in the open or "spot" market. In a traditional market, one in which contracts for future supplies at a set price are honored, the spot market would provide a commercially based trading price reflecting market conditions. Furthermore, before the Iranian oil shortage, the spot market constituted only 5–8 percent of total oil trade. Companies and traders exchanged single cargoes of crude oil and product to smooth out individual demand. However, in the Iranian oil shortage, the spot market expanded to as much as 25 percent of international oil trade as producer governments and traders used it as an auction block for crude sales to panic buyers. As a result upward spiraling spot prices started to set prices for the entire market. Under depressed market conditions such as obtained in early 1981, when supply exceeds demand, spot prices are lower than official prices (plus individual premiums) and consequently help in forcing producers to reduce prices.

EXPORT RESTRICTIONS

In addition to unpredictable breaches of contract affecting both supply and prices some producers both inside and outside OPEC also interfere with oil trade by restricting the resale of oil cargoes by commercial firms that have supply contracts with the producers. Mexico, Venezuela, Algeria, and Libya all forbid resales. Kuwait sets destination and resale restrictions so stringent that sales to an affiliate of which the company with the supply contract owns less than 51 percent may be treated as a forbidden resale.

In contracts with customers (other than ARAMCO), Petromin of Saudi Arabia has dictated that "under no circumstances shall Buyer resell the said Crude Oil in its original form or blend it with any other crude oil or crude oil deliveries for purposes of resale."[3] The seller requires a certificate from the buyer that proves the cargo was discharged at the port of unloading. There are ways around these clauses, such as forging certificates and immediately reloading the cargo for another destination or resale. But the restrictions on resale impair the flexibility of companies to shift cargoes easily to match up crude oil quality and supply needs.

In addition to restrictions on resale, many countries forbid the shipment of oil to certain countries, notably South Africa or Israel, and mandate the shipment of the same cargo to other countries. For example Saudi Arabia requires that the ARAMCO partners supply certain less-developed countries with their full contract volumes even though Japan, Europe, and the United States must accept reduced supplies because volumes available to ARAMCO have been curtailed. Furthermore OPEC is considering a plan of global petroleum allocation that would grant preferential treatment to developing countries and allocation of remaining supplies among the industrialized countries. According to a report of the OPEC Long-term Strategy Committee, "OPEC should formulate and declare as a general policy a preferential treatment of developing countries as far as security of supplies is concerned. A specific mechanism within OPEC should be worked out and agreed upon to ensure the implementation of such supplies at official prices of OPEC member countries."[4]

Finally, the OPEC countries are beginning to subject customers to political criteria to determine whether or not their supply contracts will be honored. For example, in 1980 Denmark signed an agreement with Petromin for delivery of 200,000 barrels per day of oil. Clause 8.1c of the contract states that the buyer "or such government or any such department or instrumentality" will not "conduct itself in such a manner as to bring the kingdom of Saudi Arabia or any of its departments or instrumentalities into disrepute in the international oil community or in any manner whatsoever." Petromin also reserves the right "in its absolute discretion" to "determine that there has been any breach by the buyer," in which case it can suspend the contract.[5] Denmark's Energy Minister Poul Nielson was careful to point out that Denmark is "not planning to do anything to bring Saudi Arabia into disrepute any way"; nonetheless the implications of the contract cannot be as readily understated: the oil importers must avoid political or media criticism of Saudi Arabia or risk a suspension of oil shipments.[6]

To sum up, the producing countries in a relatively brief period of time have managed to gain ownership or control of nearly all of the crude oil that the major oil companies previously produced and controlled. This "oil power" has given the governments of the producing nations unprecedented leverage over world trade. They can restrict exports, raise prices, break contracts at will, and interfere with the resale or destination of oil cargoes. Although none of these actions alone can interrupt the flow of oil, each can interfere with the smooth distribution of oil in normal times and enormously complicate the allocation of supply during shortages. Under various conditions, restrictions on the resale of oil could limit the flexibility of companies to meet regional shortages. Furthermore, as the OPEC nations expand downstream and refine more of their own crude oil, the availability of crude oil and products could become greatly limited during an emergency. Before examining the impact that OPEC state company control could have on the commercial response to an oil crisis, it is useful to examine the development plans of the producing nations.

DOWNSTREAM EXPANSION

A long-standing objective of the OPEC nations has been to build up their own refining, transportation, and marketing operations. For the OPEC producers expansion into downstream activities represents long-term economic and political survival. They consider the existence of excess refining, petrochemical and tanker capacity in the rest of the world irrelevant to their development plans. As one OPEC analyst notes,

> The desire of OPEC Member Countries to participate in downstream operations has been confronted with similar criteria and standards to those faced by other raw material producers. Every step in this direction has been met with the concept of the existence of over-capacity which renders most projects unfeasible and uneconomical or any change of the established ownership and control, contrary to consumer interests. What is neglected, therefore, is the "national approach" according to which along with the concept of return on investment, the producer countries are also concerned with creating employment, substituting imports and being self-reliant, especially in the long term.[7]

Thus, the OPEC nations will not be easily deterred from building their own refineries, petrochemical plants, tankers, and marketing organizations. Their strategy, however, is still evolving. How will they attain this goal in a world market already overcrowded by downstream operators?

The main obstacle the producing nations face in developing vertically integrated oil industries is a shortage of skilled management personnel among their own people. This has been a consistent problem since the producers began to seek control over the oil companies. In the 1950s, for example, Venezuela, then the most advanced of the producing nations in upstream an downstream operations, had trouble breaking into the established oil industry. As Franklin Tugwell, historian of the Venezuelan oil industry writes, the government oil commission "was never able to keep close enough track of the companies' marketing decisions. Its leaders, though highly trained, lacked experience, and the agency itself lacked the staff and facilities needed for the complex job it had taken on."[8] Several of the OPEC nations today find themselves in a similar position as they attempt to gain experience in the complicated logistical and technical skills that the companies have developed in product marketing. To acquire experience in refining and marketing, activities still dominated by the major companies, the OPEC states need to learn the ropes from established firms that operate in the major markets. Thus, over the past few years and especially since the Iranian oil shortage the OPEC countries have sought special arrangements with foreign refineries or marketers that would allow the producers not only to realize some profit on downstream operations outside their domestic markets but to gain experience in international product trade.

Recently the main tactic for downstream expansion has been the crude processing agreement. Under these contracts European refiners process a certain amount of crude oil and either sell the products on behalf of the producer or the producer state company markets the products. In a variation of this strategy, state companies are also trying to acquire partial ownership of refineries in Europe and the United States. Frequently these bids offer assured supplies of crude oil from the producer country to the refinery. This move would achieve two goals. By becoming principal shareholders producers would capture some of the total value added to the crude oil by processing and sales. Furthermore they could acquire financial and marketing expertise either by association with the firm or, as principal shareholders, by requiring that the firm employ some of their nationals in refining and marketing.

Because of their proximity to Europe, Libya and Algeria have long processed a certain amount of crude oil in Italy for their own use. Since 1979 the Persian Gulf states have started to contract European refiners to process crude oil and sell products on their behalf. Saudi Arabia has arranged for roughly 170,000 barrels per day to be processed by BP (50,000 bd), Mobil (35,000 bd), Latsis refinery in Greece (10,000–15,000 bd), and Bapco in Bahrain (20,000 bd). Some of the products, such as the middle distillates, will be shipped back to Saudi Arabia for internal use; Petromin has planned to market other products directly in Europe. Some of the companies involved in these deals sell the products on behalf of the companies and turn the revenues over to Saudi Arabia.

Since February 1979 Kuwait National Petroleum Company has upgraded 15,000 barrels per day of Kuwait-refined fuel oil into lighter products in Sicily at the Monti Group's Milazzo refinery. Furthermore Kuwait is interested in acquiring shares in European refineries as part of future processing deals. Although some small independent refineries have expressed interest in such arrangements with the producing states, the major oil companies have tended to resist bids for partial ownership. BP, for example, refused Kuwait's proposal to acquire an equity interest in its refineries. The penalty for refusal was payment of a $3.50 per barrel premium for one-half of the 150,000 bd that BP receives from Kuwait.

OPEC nations have thus far restricted their downstream activities to Europe. They are beginning to investigate opportunities in the United States, however. As a result of crude oil decontrol, many smaller U.S. refineries have lost government subsidies under the old entitlements program that helped them to compete with larger companies. Like their European counterparts, these small independent refiners would welcome an infusion of OPEC money and crude oil into their systems. As one small refiner has stated, "If the foreign groups don't invest downstream in the United States, they will do it in their own countries. And if they do, we will be importing more refined products. It's better to have the dollars invested in this country."[9]

In the short term some refiners would benefit from joint ownership with OPEC producers, but in the long term such deals could help undermine commercial refiners in the industrialized countries. Crude processing deals and joint ownership of companies provide an opportunity to learn the oil business with very little risk to the producer. According to recent reports, the OPEC companies that seek joint ownership do not plan to sink any capital into the plants (for upgrading equipment and other improvements) nor to assume any direct role in management.[10] Yet as a major stockholder the producer could gain access to the inner workings of the firm. Once producers learn what they need to know about refining and marketing, they are likely to sell out and apply their new knowledge to their own downstream operations. Producers would have everything to gain and nothing to lose by acquiring part-ownership of a refinery outside their own country.

In the short term the refiner can take advantage of crude oil and the financial benefits of a favorable sale of stock but gains little in the long term. Not even greater security of supply is acquired, since recent experience has revealed the ease with which OPEC state companies break contracts. Moreover, OPEC producers may well sell their stock in refineries as soon as it has served their purpose. If, for example, a refinery was only able to survive and turn a profit because it had access to supply at official prices, the refinery could well go under once the OPEC producer relinquished ownership and revoked the supply contract.

The difficulty that OPEC producers have had in gaining expertise in refining and marketing also applies to transportation, again because the OPEC fleet lacks adequately trained officers and management personnel.[11] Furthermore, even though shipping has not been the exclusive domain of the multinational oil companies, the excess of tanker capacity worldwide indicates no real demand for new tankers in the immediate future. Only if OPEC began to require that its oil be shipped in OPEC-owned and operated tankers could it attempt to build up a competitive fleet. However, since OPEC tanker capacity currently comprises only 3.5 percent of world tanker capacity, OPEC could not attempt this strategy for many years to come. OPEC countries currently have about 12 million deadweight tons (Dwt) in tanker capacity, which could carry only about 230,000 bd of oil, or roughly 1 percent of total OPEC crude oil output. Hence OPEC producers must continue to use commercial tankers for crude oil transport.

OPEC REFINING CAPACITY

In 1980 OPEC members had the capacity to process 6.25 mmbd of crude oil; they added nearly 1 mmbd of that capacity in that year alone. OPEC expects to construct an additional 2-3 mmbd of capacity over the next few years, so by 1985 total refining capacity could be 8-9 mmbd. At the same time OPEC officials expect that internal oil consumption, which is currently 2.4 mmbd, could increase to 3.9 mmbd by 1985.[12] The construction of OPEC refining capacity could help OPEC meet its own expanding petroleum product needs.

Although the OPEC producers may initially lack downstream expertise, their exclusive access to crude oil will give them an extraordinary advantage over the major oil companies in the product market. Furthermore, they could force customers to accept both refined products and crude oil. Before the Iran-Iraq war, Iran was requiring crude oil purchasers to buy surplus fuel oil equivalent to 20–35 percent of crude oil volume at a premium over market value. With their strong position in crude oil and a growing refining capacity, the producer nations are likely to become major exporters of oil products by the end of the 1980s.

Although some American refiners have been concerned about an influx of fuel imports from OPEC countries to the United States, the most likely outlet for OPEC products will be Europe. Product transportation requires specially designed clean tankers that tend to be far smaller than crude oil supertankers. Consequently Middle East producers would lose the economy of scale offered by supertanker transport if they attempted to ship products instead of crude oil to the United States. If Middle East producers forced the United States to accept some products as well as crude oil, the total price of these imports could become high enough to encourage development and use of synthetic fuels or shale oil. Hence OPEC nations, with the exception of Venezuela and Ecuador, are unlikely to target the United States for product exports.

By contrast the economics of shipping products to Europe encourage Middle Eastern and African producers to build up refining and marketing operations. Before the closure of the Suez Canal from 1967 to 1974), Persian Gulf producers sent crude oil to Europe on relatively small tankers by the short route through the Gulf of Aden, the Red Sea, and the Suez Canal. With the closing of the canal and the development of supertankers, the Middle East countries started to send oil to Europe by the longer route around the Cape of Good Hope. The reopening of the Suez Canal to oil tanker traffic has allowed the economical transport of both crude oil and products by the short Mediterranean route.

To take advantage of the canal Saudi Arabia is building major refineries along the Red Sea. For example, the Greek conglomerate, the Latsis Group, in a joint venture with Petromin, will construct a 325,000 bd refinery, as large or larger than the major refineries in the United States, at Rabigh on the Red Sea, 120 miles south of the new crude oil pipeline terminal and refinery complex at Yanbu. By 1982–83 this refinery could be producing fuel oil for export primarily to Europe.

The Europeans have long recognized that a flood of oil products into their markets could force many refineries out of business. In

1981 Western Europe could process roughly 20.5 mmbd but refined only 13–14 mmbd of crude oil. Higher oil prices and depressed product sales have forced most refiners to cut production or to close down plants altogether. At the same time, however, Europe has net product imports of 700,000 barrels per day. If those imports grow because Middle Eastern producers start to require Europeans to import products as well as crude oil, many more European refineries would go bankrupt.

The European refining problem remains an important item on the agenda of discussions between the European Economic Community (EEC) and OPEC. In 1978 the EEC initiated talks with OPEC in order to develop a common approach to refining issues. Several obstacles surfaced immediately. In December 1978 Secretary General Dr. 'Ali 'Atiga of the Organization of Arab Petroleum Exporting Countries (OAPEC) stated that from the Arab standpoint "what the common policy is aiming at is a coordinated approach towards the marketing of the products of such [Arab] refineries. In brief, the objective is to ensure free and fair access for Arab refined products to the EEC and other major consuming areas, unhindered by the present tariff and quota barriers."[13] Dr. 'Atiga also stated that Arab exporters might find it necessary to link the marketing of products with that of crude oil. The Arabs have turned a blind eye to the European problem of excess refining capacity.

Because of fundamental disagreements over refining policies and other pricing or export issues, the EEC and OPEC have been unable to strike up a meaningful dialogue on common economic and energy problems. Indeed, OPEC suspended EEC-OPEC talks abruptly after Guido Brunner, then EEC energy commissioner, accused OPEC of practicing "economic brinkmanship" in an interview with the *International Herald Tribune* in June 1979. "Most of all, the OPEC countries," he argued, "think that they can limit production slightly below demand in order to maintain prices and spur energy conservation— without stopping reasonable growth in the world economy . . . If they miscalculate the oil gap, it could push the world economy off the tightrope, causing recession, destabilizing the world monetary system and causing unemployment with grave social repercussions."[14] Thus what began as a discussion of refining problems quickly degenerated into acrimony. By 1981 there was little prospect of resurrecting formal talks between the EEC and OPEC on the major issue of OPEC down stream expansion and product exports.

IMPLICATIONS FOR SECURITY OF OPEC DOWNSTREAM EXPANSION

OPEC economists have written that "the oil industry operates more economically when it is vertically integrated . . . Thus, it follows that the natural complement to the control and ownership of crude oil production is transportation and refining of petroleum, and ultimately, distribution of petroleum products and gases by the producers and consumers in a more equitable and fair proportion than exists today."[15] Other economists outside OPEC have also suggested that the development of vertically integrated companies in the producer nations would have positive effects on the market. Thomas L. Neff argues in *Energy and Security* that

> Downstream producer involvements, another source of reduced flexibility [to private companies], may also benefit consumers. If producers become extensively involved in refining or product markets abroad, they will have a stake in the efficient and undisrupted functioning of these markets. Such involvement may also help moderate prices. If crude and product prices rise too much and demand slackens, the downward pressure on prices is first felt in product markets. If producers are not involved in product markets, they can hold crude prices up longer, letting the intermediary companies suffer the erosion of profit margins. But if producers are involved, they will feel the demand effects more directly.[16]

Economic theory may support such arguments, but the economic reality of world oil trade today does not. It is unlikely that the creation of vertically integrated oil companies in the OPEC countries will help to moderate prices, reduce the risk of disruptions, or increase market efficiency. As noted throughout this chapter, the OPEC state oil companies do not behave in the same manner as private oil firms. The crux of the matter is that they do not recognize or honor the forward contract, which is the basis of traditional commercial transactions. Instead they operate according to a new type of contract, the "forward spot" contract. Whereas a normal forward contract would establish the future delivery of oil at a price and in a volume previously agreed upon, OPEC's contracts establish the future delivery of oil at a price and in a volume that is always subject to change. Furthermore OPEC producers violate the fundamental commercial character of trade (as has the United States on occasion) by forbidding sales to certain customers for political reasons and resales of oil for economic or logistical reasons. The OPEC producers have thus turned the oil market into an oil bazaar.

If the oil-producing nations succeed in duplicating the downstream services now provided by the major oil companies and continue their noncommercial practices, they could force many commercial refiners and marketers in the consuming countries out of business, especially in Europe. The Seven Sisters would be particularly affected since European refineries represent roughly 73 percent of their refining capacity and marketing operations outside the United States. The loss of the European market to OPEC state companies would eliminate the multinationals from international trade and restrict their activities to the western hemisphere.

The retreat of the Seven Sisters from the world oil market would have profound consequences for the United States and its European allies. In the past the multinational oil companies had the flexibility not only to smooth out regional distribution problems but also to handle government allocation plans during emergencies. However, if the companies are forced to close large segments of their European operations because of OPEC competition, European governments, state companies, and independent marketers would become captive to the capricious export policies of the producing states. If one OPEC nation suspended product exports because of internal disruptions or for political and commercial reasons, other OPEC nations could not always be relied upon to fill the gap. Furthermore the creation of rigid supply channels between state companies in the Persian Gulf and North Africa area and state marketing agencies in Europe would vastly complicate if not paralyze the process of supply reallocation in a major shortage. The commercial changes effected by OPEC's downstream expansion would have dire strategic consequences for the oil-consuming nations.

There has been a tendency in the United States to distinguish between the strategic and commercial aspects of maintaining access to world oil supply. This distinction becomes invalid when the survival of national economies depends on the continued strength of commercial activities. The changing terms of commercial access to oil have jeopardized the ability of the major oil companies and the countries they serve to react effectively to a global oil shortage. Without strong commercial firms in place to serve many markets, the IEA supply-sharing agreement simply may not work. If the European market were managed by state marketing agencies importing largely refined products from OPEC, the IEA supply-sharing agreement would become a worthless scrap of paper.

The companies and the oil-importing countries need to resist OPEC's expansion into downstream operations. Since OPEC is still in the learning stage companies should reduce opportunities for OPEC members to master marketing techniques outside their regional market. Companies should resist OPEC bids for joint ownership, extensive crude processing deals, and other arrangements that would give OPEC producers a direct hand in the consuming nations' oil markets. Whenever the OPEC producers seek to gain access to an established refining and marketing firm with offers of assured crude oil at official prices or special financial terms, the company should resist in the interest of long-term security.

In the face of mounting OPEC control over petroleum refining and marketing, the consuming nations must do what they can to maintain the competitiveness of the commercial companies. The survival of these firms in the face of OPEC competition depends not only on access to petroleum but on financial strength. As long as the major companies have the natural and financial resources to counter OPEC, they can preserve their logistical superiority and control over downstream activities. In this respect the consuming nations in which the companies are based should consider the strategic and financial implications of measures that are designed deliberately either to weaken their marketing operations (vertical divestiture, nationalization) or to curtail their freedom of economic action (restrictions on investment in non-energy-related businesses, onerous taxation). While such measures may achieve certain political goals, they could also curtail the overall financial strength needed to offset the growing power of the OPEC nations to compete with the majors for product markets. The major companies at this time appear to be in no danger of going under, with the possible exception of the British Petroleum Company. Yet consuming nations need to design energy and economic policies that will not undermine their strength in the long term.

CONCLUSIONS

Control over crude oil production represents only half of the battle to maintain global access to energy. Refining, transportation, and marketing are also important elements of world oil trade. Control of these downstream operations represents considerable power in the oil market. Although the OPEC nations have greatly impaired the power and flexibility of commercial oil companies by nationalizing oil production, the private companies are still in a position to compete sharply for control of the downstream end of the industry.

In the 1980s it is vital for the oil companies to maintain their hold over these operations. The companies need to resist the efforts of the Middle East and North African producers to gain a foothold in the major consuming markets of Europe and the United States. The consuming nations must make every effort to support the companies instead of enacting policies that undermine their strong financial position and flexibility of response. The governments of the consuming nations must realize that even though the majors may be politically unpopular, life without them could be disastrous from the strategic standpoint.

As long as the companies have a hold over the logistics of world trade and downstream operations, they have some ability to respond to a world oil shortage. If exports are restricted and access to crude oil is limited, in a crisis the companies may be able to shift around only marginal amounts of crude oil under the IEA supply-sharing agreement or their own allocation schemes. With limited commercial supplies of crude oil and contractual constraints on crude flows the consuming nations must build up their stockpiles of crude oil for use in an emergency. This is a powerful argument in favor of the strategic petroleum reserve. Without assured supplies of crude oil from the SPR the companies may not survive the next oil crisis, and OPEC will be free to take over control of the world oil market.

NOTES

1. Louis Turner, *Oil Companies in the International System* (London, 1978), p. 93.

2. Ian M. Torrens, *Changing Structures in the World Oil Market* (Paris, 1980), pp. 9–10.

3. "Text of Saudi Arabia's Oil 'Incentive' Contracts," *Petroleum Intelligence Weekly,* Special Supplement, August 25, 1980, p. 3.

4. Quoted by Francisco R. Parra, ."Allocation, Next Big Change in World Oil Trade?," *Petroleum Intelligence Weekly,* Special Supplement, September 15, 1980, p. 3.

5. Quoted in "Death of a Minister, Denmark and Saudi Arabia," *The Economist,* May 31, 1980, p. 91.
6. Ibid.
7. Fironz Azornia and Ivan Bejarano, "OPEC's Share in Downstream Operations: The Transportation Case," *OPEC Review* 3 no. 2 (Summer 1979): 75.
8. Franklin Tugwell, *The Politics of Oil in Venezuela* (Stanford, 1975), p. 59.
9. Quoted in "Oil Exporters Press Move into Downstream Areas," *The Oil and Gas Journal,* August 11, 1980, vol. 78, no. 32, p. 30.
10. Ibid.
11. *OPEC Review,* p. 77.
12. "OPEC Warns its Oil Needs May Cut Exports in 1990s," *Petroleum Intelligence Weekly,* September 8, 1980, p. 2.
13. Quoted in *Middle East Economic Survey,* December 18, 1978, vol. 22, no. 9, p. 2.
14. Reprinted in *Middle East Economic Survey,* July 9, 1979, vol. 22, no. 38, p. 2.
15. *OPEC Review,* p. 75.
16. Thomas L. Neff, "The Changing World Oil Market," in *Energy and Security,* ed. David A. Deese and Joseph S. Nye (Cambridge, Mass.: Ballinger Publishing Company, 1980), p. 35.

7 THE FINANCIAL CONSEQUENCES OF IMPORT DEPENDENCE

The first oil shortage, the embargo of 1973–74, activated massive flows of money across foreign exchanges. Within twelve months the share of fuels in world trade rose from 12 to 20 percent,[1] and the current-account balance of the OPEC countries increased sevenfold.[2] Unspent petrodollars were deposited in large international banks and despite warnings of financial chaos or collapse the international financial system successfully recycled the funds, lending them to countries that chose to maintain high growth rates rather than deflate their economies in response to oil-induced balance-of-payments deficits. The rapid-growth countries that borrowed heavily were the non-oil-producing less-developed countries (LDCs) and the smaller industrial countries, such as Spain, Austria, and Sweden. So successfully did the international financial system cope with the flood of petrodollars that by 1979 OPEC's surplus had disappeared. From over $60 billion in 1974 the OPEC balance-of-payments surplus (before official transfers) had been reduced to $7 billion by 1979.

The successful adjustment of the world economy to the sweeping changes of the 1970s cannot be credited solely to the international commercial banks. The OPEC countries themselves astonished everyone with their ability to absorb imports. Between 1973 and 1979 their spending on imports increased at an average annual rate of 15 percent.[3] Equally important, heavy borrowers were willing and able to go into debt at commercial rather than concessional rates of interest to maintain their high growth rates. Indeed, they borrowed money primarily to expand export capacity, which provided the additional foreign exchange they needed to service their external indebtedness. Finally, the adjustment of the world economy and financial system was accelerated by a decline after 1974 in the real price of oil. By 1978 the oil-exporting countries' terms of trade with the industrial world were nearly 20 percent below 1974 levels.[4] Most important, the real price of oil did not increase further.

CHANGED CIRCUMSTANCES OF THE 1980s

Although oil prices increased only 150 percent in 1979–80 compared with 400 percent in 1974, the smaller increase occurred at so much higher a level (roughly $13 a barrel instead of $3) that the dollar effects has been nearly as great. The outlook for adjustment to the more recent price jumps is not nearly so favorable as it was in 1974. For one thing, the OPEC countries themselves are less likely to follow policies that will ameliorate the effects of the 1979 price jump.

The producers appear to have learned from the experience of the intervening years the lessons of demand-inelasticity and "money illusion." When consuming countries panicked about security of supply after the Iranian revolution, OPEC members came to realize that they could achieve higher revenues by selling less oil rather than more. In 1980 almost all OPEC producers curtailed their production rates as demand in consuming countries dropped off.[5] Most of them, not having Saudi Arabia's rich resources, had become truly concerned about the limits of their national treasure and wanted to make it last.

Moreover the difference between money income and real income had been graphically illustrated to them when their terms of trade declined sharply in the 1970s. In the face of rising import prices, they had to export more oil to pay for the same volume of imports. They will probably be able to avoid such a decline in the 1980s, when world demand and supply are likely to be much more closely balanced (see Chapter 1).

OPEC's demand for exports from the industrialized countries (and therefore their requirements for income from oil) grew at a rate of 15 percent between 1974 and 1979. OPEC demand is unlikely to grow at the same rate in the 1980s. Chastened by the Iranian revolution, many world leaders, including heads of OPEC states, have begun to realize that the social strains that accompany a rapid growth rate threaten a regime's stability; prudence dictates a more moderate growth rate. This is not to say that growth will not be substantial but, rather, that there will be a new emphasis on social services such as education and rural development, which are less import-intensive than major industrial projects and thus require less foreign-exchange income.

The oil-exporting countries more and more view "oil in the ground" as preferable to an accumulation of financial assets, not only because inflation reduces money's purchasing power but also for political reasons. The freeze on Iranian assets in American-controlled banks, the U.S. embargo on trade with Iran, and the cutoff of U.S. exports to the USSR of grain and high-technology products have made the OPEC surplus countries doubtful about the security of their financial holdings in, and trade relations with, the United States.[6] By making the OPEC nations aware of the risk of blocked assets and other means of economic warfare, the United States in its dealings with Iran and the USSR has made the future of oil supplies somewhat less secure.

If the OPEC countries are successful in implementing their long-term strategy to adjust the price of oil to prices in the industrialized countries plus the latter's growth rates, the real price of oil will probably increase an average of 2 to 3 percent annually. Even such an apparently modest increase in the real price of oil would probably make it impossible to eliminate the petrodollar surplus and therefore the unstable balance of international payments. What is more, any major supply interruption could seriously exacerbate the payments deficits of the consuming countries and increase the surplus of the exporting countries.

Only if there is no change in the real price of oil or a decline in real price is there any hope that the world economy and the balance of international payments will adjust as well in the 1980s as they did in the 1970s. Even under the most favorable conditions, however, the recycling mechanisms will change considerably. In the 1970s it was essential that borrowers be able to borrow and that international banks be able to lend. The very success of recycling in the 1970s, however, implies difficulties in the 1980s. International banks are now reassessing their loan exposure among many LDCs while some LDCs are fully indebted, that is the size of their debt equals their ability to repay.

During the 1970s the industrial countries sought for the most part to control inflation through deflationary fiscal and monetary policies, while a number of developing countries went into debt to maintain high growth rates. After 1973 the GNP of the large industrial countries grew an average of only 3 percent, while the GNP of the non-oil-producing LDCs grew about three times as rapidly.[7] While world trade was growing less than 5 percent on the average between 1973 and 1979,[8] the increase in non-oil LDC exports of manufactured goods averaged more than 10 percent. In 1979 exports of manufactured goods from the non-oil-producing LDCs exceeded exports of raw materials for the first time.[9] To achieve this remarkable record the developing countries increased their cumulative external indebtedness from $95 billion at the end of 1973 to $315 billion in 1978 and nearly $400 billion in 1980.[10] More than three-fifths of that total was borrowed from commercial banks. The non-oil-producing LDCs accounted for nearly 60 percent of all new Eurocurrency credits in 1979 compared with 35 percent in 1974. Service charges on their external debt rose from about 9 percent in 1973 to over 17 percent of foreign exchange receipts in 1979.[11] More important, their interest rates, which averaged about 4 percent in 1973, soared to nearly 20 percent at the end of 1980. Since roughly one-quarter of their debt is carried at floating interest rates, every 1-point rise in the benchmark rate increases their annual interest charges by $1 billion.[12]

Two things are important here. First, the bulk of LDC borrowing in the 1970s financed new productive capacity, either directly or indirectly, resulting in an increase in exports and foreign exchange receipts. Second, as the Bank for International Settlements has pointed out, "financing a persistent balance of payments deficit is a different proposition from financing a temporary one."[13] During the 1970s the world assumed that an oil price shock of the magnitude experienced in 1973–74 was a one-time event and that any future oil price rises would be minor. People were forced to disabuse themselves of this notion in 1979–80. Moreover as Rimmer de Vries, the respected vice-president of the Morgan-Guarantee Trust Company, has written, the rate of increase in the relative price of oil during the 1980s would have to be closer to zero than to 3 percent for non-OPEC balance-of-payments deficits to disappear.[14] As we have seen, real oil prices are not likely to be stable, so OPEC surpluses will probably continue, rather than disappear as they did in the 1970s, even if there are no more "price shocks," and the high level of non-OPEC LDC debt will remain. Thus countries that borrowed heavily in the 1970s will probably be less willing or able to borrow heavily in the 1980s.

More than 80 percent of all Euromarket loans to LDCs from 1974 to 1979 went to just twenty countries; over 40 percent went to five countries: Brazil, Mexico, Argentina, South Korea, and the Philippines.[15] Among the major borrowers, the burden of oil imports and debt service charges in relation to foreign exchange income varies greatly. Brazil, the largest borrower, had a cumulative debt of $55 billion in 1980, including $37 billion to private banks. Oil imports and interest payments alone accounted for about 80 percent of Brazil's foreign exchange receipts from exports of goods and services; amortization charges exhausted the other 15 percent. The Philippine burden of national overhead (oil imports plus interest charges) was almost as staggering at 70 percent. For Thailand it was 50 percent; for Turkey, 40 percent. (These figures do not include amortization charges, which became especially heavy in the early 1980s.)

Under these conditions maintaining imports of essential goods and services is possible only by drawing down foreign exchange reserves. The only alternative is to reduce the country's demand for imports by reducing growth rates or by directly controlling imports. In 1980 the LDCs did all three, and, as the 1980s progress, they are likely to rely more on slower growth to reduce their payments deficits. In fact, the World Bank's 1980 projection for annual LDC growth rates for the 1980s was 2.2 percent, substantially lower than its earlier estimate of 5.6 percent.[16] The bank assumed that the world recession would diminish demand for LDC exports and that real oil prices would increase an average of 3 percent a year through the 1980s.

Insofar as the LDCs reduce their payments deficits by reducing their growth rate, the burden of the persistent OPEC surpluses will be borne by the industrial countries, whose deficits will climb as exports to the LDCs decline. The depressing outlook for the non-OPEC world-stagnation of real growth, contracting world markets, and inflation—has inspired so many suggestions for coping with the recycling problems of the 1980s that the *Financial Times* headlined one article "Recycling a la Rube Goldberg."[17] The suggestions cluster around two ideas: getting OPEC to lend funds directly to the LDCs and getting the IMF to support "structural adjustment lending" and more flexible terms for balance-of-payments support.[18]

Even new mechanisms will not prevent recycling problems if the real price of oil continues to rise. Interest burdens will grow and the difficulties of repaying principle will become acute. And the basic problem of the LDC borrowers will remain: They will be borrowing not to increase productive capacity but to maintain levels of output already achieved. Their problems, like those of all oil importers, are structural in nature, and any structural adjustments they undertake will tend to be inadequate if real oil prices continue to rise.

A DIGRESSION ON FORECASTING
THE REAL PRICE OF OIL

The early 1980s are a time of uncertainty in forecasting demand-supply energy balances and in predicting the future of real oil prices. Additional uncertainties stem from unexpected large declines in consumption in the major western oil-consuming nations. In 1980 and 1981, major institutions projecting oil supply-demand relationships reduced their estimates of demand in the OECD countries. These projections flowed from the unanticipated low levels of actual consumption and reflected unexpectedly high actual price elasticities of demand.

This high responsiveness should not be surprising. Economists recognize that long-run elasticity is higher than short-run since consumers adjust gradually as equipment must be replaced. Gas-misers replace gas-guzzlers; homes are insulated or made fuel-efficient; machinery is replaced or plants redesigned to be fuel-efficient; new forms of energy are employed.

The world in the early 1980s had entered the long-run in relation to the 1973-74 oil price hike; hence, price elasticities rose. They also increased from the 1979 price jump that sustained the rising measures of elasticity. The influence of the 1979 price hike will strengthen through the decade.

The world now operates in an unprecedented range of *relative* energy prices. No basis in historical fact exists for measurements of the current price elasticity of demand for energy, short- or long-run. Estimates are thus judgmental. Oil consumption projections are more subject to error than previously, even if relative oil prices remain at their present level.

IMPLICATIONS FOR NATIONAL SECURITY

Any country that, like the United States in the 1960s, experiences a shift from relative self-sufficiency to increasing import dependence in a commodity as important to the economy as petroleum, experiences a diminution of national security. During the 1970s the United States was more vulnerable to pressures from abroad than it had been since the first half of the nineteenth century, primarily because of its need for oil. National security may improve in the 1980s but almost certainly not to the levels the country knew in the 1950s or 1960s.

The chief danger to U.S. national security of rising real oil prices is that they diminish the nation's ability both to influence external events and to resist being influenced by them. Impact of rising oil prices on U.S. inflation, in particular, is nearly impossible to avoid. Informed policymaking may ameliorate any problems that arise, but so long as the United States depends on foreign sources of oil to any significant degree, U.S. domestic economic policy will be influenced by external developments. Similarly depreciation (or appreciation) of the dollar's foreign exchange value because of oil price increases affects U.S. competitiveness in the export market, domestic incomes and employment, and the ability of domestic firms to compete with imports.

Escalating world oil prices also affect the country indirectly. Unspent petrodollars have been invested chiefly in dollar assets: in bank accounts as U.S. dollars, in U.S. securities (both industrial and government), and in U.S. real estate. Meanwhile, U.S. international banks at home and abroad receive dollar deposits from the low-spending oil exporters (primarily Saudi Arabia, Kuwait, and the United Arab Emirates) and relend them, increasingly, to the rapidly growing LDCs. This recycling process itself increases the vulnerability of the United States, as we shall see.

First, the recycling process in the short run can increase domestic inflation if the larger volume of U.S. exports that it stimulates is not counterbalanced by reduced domestic consumption at full employment. If there is full employment domestic consumption must be reduced by an amount equivalent to exports if prices are not to rise or unless the situation is counteracted by deflationary fiscal and monetary policies. Rising domestic prices, moreover, tend to cause the dollar to depreciate, making all imports but oil (which is paid for in dollars) more expensive and boosting inflation further. This energy-induced vulnerability was apparent in the late 1970s when, in terms of relative prices and the degree of industry obsolescence prevailing at the time, the U.S. economy was probably operating at full capacity and excess demand.[19]

The recycling process increases U.S. vulnerability in another way as well. Some of the large international commercial banks have extended so much credit to a small number of developing countries that they have exposed themselves to an unprecedented number of "country risks." Probably not since the nineteenth century have private banks financed the external needs of sovereign governments as much as they did in the 1970s, governments moreover that are much more politically insecure than the industrial democracies of the developed world. True, the major borrowers—Taiwan, Korea, Brazil, Mexico, and the Philippines, for example—were on the whole politically stable, but recent events in Iran and Korea have alerted the banking community to the difficulties of assessing political risks and made them more aware of their own vulnerability to political upheavals abroad.

Although the loans from U.S. banks to the LDCs represent a small fraction of the banks' total assets, it is difficult to assess the degree of political and economic risk they entail. Banks all over are reexamining the meaning of "prudence." Added to the traditional hazards of lending is the unprecedented degree of interdependence between international banks and between international and domestic financial systems. Bankers and other international financial experts are uneasy about how little they understand the Euromarket, a largely uncontrolled mass of dollars and other currencies on deposit in countries outside their home countries. Experts debate whether the Euromarket is too large, whether it contributes to money supply growth and inflation, and whether or not it should be controlled. They all agree, however, that because no outsider knows how much any single bank might lose if another participating bank fails, a crisis could bring all banks under suspicion and the world might panic before central bankers had time to confer.[20] In conversations in June 1980, several "gnomes of Zurich" revealed that the banks themselves have no contingency plans; they all assume that "the Fed" (the Federal Reserve Board in Washington) would cope with whatever world crisis might appear. So unbounded are the hazards and so unfamiliar that Western monetary officials recently devoted a set of meetings at Alpbach, Austria, to the question of whether economic crisis is likely in this decade.[21] The international financial system and the value of the dollar are vulnerable not only to the mounting indebtedness the developing countries must incur to pay for essential imports but also to the greater risks that arise because the rising burden of debt service charges makes the borrowing countries politically more unstable. And austerity measures forced on the countries so they can meet interest and amortization charges might well create an environment in which populist demagogues would flourish. "Why should we export the product of our labor to benefit multinational bankers who seek only to exploit our weaknesses?" an ambitious politician might ask. In a country accustomed not to belt-tightening but to rapid growth, the appeal of a nationalistic economic policy that denies the validity of existing indebtedness could be contagious. Political relations between the developed and developing world might deteriorate seriously, increasing the possibility of widespread terrorism, economically induced migrations from South to North, and politically caused financial crises.

The greater the likelihood of an increase in the real price of oil, the greater is the probability of economic stagnation and political instability in oil-importing developing countries, economic stagnation and unemployment in the OECD countries, and a crisis in or the collapse of the international financial system. The greater the economic difficulties of the oil-importing countries, the less likely is an increase in the real price of oil, but the greater the risk of political instability. The higher growth rates are, the lower unemployment will be in oil-importing countries and the smaller the risks of political instability, but the more likely a rising real price of oil. The higher the real price of oil, the more intractable recycling problems become and the greater the risks of financial instability. And the ability of the United States to influence these events will be limited so long as it remains dependent on imported oil to any significant degree.

What are the possible solutions to this dilemma? The United States is not without influence if it uses its strengths rationally. The risks of political instability in the developing countries and of an international financial crisis can be minimized if commercial banks are used less in the recycling process. To strengthen their resources for coping with the structural problems of the LDCs, the International Monetary Fund (IMF) and the World Bank could draw more on the resources of the OPEC countries. However, to get large holders of petrodollars (mainly Saudi Arabia, Kuwait, UAR, and Iraq) to lend money to them rather than to the commercial banks, the Bank and the IMF must make their terms at least as attractive as those available from the private banks. What is more, the oil exporters are likely to demand and obtain a greater role in decisionmaking within the IMF: Witness the controversy over admitting the Palestine Liberation Organization as an observer at the annual IMF meetings in Autumn 1980.[22]

Giving the international financial organizations a larger role in the recycling process seems more feasible than counting on further bilateral aid from the OECD countries. The United States is not the only donor of economic aid to have lost its enthusiasm for such resource transfers. And the outlook for stagflation in the industrial countries being what it is, this lack of enthusiasm is not likely to be reversed soon.

Theoretically, OPEC and the major oil importers—the United States, Japan, and the European Economic Community—could agree on security of supply in return for *scheduled* price increases related to OPEC's terms of trade. Before this could be done, however, the members of the European Economic Community would have to agree on a common energy policy, an achievement they have not found possible in six years of desultory attempts. The United States should continue to press its allies for the concerted action that would strengthen the oil consumers' negotiating position.

A concerted effort by the major oil consumers to negotiate with OPEC as a group is more likely to be effective now because of OPEC's increasing dependence on the industrial countries. Nearly a decade of rapid economic growth and rising incomes has heightened the expectations of citizens in the OPEC nations, who have developed a taste for many goods and services that are not available in sufficient quantity or quality from other than Western sources. If the United States, the European Economic Community, and Japan could present a credible united front, the dangers of another oil embargo by OPEC would be greatly diminished, because the OPEC countries that consume many imports would probably break ranks quickly, out of fear that austerity would generate domestic unrest.

If the United States does not succeed in getting its allies to agree on a common approach, can it wield any influence unilaterally? Probably so. A debtor always has a bargaining advantage over a creditor, whose resources are being used by the debtor and are therefore at risk. Indeed, the larger the debt, the greater the debtor's bargaining advantage, and the United States is very much OPEC's debtor, having borrowed petrodollars from the OPEC countries whose relative inability to absorb imports has made them willing to deposit funds with U.S. banks and purchase U.S. government securities, real estate, and industrial properties. It is in those countries' interests to support policies that make the United States economically healthy and politically stable. The Saudi Arabians have shown themselves to be aware of these realities.

The creditor's vulnerability to economic sanctions was vividly illustrated to the world by U.S. initiatives taken in 1979 in response, first, to the Iranian seizure of U.S. diplomats in the U.S. embassy in Teheran and, second, to the Soviet invasion of Afghanistan. The blocking of Iranian owned dollar accounts in U.S. banks (including foreign branches of U.S. banks) so startled the financial world that the price of gold rose to the unprecedented height of $850 per ounce, while the foreign exchange value of the dollar declined, which was attributed by some observers to apprehensive private Arab investors diverting dollar investments into gold.[23] The U.S.-initiated economic sanctions against the USSR underscored the vulnerability of foreign importers to U.S. sources of supply.

Such use of U.S. economic power is not free of cost. Trusting the sanctity of contracts is essential to the smooth flow of trade, particularly when large volumes are involved. Abrogating an existing contract for political purposes is likely to weaken the competitive position of the country breaking the contract, at least in the short run. It is a measure that should be employed only as a last resort and only in situations of the highest priority. Taking Americans with diplomatic immunity prisoner in an invasion of a U.S. embassy is by no means a minor matter, but the taking of hostages in Iran was not sufficiently dangerous to our national security to warrant such an abrogation of contracts in the volatile Middle Eastern setting, especially when we could have shown our concern in equally effective but less self-damaging ways. We can never know how much that untimely use of economic power damaged our national security, if only by diluting the potential effectiveness of economic sanctions in circumstances where the threat to our national security may be greater.

Not only have the sanctions against Iran and the USSR retarded the growth of OPEC dependence on the U.S. economy, they were of little avail on their own terms. The blocking of Iranian dollar accounts hurt Iran, but Iran by itself is not that important, and the economic sanctions against the USSR were so widely circumvented that their effectiveness was probably negligible.

In the long run any technological innovation that helps make oil obsolete will strengthen U.S. national security. Such research and development was retarded for the six years of national debate on a proper U.S. energy policy that left the U.S. business community in total doubt about what the future price of oil and energy would be in this country. The 1980 energy bill, simply by making it clear that domestic oil prices will rise to the international level, did much to stimulate research and development. In addition, it provided for federal support of research into alternative energy sources, although that support has been reduced by the new administration. Until new fuel substitutes appear, U.S. vulnerability to oil shortages can be minimized only by astute policymaking.

The United States should also work with Europe, Japan, and the LDCs to seek less crisis-prone solutions to the international financial problems of the developing countries. Together they should find ways to rely less on the commercial banks for recycling, to minimize the risks of an international financial collapse. The big borrowers among the developing countries can restructure their economies to eliminate import restraints and currency controls and make their markets even more important to the industrial economies than they have become. Above all, the United States should encourage and strengthen its *growth* industries, which are important for export, and help to phase down those domestic industries that cannot compete with labor-intensive imports from the developing countries.

NOTES

1.   *IMF Survey,* March 3, 1980.
2.   *CEA Annual Report,* January 1980.
3.   *The Economist* (London), March 8, 1980.
4.   J. Amouzegar, "Petrodollars Again," *Washington Quarterly* 4 no. 1 (Winter 1981): 132; George Ecklund, *World Oil,* January 1980.
5.   *Petroleum Intelligence Weekly,* August 18, 1980, p. 1.
6.   *World Business Weekly,* November 3, 1980.
7.   *The Washington Post,* June 6, 1980; *The Economist,* April 5, 1980.
8.   *IMF Survey,* March 3, 1980.
9.   *The Economist,* December 20, 1980.
10. Chase Manhattan Bank, *International Finance,* February 16, 1981.
11. *The New York Times,* March 3, 1980.
12. Morgan Guarantee Bank, *World Financial Markets,* December 1980.
13. *Financial Times* (London), July 25, 1980.
14. "OPEC Surplus and Oil Prices," *The New York Times,* August 6, 1980.
15. *The Economist,* November 3, 1979.
16. *Financial Times* (London), August 8, 1980.
17. Ibid., August 11, 1980.
18. Ibid., July 25, 1980.
19. Henry Wallich, "Monetary Policy during High Inflation"; remarks to the Swiss-American Society, Basel, Switzerland, June 1980.
20. *Wall Street Journal,* July 18, 1980.
21. Ibid., September 2, 1980.
22. *The New York Times,* September 5, 1980.
23. *The Economist,* March 22, 1980; and *The New York Times,* March 25, 1980.

8 SECURITY RISKS TO ENERGY PRODUCTION AND TRADE

Since World War II fuel production and transport has become the object of political manipulation and sabotage. Various actions, including political embargoes, air raids, strikes, and terrorist attacks, can disrupt the energy logistical system. Depending on the extent of damage or the duration of the disruption, such interference can throw the market into chaos for weeks if not months.

Examples abound of attacks on energy facilities in times of war. Toward the end of World War II the allies bombed the Germans' synthetic fuel plants and thus destroyed one of their most important strategic assets. In the Suez Crisis of 1956 the closure of the canal to oil tankers forced international oil companies to quickly reroute cargoes and stretch inventories to prevent a shortage in Europe. During the 1973 Middle East war the Israelis bombed power stations, refineries, and pipelines in Syria and the Arab oil embargo set off the first major international oil shortage since World War II. The Iranian revolution of 1978–79 revealed the vulnerability of oil production to strikes by oil workers while in the Iran-Iraq war in 1980, each side crippled the other's export operations by bombing oil ports and refineries.

As energy becomes a subject of more heated political debate or an instrument of political conflict, energy systems such as oil or gas wells and pipelines, nuclear power plants, and conventional electric generators could become a common target of sabotage. In the United

States there have been frequent though relatively ineffectual attacks on power stations and fuel pipelines. For example, from 1975 to 1978 the New World Liberation Front, a radical group in California made at least eight assaults on power plants or company headquarters to protest rate increases.[1] Energy firms have had the flexibility to overcome these disruptions so that no single act of sabotage could force the system to shut down. Private companies do not have either the finances or the manpower to guard every portion of the logistical system against terrorist assault, however.

Although all energy installations can be considered potential objects of sabotage, the security risks to international oil production and trade pose a particularly critical dilemma for the industrialized countries. On the one hand, any significant threat to the oil installations of the Middle East, principally of Saudi Arabia would provoke a military response from the United States and its allies. On the other hand, the West would risk a pyrrhic victory if in the course of intervention armed forces destroy the prize that they aim to preserve.

Much has been said about the need for an allied military presence in the Middle East, but less has been said about the ability to protect—or repair—key oil installations. Can the military defend oil wells and ports against air or land attack? If oil facilities were destroyed, could the armed forces and a corps of engineers put them back to work, and at what cost? Although there are no easy answers to these questions, it is possible to characterize the principal risks to the oil logistical system and draw some conclusions about how or if the network can be secured.

Close to 30 million barrels of oil (mmbd) is traded internationally every day, more than half coming from the Middle East. To handle this immense volume of petroleum international companies have built up a vast logistical network centered in the Persian Gulf and spreading out worldwide. At the "up-stream" end (exploration and production) key facilities are on- and offshore wells, pumps, gas-oil separators, water processing plants, and pressure maintenance equipment. At the "downstream" end (refining and marketing) the major facilities are pipelines, pump stations, storage tanks, tankers, oil ports, and industrial plants that use natural gas or oil, such as refineries and power stations. The focus of this analysis is on Saudi Arabia, which accounts for nearly one-third the oil traded internationally.

Oil production like any other form of mineral extraction or industrial activity is subject to a combination of political, economic, and technical conditions. First, unless companies can explore for new petroleum resources, known reserves will decline. So, denial of access to oil-bearing areas can pose a long-term threat to world oil supplies. Furthermore, when oil recovery is interrupted suddenly or poorly controlled, the productivity of oil fields can be impaired. The tap cannot be turned off and on arbitrarily without technical and economic consequences.

Contrary to popular belief, an oil reservoir is not an underground lake full of petroleum. If it were, the oil would be easy to suck out. Instead, the reservoir resembles a hard sponge from which oil must be squeezed. Rock formations (*petroleum* literally means rock oil) hold oil, water, and gas trapped in microscopic pores. To extract oil, engineers must drill a well into the rock to provide an outlet for the oil and gas in the formation. Initially the oil flows down into the well under its own weight and rises naturally to the surface. As oil and gas leave the reservoir, however, natural pressure is reduced and the flow slows down. So the key to oil production is to maintain pressure in the reservoir artificially.

In the Middle East many but not all oil fields flow under natural pressure. In Saudi Arabia, for example, Dammam no. 10 on the Persian Gulf has flowed naturally since its discovery in 1938. However, Saudi Arabia produces the greater part of its oil by artificially maintaining the pressure in the reservoir with water injections. In support of 9.5 mmbd oil output, ARAMCO (the Arab-American Oil Company) injects 11.8 mmbd of water into major oil fields.

Before injection the water must be treated to remove seaweed and other debris. The largest seawater treatment plant in the world is located at Qurayyah near the Ghawar oil field. Processing removes some of the contaminants, but total desalination would not be economical. Hence salt steadily encroaches on the edges of the reservoirs. Oil with an excessively high salt content must be processed before shipment. ARAMCO now has the capacity to desalt just under 500,000 barrels of oil a day but plans to construct desalting and dehydration plants at the Ghawar, Abqaiq, and Shedgum fields that together could treat as much as 7 mmbd of oil. Water yielded from dehydration would be reinjected for pressure maintenance.

As oil and gas rise to the surface, they must be segregated by special gas-oil separators. In Saudi Arabia, a total of fifty-eight gas-oil separators are in operation, each processing some 50,000 barrels a day at least. A giant plant with capacity of 300,000 barrels a day is located at the Abqaiq field, where a previous unit burned down in 1978. Gas is either flared, stored, or piped to industrial facilities for immediate use. In 1975 ARAMCO began construction of a master gas system to collect and process associated gas for fuel use, as well as petrochemicals. Gas also is used to generate electricity for the eastern oil-bearing province. The power plants are located in various parts of the region and should have a generating capacity of 5,000 megawatts by 1982.

From the oil fields petroleum flows through pipelines to field storage tanks and onto storage tanks at refineries and oil ports. These pipelines must be entirely filled before oil can be transmitted through the lines. Pumps, usually automated by computer, force the oil through the line at roughly 3–5 miles per hour. The flow of oil can be slowed down, but it cannot stop entirely without also bringing to a halt the flow of oil from the wellhead. In short, production and pipeline transport are parts of a continuous operation. An interruption of one has an immediate impact on the other.

As Figure 8–1 illustrates, there are five major crude oil pipelines from the Persian Gulf countries to the Mediterranean. Although in recent years only three have been in use, together these five lines could pump as much as 4.6 mmbd of oil, just over one-quarter of Middle East oil output. Three lines run from the Kirkuk oil fields of Iraq to Banias in Syria, Tripoli in Lebanon, and Dortyol in Turkey, all oil ports on the Eastern Mediterranean. The line to Turkey can pump 500,000–700,000 bd; the parallel lines to Banias and Tripoli can transmit 700,000 bd and 500,000 bd, respectively. Thus, Iraq could export about 2.2 mmbd, two-thirds of its usual output, by pipeline to the West.

The other east-west lines in the region transport crude oil from Saudi Arabia. In the 1950s ARAMCO built a 754-mile line known as Tapline from the Qaisuma fields through Jordan to the port of Sidon near Beirut. The line has a capacity of 470,000 bd. In the past few years the Saudis have shipped only a small amount of oil through this line to supply Jordan and Lebanon. However, the portion of the line running to Sidon has frequently been ruptured or closed in the course of armed combat within Lebanon or more recently by Israeli air raids on southern Lebanon in 1981.

The other Saudi crude oil line that has been under construction since 1977 began operation in July 1981. The line runs from the Abqaiq

Figure 8-1. Major Middle Eastern Oil Pipelines.

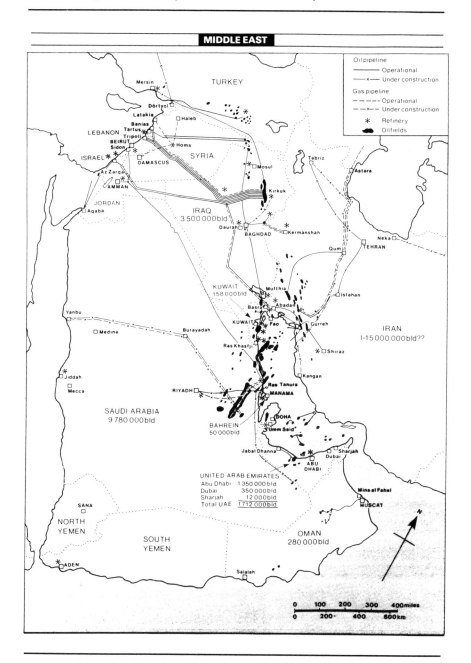

Source: *International Petroleum Times,* August 15, 1980.

oil field for roughly 750 miles to Yanbu on the Red Sea. The line has an initial capacity of 1.85 mmbd and could eventually pump 2.45 mmbd or about 20 percent of Saudi output. The line feeds oil to the refinery at Yanbu and at Jeddah, which together have a capacity of just over 200,000 bd. From Yanbu oil shipments go north through the Red Sea to the Suez Canal or through the Suez-Mediterranean pipeline to Alexandria for transit to ports in southern Europe.

The Red Sea and the Mediterranean could become an important alternate route for Middle East oil exports to Europe. The Saudis plan to build a second line from the Ghawar oil field to Yanbu and in September 1981 gave Iraq permission to construct a new oil pipeline for its exports across the Saudi desert to a terminal slightly north of Yanbu. Since Iraq already can pump just over 2 mmbd through existing lines, the new conduit could allow it to divert all oil away from the Persian Gulf route.

The ability to ship oil through the Red Sea and up through the Suez Canal has two major advantages: It relieves pressure on the Strait of Hormuz and creates an important commercial and strategic relation between Egypt and Saudi Arabia. Since Saudi Arabia will be able to send at least half its oil and Iraq nearly all its oil west by pipeline, the Strait of Hormuz would cease to be the principal choke point at which a hostile power could pinch off the flow of oil. The Red Sea route also allows European importers to use smaller tankers at rates that are less than the cost of supertanker shipments to Europe via the Cape of Good Hope. Finally, the extra shipping business that Egypt receives from the new tanker traffic should give Egypt a strong incentive to patrol the upper portion of the Red Sea between Yanbu and Suez and cooperate with Saudi Arabia and Iraq to preserve the route's security.

For other Middle East producers the Mediterranean may not become a major trade route. The eastern and southern Mediterranean ports are considerably smaller than those in the Persian Gulf and cannot accommodate supertanker traffic. The cost of using smaller tankers to go through the Mediterranean to the Western Hemisphere or around Africa to Southeast Asia would be prohibitive. Above all, political tensions in the area frequently interrupt fuel transmission. The pipeline from Saudi Arabia to Lebanon, the lines from Iraq to Syria and from Iraq to Turkey have been objects of sabotage. As long as the conflict between Israel, Syria, and Palestinian forces in Lebanon persists, the lines running across these territories cannot be considered reliable.

Because of the limited capacity of east-west lines and Mediterranean ports, the Persian Gulf will provide the principal route for oil cargoes in the foreseeable future. This waterway and its oil loading facilities now forge the critical link in the worldwide oil delivery system. The oil loading terminals have been designed to receive oil from specific fields as well as blends of oil from different wells. Blended and segregated supplies of oil are stored in tanks on shore from which underwater pipelines carry oil to loading terminals. These terminals are either fixed docks with berths or offshore facilities consisting of large circular moorings that can handle either one or several ships at the same time. In either case underwater pipelines link the tanker to the storage tank. Pump stations for these lines rest on floating platforms.

In the Persian Gulf many of the loading terminals for Saudi Arabia and the lower Gulf states are offshore, where greater depths can accommodate supertankers. The depth of the harbor and the size of the tanker that a port can handle determine the volume and route of oil cargoes. For example, very large or ultra large cargo carriers (VLCCs, ULCCs) of 250,000 to 500,000 deadweight ton (DWT) could not be used in the Mediterranean because most of the ports are too shallow for them. They also cannot dock at the older fixed terminals at Ras Tanura in Saudi Arabia, which receives tankers of up to 70,000 DWT only. Thus, while supertankers are ideal for moving large volumes of petroleum over long distances, smaller tankers have the advantage of being able to move in and out of any port.

The flow of oil out of the Persian Gulf requires careful coordination. As one specialist notes, "for the system to work, oil must go to precisely the right port and in the right mix of crude and product types as well as in the right total amounts. A shift in crude flows or product types or a shift in ports, can disrupt the web of tanker movements, refinery outputs and product distribution systems upon which every nation depends."[2] Thus, even when supply matches demand, sudden upsets in the scheduling of tankers or the availability of specific crude oils can create a temporary shortage for customers in the world market.

The Strait of Hormuz provides the only passage in and out of the Persian Gulf. Each day as many as 300 vessels of various sizes including tankers carrying two-thirds of the world's oil go through this narrow waterway. The strait is about 25 miles long, and the channel for supertanker transport is only 2 miles wide.

There has long been speculation that the strait could be closed by a blockade, mines, or a few sunken or damaged tankers in midchannel. Even though the sinking of two or even three tankers would not prevent passage of other vessels, the psychological impact would send insurance fees skyrocketing and as a result, tanker traffic through the Persian Gulf would slow down. The greatest threat to the strait, however, would be the placement of mines in the channel. According to one estimate, "only 200 mines would be required to close the 25-mile strait. Another 50 mines might be added to this requirement to hedge against technical failures, misplaced drops and similar errors."[3] Mines could be planted by submarines or aircraft. Furthermore, the threat of mining could be as disruptive as actual mines. If planes or ships appeared to be mining the strait (with large chunks of concrete, for example), ships would refuse to pass through the channel until a minesweeper declared the region safe. However, since such an action would not slow tanker traffic for very long, it could not set off a shortage in the world oil market.

The Iranian revolution of 1978–79 and the Iran-Iraq war vividly illustrated how vulnerable the entire production and distribution system is to political or military interference. Not only can such events immediately suspend oil exports, but they are likely to have a long-term impact on the economies of oil-producing countries and the world market. When Iranian oil workers first went on strike in late October 1978, Iranian oil output was roughly 5.5 mmbd but dropped within two months to just over 1 mmbd. Furthermore, even though Iran has proved reserves of 58 billion barrels—twice as much as the United States—its production remains less than half of U.S. oil output. The main problem is a shortage of technicians and inadequate pressure maintenance in the reservoirs.

Before the revolution the shah of Iran had planned massive secondary recovery programs to reverse the decline in oil production. In 1977 output peaked briefly at 8 mmbd but dropped thereafter because of declining pressure in the principal fields. When the shah was deposed, however, the new regime abandoned his plans for installing major water and gas injection equipment and expelled most of the foreign oil technicians in order to pursue a policy of an "all Iranian" oil industry.[4] Although the new government planned to keep production at 4 mmbd, productive capacity could not be sustained.

The Iran-Iraq war not only damaged the oil ports in the Northern Gulf but called attention to the vulnerability of Saudi export facilities.

At the time of the conflict, there was speculation that the war would spread through the region and place Saudi oil ports in jeopardy. To help protect these installations from air attack, the United States sent electronic surveillance aircraft known as AWACS (airborne warning and control system) and a military support team to Saudi Arabia in September 1980. The AWACS aircraft can detect low-flying airplanes and missiles within a range of roughly 360 miles. This early-warning system allows time to mobilize fighter aircraft to intercept an attack on the oil fields. The United States had previously deployed an AWACS in 1979 to monitor the Yemeni war on Saudi Arabia's southern border.

Political instability in and around the Persian Gulf raises serious questions about military threats to oil installations and the ability of producers and their western allies to deter those threats or repel actual attacks. The list of regional conflicts is well known: the Iran-Iraq war, skirmishes between North and South Yemen, the ongoing conflict between Israel and its Arab neighbors. Internal political and religious conflicts could also arrest the flow of .oil. Terrorist groups could use the threat of sabotage or actual sabotage to achieve their ends. Moreover, rival groups could start to do battle in or around the oil fields. For example, in November 1979 pro-Ayatollah Khomeini Shi'a Muslims exchanged shots with the Saudi National Guard close to the Persian Gulf oil terminals. Since the Shiites are concentrated in the area around the Ghawar oil field, an escalation of hostilities could affect petroleum operations.

The growing Soviet presence in the Middle East complicates an already explosive internal situation. Soviet military advisors are in Iraq, Syria, and South Yemen. Above all, the Soviet invasion of Afghanistan in December 1979 aroused fears that the Russians were poised to invade Iran and so be in a position to control the Persian Gulf. In response to that display of arms, President Carter stated that "any attempt by any outside force to gain control of the Persian Gulf region will be regarded as an assault on the vital interests of the United States . . . and will be repelled by use of any means necessary, including armed force."[5]

With that warning President Carter made a strategic commitment to the region that the Reagan administration has accepted and that the U.S. Congress and armed services must be prepared to fulfill. It is beyond the scope of this chapter to examine how the United States might execute a military campaign in the Persian Gulf; nonetheless, it is central to this analysis to assess whether or not the problem of oil field security has a military solution. Can conventional ground and air forces deter attacks on Saudi oil installations? By placing sophisticated weapons and radar equipment in the area, would the West promote the region's security or aggravate the threats to the flow of oil?

Because of unique geographical and demographic conditions, Saudi Arabia faces massive difficulties in protecting its territory and valuable oil installations against attack. First, the kingdom is just under 900,000 square miles or roughly the size of the United States east of the Mississippi. The oil fields and ports along the Persian Gulf cover an area of some 70,000 square miles, the size and shape of Portugal. Although this province is the principal location of Saudi economic activity, the Saudis are building up an industrial complex of refineries, petrochemical plants, and export facilities at Yanbu on the Red Sea. Thus by the late 1980s Saudi Arabia will need the capability to defend both its east and west coasts.

In contrast to the vast territory, the population of Saudi Arabia is relatively small and disparate. Roughly 8 million persons live in the kingdom, of whom only 4–5 million are native Saudis. The rest are foreign workers such as Palestinians, Pakistanis, and Koreans. Of the 4–5 million Saudis, less than 1 million men are fit enough or the right age for military service. While total armed forces amount to 47,000, the National Guard, which reports directly to the royal family, has 20,000 men. Thus, the Saudis could turn out a fighting force of just under 70,000 at the start of a crisis.[6] By contrast, Israel, which has half the population of Saudi Arabia could mobilize a force of 375,000 (male and female) in an emergency.[7]

With enormous distances to cover and limited manpower, Saudi Arabia could not guard the oil fields with its armed forces alone. It must rely heavily on air defenses to maintain constant surveillance of the eastern province and if necessary to intercept an air attack on key installations such as the oil ports. Thus if Saudi Arabia had a comprehensive radar system and a fleet of fighter aircraft, it could deter or actually intercept a limited air raid on the oil installation on the same scale as occurred in the Iran-Iraq war. Furthermore, a modern Saudi air force could withstand any air assault attempted by South Yemen. Other possible Arab aggressors such as Syria, Jordan, or Libya are too far away to fly a fighting mission in an out of the Persian Gulf.

Although a modern air force equipped with sophisticated radar systems and fighter aircraft could deter an attack on the oil fields by radical Arab states, it could not necessarily guarantee the security of commercial oil operations. Any aerial combat in the area of the petroleum fields and ports could result in damage to those facilities. Furthermore if an enemy were determined to destroy those installations, the pilot could nose dive kamikaze fashion into the port or field. No amount of antiaircraft weaponry on the ground or in the air could prevent damage to the fields below once action had broken out in the sky. Thus a sophisticated air defense system may have some deterrence value but only limited value in preventing damage to the oil fields in a military engagement.

Even with an upgraded air defense system, however, Saudi Arabia would be poorly prepared to defend the oil fields against many other possible threats. The Saudi air force alone could not intercept strategic strikes by Israel. Furthermore, no air force in the area, whether Arab or Israeli, could meet a serious threat from the Soviet Union. Finally other risks to the oil installations on the ground exist that conventional air defenses would not cover. These threats emanate from political conflict or terrorist activities in and around the Saudi oil fields.

The possibility of an Israeli attack on Saudi military and energy facilities cannot be ruled out if the Arab-Israeli conflict ever resumes and Israel perceives a security threat from Saudi Arabia. The Israelis have demonstrated their expertise in destroying enemy military and industrial facilities. In the October war of 1973, they destroyed the oil-storage depots and terminals at Banias and Tartus in Syria, actions that crippled Syria's economy. Israel bombed Palestine Liberation Organization (PLO) headquarters as well as oil pipelines and refineries in Southern Lebanon (June 1981). The attack on oil facilities created fuel shortages in the region. Finally, in a surprise air attack, the Israelis destroyed the OSIRAK nuclear reactor in Iraq (June 1981).

Israeli strategists regard such attacks as essential to a successful defense in times of crisis and in some instances to their long-term security, notably the destruction of OSIRAK. According to one report, "these analysts suggest that the commandos, and the air and naval units, should attack both military and strategic targets—army camps, missile batteries, power plants, factories, dams, bridges, air and sea ports, rail and bus terminals and city centers."[8] A steady wave of attacks would destroy the enemy's logistical network and "its economy would be ruined."[9] Israel would have great difficulty executing a series of attacks on Saudi Arabia's eastern oil province. Nevertheless, given Israel's superiority in such strategic air maneuvers, it could succeed in knocking out a few of the crucial energy installations or parts of the air defense system—airborne and ground radar equipment—that help to protect the oil fields.

To a large extent the United States has the political leverage over Israel to deter it from any kind of assault on Saudi Arabia. Where Israel's security is concerned, however, its actions can be unpredictable and possibly at odds with U.S. interests. Thus it is critical to U.S. security policy in the Middle East to provide Israel with sufficient guarantees of U.S. support and incentives not to conduct preemptive strikes against Saudi air defenses in the event of a new crisis in the Middle East.

The defense needs of Saudi Arabia would utterly change if the Soviet Union moved from Afghanistan into Iran or if Iran fell into the hands of a pro-Soviet regime. As long as the Soviets must deploy from their borders with Iran, the United States and Saudi Arabia have time to mobilize their forces to meet a Soviet attack. If the Russians had bases within Iran, they could reach the Saudi oil installations in about ten minutes flying time. From that position the Russians could gain complete control of the Persian Gulf. To protect its vital interests as defined in the Carter doctrine, the United States would send naval and ground forces into the Persian Gulf.

If the United States and the USSR deployed forces into the Persian Gulf, oil transport would effectively cease. Even though neither side actually made strikes at oil installations, the entire area would become a crisis zone. Insurance brokers would place such high premiums on tankers in the area that some cargoes might not leave the Gulf at all. Nevertheless, some tankers would still go out under military escort as long as the Strait of Hormuz remained open. If the Strait were blocked, mined, or threatened by a show of arms, tanker traffic would come to a halt.

Under these circumstances the transmission of oil by the east-west pipelines would become vital to maintaining basic energy operations in Saudi Arabia. Since oil production and transport are part of a continuous process, when transport is interrupted, production must be cut back for the simple reason that once oil is extracted, it must have somewhere to go above ground. Thus to preserve the lowest possible level of oil and gas production, the producer must have a conduit for the oil and gas. Most important, Saudi Arabia needs to keep up oil and gas production in order to have electric power. Saudi Arabia generates electricity from gas-powered turbines. Most of this gas is produced in association with oil. So in order to have a fuel supply for electricity, the Saudis must maintain a certain level of petroleum output, keep gas-oil separators in operation and gas flowing to electric generators. If the east-west pipelines were destroyed, the Saudis would not be able to maintain the minimum of oil production for generating electricity.

It lies beyond the scope of this chapter to explore if or how a confrontation between the United States and the USSR in the Persian Gulf would be resolved. It is clear, however, that the use of force by either side would totally paralyze oil operations in the area. Nevertheless, if there were enough pipelines carrying oil west to the Mediterranean, then a blockade of the Strait of Hormuz or some other show of force in the Persian Gulf would no longer be enough to halt the flow of oil. Therefore military control of the Persian Gulf would no longer constitute an intolerable threat to the region and its oil resources. Indeed, to halt the flow of oil, the Soviets would then be forced to fly well into the Saudi interior to strike at the pipelines, a mission far more difficult than simply deploying forces to the Persian Gulf. In short, the construction of east-west pipelines could prove to be a more effective defense for the oil fields than the conventional radar and weapon systems that the Saudis plan to install.

Even if the Saudis build strategic east-west pipelines and modernize their air and ground defenses, the oil fields and ports could still remain vulnerable to sabotage by terrorists. The presence of airborne or ground radar systems or of F-15 fighter aircraft will not deter a determined group of terrorists from dismantling key elements of Saudi production equipment. For example, since Saudi Arabia relies on water pressure maintenance for nearly all of its production, damage to giant water-processing plants could interrupt production. Similarly the wrecking of gas-oil separators, crucial to the recovery process, could slow down production for weeks if not months depending on the availability of parts and technicians to repair the facilities. Terrorists could knock out the system more efficiently and at far less cost than the combined air forces of Iran and Iraq. Furthermore they could do so far from the oil ports or the Strait of Hormuz on which recent strategic planning has been focused.

With its small and disparate population Saudi Arabia does not have a security force large enough or reliable enough to guard every facility against sabotage. As one Saudi security official has stated, "we can't protect every inch of pipeline. It would take all our troops."[10] Indeed, few of the key installations in Saudi Arabia are adequately guarded. At Ras Tanura one journalist reported that he was able "to drive onto one of the piers with a forbidden camera and approach an Iraqi tanker on foot without once being stopped or searched by the single guard on duty."[11]

Not only are major facilities poorly guarded. If they were damaged, there could be a shortage of parts or technicians to repair the equipment. Many Saudi production facilities are unique in their size and specifications. As one analyst points out, "this problem can only be dealt with by pre-purchasing and stocking such equipment, but no current plant exists to take these steps. Accordingly regardless of the Saudi regime, Western oil supplies will be acutely vulnerable to even low levels of paramilitary violence."[12]

Finally, as the disarray of Iranian oil production reveals, a force of skilled technicians is needed to maintain and possible restore oil recovery. If strikes by oil workers or terrorist attacks cripple oil operations in Saudi Arabia, could the United States step in to maintain both civil order and restore production? Could the United States do so without the permission of the Saudi regime, whatever that might be after such an upheaval? The United States would face massive political and military difficulties if it attempted to intervene in Saudi internal affairs. Furthermore, the U.S. government would need to conscript engineers from U.S. companies and protect this technical team in a combat zone. There is no precedent for drafting a civilian labor force of this kind; the legal and logistical implications of maintaining such a team raises a host of questions that have yet to be analyzed.

Although conventional air and ground defenses can protect the oil-producing regions of the Persian Gulf from external attack, military forces can do little to secure oil installations from internal terrorist attacks. Even if troops are stationed near the oil fields, installations remain vulnerable. Any air or ground combat in or around key facilities could destroy them inadvertently. Whereas there are innumerable ways to sabotage or accidentally damage oil facilities, there are virtually no sure ways of defending them against such attacks.

CONCLUSIONS

Energy production and distribution systems are vulnerable to military attacks, terrorism, and political interference. Although all energy facilities could become objects of sabotage, frequent attacks on such installations have occurred only in regions undergoing acute political conflict. The political instability of the Persian Gulf constantly jeopardizes petroleum production and trade. As long as the Middle East suffers from inter-Arab and Arab-Israeli hostilities, the West's oil supplies will remain at risk.

Fuel installations and energy trade routes are considered to be important strategic targets. By cutting off energy supplies, an aggressor can nearly cripple the defenses and economy of any nation. Thus if war broke out in the Middle East, the principal oil installations along the Persian Gulf including production equipment and transport facilities would be prime objects of attack. Furthermore, any military force that could control the Strait of Hormuz at the mouth of the Persian Gulf could effectively cut off the export of oil and so force producers to cease oil recovery.

It could be of considerable commercial and strategic importance for the Middle East oil producers to build east-west pipelines capable of conveying most of their oil over land instead of through the Persian Gulf. As long as two-thirds of the non-Communist world's oil supply goes through this channel, a military power can easily cut off exports to the west by deploying forces in and around the Persian Gulf. If instead producers exported much of their oil by pipeline, the same armed power would be forced to conduct far more difficult and counterproductive maneuvers on the oil installations themselves in order to halt the flow of oil. That power would need to bomb oil fields and specific pieces of production equipment or make low-flying strikes at pump stations for those east-west pipelines. Such missions pose a far higher level of risk than a show of force along the major oil export route. By diversifying trade routes and means of transport, the oil producers could greatly reduce the military threat to oil exports that reliance on the Persian Gulf incurs.

Even if the oil producers and their Western allies build up conventional air defenses, saboteurs could easily damage key oil installations on the ground. Furthermore, any armed conflict between political rivals in or around the oil fields could interfere with production.

As the Iranian Revolution vividly illustrated, strikes by oil workers can bring production to a standstill and unless the government has a technical team that can restore operations, this form of political interference can curtail output indefinitely. Military intervention by the United States or its allies would only exacerbate the crisis. It is unlikely that armed forces even with the help of a civilian technical corps would be up to the task of restoring production and trade. The problem would be particularly acute in Saudi Arabia because it has so many unique oil installations, that, if destroyed, could not be readily duplicated or repaired.

There is a general consensus that the West will remain so dependent on Middle East oil for the next twenty to thirty years, that the United States and its allies would risk going to war with the USSR if the Soviets ever tried to deny access to the region's petroleum. It should be noted that the West has managed to adapt to the loss of roughly 8 mmbd of oil, the combined output of Iran and Iraq before the Iranian revolution and the Iran-Iraq war. The United States never considered the possibility of intervening to maintain access to the oil of Iran or Iraq because to do so would have provoked a war with those countries and their possible allies, including the Soviet Union. Yet the United States still maintains the doctrine that it would use "any means necessary including armed force" to prevent the USSR from controlling the Persian Gulf or more specifically, Saudi Arabia.

The necessary conclusion is that going to war over oil would be far more perilous to the West than undergoing the economic disruption that would be created by a suspension of Saudi oil exports to Europe and Japan. While helping Saudi Arabia to build up its military defenses and increasing the allies' capability to reach the Middle East rapidly, the United States must regard such measures as solely deterrent. Under no circumstances would an open battle between the United States and the Soviet Union or the United States and any regional forces help to preserve the flow of oil. It would immediately halt exports and probably do enough damage to the logistical network to halt production for several years thereafter. In short, there is no military solution to the problem of securing oil supplies.

Ultimately the security of the oil fields must be treated as a political, not a military, problem. The external and internal threats to oil operations are a function of the political instability of the entire Persian Gulf. Thus the United States must assume that while military actions, both preventive and reactive, can help defend the territory or the regimes of the Persian Gulf against external threats, conventional defenses may not be able to keep the logistical system intact or restore exports to the West.

The oil producers and the United States need the "early warnings" that timely intelligence and political analysis of regional and internal affairs can provide about impending threats to the flow of oil. While helping Saudi Arabia and other conservative states to build up internal security, the United States must also have a realistic view of these nations' own political stability. The West cannot afford another Iran. Above all, measures must be taken to defuse the charged political atmosphere of the region. The next chapter examines some of the diplomatic and foreign policy measures that the United States can take to help stabilize the Persian Gulf and thus lower the risk of politically inspired attacks on the oil logistical system.

NOTES

1. Energy and Defense Project, *Energy, Vulnerability and War* (Federal Emergency Management Agency, December 1980), p. 16.
2. Abdul Kasim Mansur, "The Military Balance in the Persian Gulf: Who will Guard the Gulf States from Their Guardians?" *Armed Forces Journal International* (November 1980): 83.
3. Barry M. Blechman and Arnold M. Kuzmack, "Oil and National Security," *The Naval War College Review,* 26 no. 6, sequence 249 (May-June 1974): 12-3.
4. Joseph P. Riva, Jr., "Iranian Oil Resources and Production," in *Economic Consequences of the Revolution in Iran,* a compendium of papers submitted to the Joint Economic Committee, U.S. Congress, November 19, 1979, p. 112.
5. Terrence Smith, "President Says U.S. would use Military," *The New York Times,* January 24, 1980, p. 1.
6. The International Institute for Strategic Studies, *The Military Balance 1980–1981* (London: IISS, 1980), p. 47.
7. Ibid., p. 43.
8. Benny Morris, "New Strategic Thinking in Israel," *Armed Forces Journal International* (September 1980): 84.
9. Ibid.
10. Walter S. Mossberg, "As Mideast Heats Up, U.S. Frets over Peril to the Saudi Oil Fields," *Wall Street Journal* January 21, 1980, p. 1.
11. Ibid.
12. Mansur, "Military Balance in the Persian Gulf," p. 75.

9 ENERGY AND NATIONAL SECURITY: IMPLICATIONS FOR U.S. FOREIGN POLICY

The United States stands at a crossroads in formulating a new strategic doctrine that relates energy to national security policy. The preceding chapters have demonstrated that the nature of the challenges posed to the global community make it impossible to view this nation's energy dilemma either within a parochial domestic political context or as an isolated economic, political, or strategic issue.

The energy crisis is global in scope. It affects the world environment through degradation of forests, landscapes, and air quality. The movement of acid rain across frontiers will become a significant issue for international diplomacy during the 1980s. The energy crisis affects the international economy through vast transfers of petrodollar wealth among nations and by depleting the resources available to poor Third World nations to finance social and economic development programs.

Since 1973 the non-oil-developing countries have had to borrow almost $350 billion to finance their balance-of-payments deficits, largely as a result of the soaring price of imported oil. The Third World nations now require about $70 billion a year of new credits simply to pay for their oil imports, almost triple the $26 billion level of 1978. Since 1973 the annual debt-servicing requirements of these nations have risen to a staggering $75 billion. Debt-servicing obligations and new oil-import expenditures now consume almost 50 percent of

173

the total exports earnings of the Third World nations. These nations have entered an economic cycle where they must either continue to borrow heavily or reduce the level of their imports and see their living standards drastically curtailed. The Third World nations are heavily indebted to Western banks. Indeed, the nine largest U.S. banks have almost twice the amount of their total real assets in loans to Third World nations. As noted in Chapter 7, the debt of Third World nations to international banks is growing at 25–30 percent per year and is sustainable only as long as the rapid rate of inflation steadily reduces the real burden of their accumulated debt. If growth should cease, the short-term political temptations for a nationalistic leader in an endemically poor nation to repudiate the country's debt could prove overwhelming.

The rapid rise in oil prices has had other effects on the economies of Third World nations. The very rapid rise in the import price of petroleum-derived fertilizers has led to chronic food shortages as fertilizer imports have been curtailed. Attendant migrations of people within nations and across international frontiers has sparked social, economic, and political tensions that threaten local, regional, and global stability.

The energy crisis has sparked incidents of international terrorism by disaffected groups against energy facilities so important to the maintenance of advanced industrial societies. Among these incidents have been attacks against nuclear installations, threatening to unleash a new dimension in international conflict. The energy crisis has led to seizures of territory deemed rich in resources by states desiring the acquisition of such resources.

The energy crisis has generated changes in political alliances and has engendered the need for new political relationships with states sometimes hostile to allies of longer standing. In its effort to effect new understandings with the Arab oil producers, the United States has found that the consummation of such relations generates antagonism from Israel. In its effort to balance its relations with the Arab world and Israel, Washington often incurs the anger of both camps as well as that of its major allies, who see U.S. policy as threatening their strategic interests.

Finally the energy crisis has added a new dimension to the global rivalry between the superpowers. The specter of rising Communist bloc dependence on imported oil from the Persian Gulf during this decade poses profound questions for the United States and its major allies over the proper policies to adopt toward Moscow's burgeoning energy crisis. Likewise, given the importance of oil to the economies of the industrialized world, the United States is confronted with the necessity of spending billions of dollars in military equipment and installations to ensure its ability to preserve the flow of oil from the Middle East.

Despite the urgency of the challenges posed to U.S. foreign policy by the energy crisis, there is a dangerous tendency in this nation to be complacent about our energy situation. Many financial institutions by 1981 were proclaiming the energy crisis to have passed. Reports of the so-called "oil glut" permeated the press. Some leading oil companies were once again encouraging consumers to buy gasoline and see America. This attitude represents an abnegation of industrial statesmanship, which can only breed cynicism among the American people.

Because of the unresolved problems affecting accelerated U.S. domestic energy production (see Chapters 1 and 3), the United States will not be able to produce its way out of the energy crisis in the short run. Until about 1995 the United States and its major industrial allies will remain vitally dependent on imported energy (coal, gas, and oil) for a significant proportion of energy supplies. Certain critical energy and foreign policy issues are likely to confront the nation during this time.

In many scenarios policies in one area may constrain or even contradict foreign policy options in others. For example, in the attempt to cement relations with Canada, the United States embarked on the construction of a costly pipeline to carry natural gas from Alaska through Canada when other options might have made more sense from purely economic considerations. Likewise, in the rush to accelerate domestic coal utilization, the United States caused a reduction of residual oil imports from Venezuela, historically one of our most reliable oil supplies, thereby thwarting some part of our efforts to create a hemispheric energy system. This demonstrates the complexity of energy policy formulation that confronts our nation in this decade.

RELATIONS WITH PERSIAN
GULF COUNTRIES

After the first oil embargo, U.S. energy policy was predicated on two assumptions: that over time the United States would reduce its import dependency by developing alternative energy sources and that through large-scale arms and technology sales to Iran and Saudi Arabia it could create ties that would reduce the risks of new oil-supply disruptions in the Middle East.

These assumptions were shattered by the fall of the shah of Iran in 1979, the demise of the U.S. security treaty with Iran, the advent of Ayatollah Khomeini's Islamic revolution, and the rejection by Saudi Arabia and the other moderate oil producing states of the Camp David accords.

The consummation of the Egyptian-Israeli peace treaty, albeit a notable diplomatic achievement for the United States, poses serious problems for the Arab states of the Persian Gulf, on whom the United States and its major allies, Japan and the Western European countries, depend for oil supplies. With Egypt at peace with Israel, the moderate Arab states realize that they would have no credible military response should new hostilities break out and that the Israeli government now feels less urgency to negotiate on the West Bank settlements and Jerusalem or to pursue new peace initiatives with Jordan or Syria.

This worries the moderate Arab regimes, especially Saudi Arabia. The United States sees access to Persian Gulf oil as a separate issue from resolution of the Arab-Israeli dispute, but Arab leaders feel otherwise. Viewed from Riyadh, no issue, including the possibility of Soviet intervention in the Gulf, threatens Saudi security more than the failure to resolve the Palestinian problem.

All Gulf states except Oman have large populations of Palestinian expatriates. Unlike their brethren in the refugee camps of Lebanon, Syria, Jordan, and the Gaza strip, these diaspora Palestinians are financially secure and vitally important to the economies of their host countries. However, they remain politically disenfranchised and unassimilated into the local cultures and are staunch supporters of the Palestinian movement. Any Arab government that seems unsupportive of the Palestinian cause runs the risk of serious political disturbances. Not all Palestinians would return to an autonomous homeland or an independent Palestinian state, but the political status of Palestinians living in the Gulf countries could be resolved if these people acquired a national homeland.

In the Arab view the Camp David peace accords accomplished in one stroke what Israel had always tried unsuccessfully: They divided the Arab camp. Jordan and Saudi Arabia are disturbed that the peace treaty left the future status of the West Bank, Gaza, and East Jerusalem ambiguous. The Egyptians believe that the five-year peace transition process will end with Palestinian autonomy, but it is increasingly clear that the government of Menachem Begin links increased Palestinian political rights with continued Israeli territorial control. Finally, the treaty does nothing to reduce the threat to national security that the Palestinian diaspora poses for Jordan, Kuwait, the United Arab Emirates, and Saudi Arabia.

U.S. policymakers tend to argue that strong public support by moderate Arab regimes of the Palestinian cause is designed for intra-Arab public consumption, and that the Arab states really fear that an independent Palestinian state on the West Bank would be a destabilizing element in the Middle East. Some Arab leaders, especially King Hussein of Jordan, do fear this possibility, but they worry more that if resolution of the Palestinian problem does not seem to be underway, any Arab leader who supports the Camp David accords or leans too strongly toward Israel's chief military supplier, the United States, risks assassination or internal political disturbances either by radical Palestinian nationalists or extremist Islamic political groups.

U.S. policymakers should not dismiss the emotional and religious significance of East Jerusalem to many Arab leaders. It is highly unlikely that even moderate Arab statesmen will ever agree to permanent Israeli control of the city without firm international guarantees of free and unfettered access to East Jerusalem for all Arabs, Jews, and Christians.

The U.S. signing of a peace treaty that Saudi Arabia and other conservative Arab regimes were unable to support, plus erosion of Saudi Arabia's position in Yemen, Ethiopia, Iran and Afghanistan, has left the Saudis feeling isolated. The fall of the shah of Iran profoundly affected Saudi strategy. Riyadh was incredulous when the United States watched its military bulwark in the Middle East collapse without providing assistance. The prospect of full-scale Soviet intervention in the Gulf during the Yemen crisis of February and March 1979 and in Iran all year and the threat of Islamic fundamentalism spreading from Iran to Saudi Arabia or the smaller Gulf sheikdoms made that kingdom feel even more vulnerable. Their concern peaked after the seizure of the Great Mosque in Mecca in October 1979 and the Soviet intervention in Afghanistan in December.

As their strategic position deteriorated the Saudis had little choice but to join their traditional adversary, Iraq, in rejecting the Camp

David accords. Considering how little reason the kingdom had to take actions favorable to the United States, it is remarkable that Riyad continued in 1979 to serve as a price moderator in OPEC councils and to keep oil production up enough to offset Iranian cutbacks.

U.S. policymakers seem unable to realize that Saudi foreign policy revolves around five major concerns:

1. Resolving the Arab-Israeli problem, especially the Palestinian question;
2. Stemming the tide of Islamic fundamentalism;
3. Avoiding entanglement in Arab factionalism and reducing Arab-Iranian tensions;
4. Preventing superpower rivalry in the region while at the same time maintaining good enough relations with the United States to feel secure;
5. Keeping oil production and prices at a level that protects the long-term market but does not threaten global economic and political stability and thus endanger Saudi assets abroad.

None of these policy objectives is independent of the others, and many of them overlap. If the Saudis were alarmed by the Soviet intervention in Afghanistan, they and their neighbors were equally concerned about the United States creating a rapid deployment force for the Middle East in February 1980 and about the policies that the Carter and Reagan administrations have evolved to thwart Soviet penetration in the Persian Gulf. The moderate Arab states, all of which raised oil production in 1979 to alleviate energy problems in the industrialized world, are concerned that Washington is exaggerating the Soviet threat to the Gulf as a way of moving the unresolved issues of the Arab-Israeli dispute out of the limelight.

So much has the U.S. strategic debate over the last two years focused on U.S. military capabilities in the Gulf that some conservative Arabs fear the United States would rather seize the Gulf oil fields than have to defend the Gulf against external attacks. This view was articulated by President Saddham Hussein of Iraq, who, after Camp David, asked all of the Gulf states to sign an Arab National Charter agreeing not to allow any foreign powers to establish military facilities in their territory. All of the small Gulf States except Oman, which endorsed the Camp David accords, have signed the charter.

The Arabs are to some degree justified in their concern about U.S. policy. Since 1973 various U.S. strategists and government officials have advocated or threatened seizure of Middle Eastern oil fields. Henry Kissinger as secretary of state, James Schlesinger as secretary of defense and of energy, and General Bernard Rogers as commander of NATO forces have all warned that the United States might use military force to protect its access to Middle Eastern oil supplies.[1] Military intervention in the oil fields has also been the subject of several congressional studies.

Although most of the highest level officials of Persian Gulf nations do not fear U.S. military seizure of the oil fields, many midlevel officials are deeply concerned about U.S. motives. The Saudis are increasingly concerned that most of the $30–35 billion the kingdom has spent on U.S. military goods and services has not gone toward arms purchases. This concern was exacerbated by the protracted nature of the U.S. congressional debates on arms sales to the kingdom, especially the sale of F-15 fighters with bomb racks and extra fuel capacity, which would allow them to serve as attack aircraft as well as defensive aircraft, and more recently of AWACS (Airborne Warning and Command System). The fact that the Israeli government opposed these transactions has not allayed Saudi concerns about the possibility of a well-orchestrated disinformation campaign about Saudi internal stability.

The Saudi military forces and National Guard are almost totally dependent on U.S. military equipment, advisors, and contractors. Concerned about this degree of dependence, the Saudi government has let it be known that while it is willing to give the Reagan administration time to formulate its Middle Eastern policy, it is making the sale of the F-15s and AWACS a test case in U.S.-Saudi relations. To demonstrate the seriousness of its intentions to reduce its military dependence on the United States, Riyadh has recently (1) awarded a $3.4 billion contract to France for the next generation of naval ships, (2) approached the Federal Republic of Germany about lifting its ban on arms sales to tense regions and selling the kingdom tanks and equipment worth $1 billion, and (3) inquired if the United Kingdom would sell it 200 Tornado fighter-bombers at an estimated cost of $7.5 billion, and (4) announced it will be a British AWACS system if the U.S. Congress vetoes the sale of U.S. equipment.

The Saudi ruling elite is deeply divided on the wisdom of reducing its dependence on the United States, but the decision to draw closer to the Europeans both for arms purchases and military technical and training assistance is a signal to Washington that the Saudis have other strategic options. They have stated that if the F-15s and AWACS are not provided they will purchase the Mirage 2000 and finance development of the French Mirage 4000.

Some of these problems may be surmounted by effective diplomacy. What bothers the Saudis most is U.S. reluctance to pressure Israel constructively on the peace front. The Begin government's policy of expanding settlements on the West Bank despite the consummation of the Camp David accords is unacceptable to Riyadh. The Saudi leaders hoped that Israeli policy might change after the June 1981 elections and were willing to wait until then and until the Reagan administration had formulated its Middle East policies to see what hope there was for resuming the peace process. But the reelection of the Begin government combined with the June 1981 Israeli attack on Iraq's nuclear facility, the ongoing crisis on Lebanon, and the announcement of a new U.S./Israeli strategic relationship substantially dimmed the prospect for peace throughout the region. The failure of the United States to take any action that was meaningful (from an Arab point of view) against Israel for the Iraqi raid, and the devastating attack on Beirut has led to a new surge in anti-Americanism throughout the Middle East.

Deteriorating relations between the United States and Saudi Arabia remain a real danger. Were Saudi Arabia to cut its oil production by 4 mmbd, it could meet all of its own revenue needs and end the current oil glut at the same time. Despite present Saudi policy, Riyadh may feel the pressure, in a slackening oil market, to reduce production by an additional 1–2 mmbd if it is apparent that Iran and Iraq are going to resume exporting oil. Whether this will happen depends to a large extent on whether the war resumes or escalates. If it escalates and Kuwait or the United Arab Emirates become involved, the chances for further disruptions of world oil supplies will increase.

There are no easy solutions to the problems disturbing relations between the United States, Saudi Arabia, and other oil-producing nations of the region. What is most disturbing is that strategic debate on the Persian Gulf area has been too parochial. The United States cannot expect cooperation about Gulf security if it does not participate forcefully and actively in the broader Middle Eastern peace process.

Recognizing potential pitfalls and without abandoning its policy of ensuring Israeli security, the United States must nevertheless move to convince the Arabs that it is serious about effecting a resolution of the Palestinian problem to which all of the major parties to the conflict can agree. Failure to help resolve the Palestinian problem will not only endanger U.S. access to Middle Eastern oil but may even cause U.S. relations with Europe and Japan to deteriorate.

The American people must realize that for the next two decades access to Middle Eastern oil is vital to the world's continued economic well-being. Not only are Saudi Arabia, Iraq, Kuwait, and the UAE important oil producers, but almost 60 percent of the world's proven oil reserves is located in the Persian Gulf. Even if the United States reduces its dependence on Gulf supplies, Western Europe and Japan are so overwhelmingly dependent on Middle Eastern oil that it will be critical for Washington to maintain an interest in the region for years to come. It is this fact and the specter of increased Soviet and Eastern European dependence on the region's oil resources during the 1980s that directly link U.S. energy and national security policy.

U.S. RELATIONS WITH JAPAN AND WESTERN EUROPE

Foreign policy differences between the United States and its chief industrial allies, Japan and Western Europe, often reflect differences in their energy needs and usually involve one of three subjects: U.S. policy in the Middle East, *detente* with the Soviet Union, and growing East-West trade, particularly in energy supplies. Historically the United States' main concern has been to maintain a strategic balance with the Soviet Union in the Middle East while honoring its security commitment to Israel. Japan and Western Europe, which are far more dependent on oil imported from the Persian Gulf (Japan gets 80 percent of its oil from the Gulf region, Western Europe 76 percent, the United States only 30 percent), are chiefly concerned with ensuring access to oil at affordable prices. Japan and Western Europe believe that continued U.S. support of Israel, especially in view of Tel Aviv's intransigence on the issue of West Bank settlements, threatens a breakdown of the peace process and the escalation of regional conflict that could threaten access to oil supplies.

It bothered our allies that the Reagan administration has down-played the necessity of resuming the Egyptian-Israeli negotiations on Palestinian self-rule and emphasized instead the need to counter the strategic threat the Soviet Union poses in the Middle East. European and Japanese officials do not share the prevailing U.S. view that the non-Communist world has suffered cataclysmic reverses at the hands of the USSR in recent years. When American analysts cite a litany of such diplomatic reverses, their allies point out that the Soviet Union has suffered its own reverses: It has lost bases in Egypt and Somalia and has suffered declining influence in Iraq, Iran, Zimbabwe, and Mozambique.

Just as Western European and Japanese leaders are alarmed by the Soviet presence in South Yemen and Ethiopia, so they were disturbed by the Soviet military intervention in Afghanistan. But in their view a de facto Communist regime had reigned in Kabul since the April 1978 coup, so the Soviet action did not alter the strategic balance as much as the United States thought it did and certainly was not worth en-dangering detente with Moscow. Although Japan and Western Europe are not happy about Syria's signing a "treaty of friendship" with Moscow, the German and French foreign ministries view the alliance as one of convenience for Syria, which fears isolation and abandonment by the West and Egypt and perceives its national security to be threatened by Israel, Jordan, Iraq, and the ongoing political crisis in Lebanon.

The Iranian revolution, the Soviet intervention in Afghanistan, and the ongoing war between Iran and Iraq have made Europe and Japan begin to realize that they can no longer automatically rely on the United States to protect their vital interests in areas not covered by the NATO umbrella. Indeed, some Europeans and Japanese are beginning to ask whether their interests and those of the United States may not diverge.

The chief concern of Europe and Japan is to maintain viable econ-omies, at the same time avoiding the acrimonious confrontations with the United States that occurred in 1973–74 and again in 1979–80 (see Chapter 1). The British and French realize that the Reagan ad-ministration will press them to contribute to a joint allied military presence in the region, and Japan believes that it will be asked to help bolster the economies of friendly states on the strategic periphery of the Middle East.

The United States' allies are not opposed to helping Washington bolster the security of oil supplies from the Persian Gulf. What bothers both Europe and Japan is U.S. reluctance to give them an equal voice in alliance affairs, particularly regarding the search for a political settlement to the Arab-Israeli dispute. Both Europe and Japan feel that the stability of the Middle East is threatened far more by internal politics and the prospect of regional conflict within the Middle East than by the prospect of a direct confrontation between the superpowers. They believe that effective alliance strategy requires creating the conditions of political and economic stability in the region and that a massive infusion of U.S. military equipment and forces will not minimize instability and may in fact exacerbate it.

In particular the Europeans believe that they cannot be assured of access to energy unless they help to effect a resolution of the Palestinian problem. They acknowledge that oil supplies are threatened by other regional conflicts such as the war between Iran and Iraq, but they reject the American position that the Arab-Israeli conflict is a separate issue from the geopolitics of energy. It is for this reason that since 1975 the Europeans have pursued a European-Arab dialogue and in 1981 launched yet another peace initiative through the European Economic Community (EEC). Moreover, it was the European leaders at the June 1980 Venice economic summit who recognized the PLO as one of the legitimate representatives of the Palestinian people, an action vigorously opposed by the United States.

The United States must realize that unless negotiations on Palestinian autonomy are resumed now that Israel has a new government, Western Europe and Japan are likely to try cementing new political relationships with the Middle Eastern oil producers (the Europeans by selling them arms, the Japanese by offering greater economic and development assistance) as a way of ensuring access to Middle Eastern oil supplies. Chancellor Helmut Schmidt's call in April 1981 for representation of the Palestine Liberation Organization (PLO) at a joint meeting of Arab and EEC foreign ministers in October 1981 demonstrates that the process is well underway.

Because of their greater dependence on Middle Eastern oil and their different perception of threats to stability in the region, the Europeans and Japanese understandably conclude that it may be impossible to construct an allied security system in the region as long as the United States, because of its own domestic politics, refuses to pressure to Israel to arrive at a comprehensive political settlement with the Arabs. The Europeans and Japanese fear that time is running out for a political settlement in the region, believe that any Arab leaders who are seen as lackeys of the United States risk being overthrown by dissident elements in their society, and categorically admonish that the outbreak of an Arab-Israeli war in Lebanon or elsewhere would lead to a cutoff of oil supplies to any state supporting Israel.

Therefore to the extent that the Reagan administration pressures Europe and Japan to become more involved in effecting a new security framework in the Gulf, the Europeans and Japanese are likely to intensify pressure on the United States to resolve the Arab-Israeli dispute. U.S. failure to respond to these pressures will lead to new peace overtures and a potential change in European-Arab relations that may work at cross-purposes with U.S. security plans. Israel, for example, would view European sales of nuclear technology and arms to Iraq as an inherent threat to peace in the region.

REACTIONS TO THE RAPID DEPLOYMENT FORCE

Announcing the concept of the rapid deployment force (RDF) in February 1980 (see Chapter 1), President Carter explained that the RDF would protect allied access to the oil fields of the Persian Gulf, especially against the threat of direct Soviet intervention in the area. The RDF is designed to be a highly skilled mobile unit that could rapidly intervene in areas such as the Persian Gulf to protect U.S. interests pending the mobilization of larger U.S. forces.

The European and Japanese, well aware of the RDF's limits and of current U.S. incapacity to oppose a direct Soviet challenge in the Gulf, have been dismayed by the amount of open debate in the U.S. press and strategic community about the RDF's inadequacies. The German and British foreign offices and the Quai d'Orsay believe that this debate may in fact have weakened the allied position in the Persian Gulf because, whether it is true or not, the region now perceives that neither the RDF nor the U.S. advisory military personnel resident in Saudi Arabia would be able to repel direct Soviet intervention.

The governments in Bonn, Paris, Tokyo, and London fear that if dissident elements in one or more of the oil-producing states doubt

U.S. ability to deter Soviet expansionism, they may wonder whether the United States can stop an internal uprising or coup against one of the kingdoms or sheikdoms of the Gulf. They suspect that even if the RDF functioned relatively efficiently, it could not arrive in time to prevent Persian Gulf oil producers or dissident elements controlling the oil fields from blowing their oil facilities up in the face of an invasion, as they have threatened to do.

A discussion of the costs and benefits of expanded military strength in the Middle East is beyond the scope of this book, but the logistics of defending the oil fields is staggering. Saudi Arabia alone has fourteen major oil fields, seven onshore and seven offshore (see Table 9-1). These fields and their supporting facilities comprise 775 active wells, three refineries, eleven loading terminals, and 2,800 miles of connecting pipeline facilities. A tight perimeter around these facilities would encompass 10,000 square miles.[2] The problems in the other major oil-producing nations in the Persian Gulf are no less staggering.[3]

Pipelines are virtually indefensible, especially in the Gulf, but oil wells are also vulnerable facilities. If the superstructure (or "Christmas tree") of a well is destroyed, it must be redrilled.[4] Wells

Table 9-1.   Oil Producing Facilities in the Persian Gulf.

	Iran	Iraq	Kuwait	Saudi Arabia	United Arab Emirates
Reserves (billion barrels)	60	36	88	150	34
Major oil fields					
Onshore	9	4	11	7	3
Offshore	2	0	2	7	5
Active wells	300	160	1,040	775	275
Number of refineries	5	7	5	3	1
Refinery capacity					
(thousands of barrels)	911	169	712	586	15
Loading terminals					
Ports	5	2	4	4	4
SBM[a]	2	0	3	7	8
Pipeline mileage	3,720	3,690	740	2,800	400

Source: Jonathan P. Stern, "U.S. Intervention in the Middle East," *Defense Communications, and Security Review* 80/1 (1979):6.

[a]Single buoy moorings or other offshore loading platforms.

are so flammable that a single unsophisticated saboteur with few explosives could do tremendous damage. If the saboteur were highly skilled the damage both above and below ground could be incalculable.[5] Loading platforms are also critical. Although minor damage to a loading platform could be repaired quickly, a sea-based surprise attack could inflict a lot of damage, reducing oil exports for a considerable time. If local refineries were destroyed, refining of Middle Eastern crude could be picked up in excess refinery capacity elsewhere in the world, but the adjustment process would still involve local product shortages and disrupt the international market, at significant cost all round. In the best of circumstances, the RDF might not be able to preserve the flow of oil.

The Europeans and Japanese, and much of the U.S. strategic community, also doubt the effectiveness of the RDF in an internal political upheaval like the one that occurred in Iran. Seizing or protecting the Iranian oil fields in late 1978 or early 1979 would have been a logistical nightmare requiring sizable forces. To have any chance of success such a deployment of force in response to an internal political situation in the Gulf might have to take place before the United States had adequate intelligence information, but a miscalculation of the country's political situation could be catastrophic for U.S. interest. Yet the Gulf Arab states believe that the internal political turmoil or subversion, whether or not it is supported by the Soviet Union or its surrogates, is far more likely than direct Soviet intervention.

This belief, as well as the security threat posed by Israel, makes the Arab regimes hesitant to allow the United States to install military bases on their soil. Arab states fear that too close an identification with Israel's main arms supplier will endanger their own security. They also worry that they might not be consulted about the use of such bases. They wonder what role the bases might play in another Arab-Israeli war or whether U.S. forces stationed within their borders would move against their armies if they mobilized against Israel or another state friendly to the United States.

Only Oman and Bahrain currently have agreements with the U.S. military. Bahrain's commercial port facilities are open to the small Middle East task force; Oman has signed but not implemented an RDF basing agreement. Some countries welcome U.S. efforts to establish an "over-the-horizon" presence, but internal and intra-Arab political considerations make it impossible for them to support the United States publicly. These states are in a political quandary: They know they may not survive without a military guarantor; they also realize that they cannot associate too directly with the United States without provoking criticism from radical Arab nations and nationalists critical of U.S. policy on Israel. They also worry that if they identify too closely with the United States, the Soviet Union will try to destabilize their societies.

Equally concerned, Europe and Japan fear that because of its preoccupation with the Soviet threat, the United States will rush to establish a major military presence in the Persian Gulf and the Indian Ocean regions without carefully assessing how to go about it. The Europeans and Japanese fear that in its haste to establish a presence in the region, the United States has neglected important local and regional political dynamics, particularly in Oman, Kenya, and Somalia, three of the states the United States is asking to provide RDF facilities.

They fear, for example, that the presence of U.S. forces in Oman could set off a social explosion. Concern about Oman centers on Sultan Qabus' isolation from the Omani masses; the maldistribution of wealth between Muscat and the rest of the country; corruption above locally acceptable levels among the expatriate officers who surround the Sultan; the lack of a clear line of succession and the expatriate military community's opposition to the leading contenders for the throne; and Oman's isolation from the Arab world because of its support for the Camp David accords. Oman appears ripe for trouble of the kind that could pose major problems for the United States.

The geopolitical issues associated with U.S. acquisition of RDF facilities on the Horn of Africa are no less complex. Somalia has been reluctant to give the United States use of its fine port and air facilities originally built by Moscow in Mogadishu, unless the United States extends military assistance, which Washington fears could extend that country's conflict with the Soviet-backed government of Christian Ethiopia. Politics in this region is complicated by the fact that in Eritrea and the Afar regions of Ethiopia along the coast of the Red Sea, Iraq, Syria, Saudi Arabia, and Kuwait are providing assistance to rival separatist groups (both Arab and Christian) fighting each other as well as the Soviet- and Cuban-backed government in Addis Ababa.

Relations between Ethiopia, Kenya, and Somalia add to the maze of cross cutting African, Arab, racial, religious, and ideological conflicts. Somalia has territorial claims against both Marxist Ethiopia and pro-Western Kenya, a fact that has led Ethiopia and Kenya to form a defense treaty against Somalia. Ethiopia and Kenya remain suspicious of Somali designs, despite the waning in recent months of some of the more extreme public pronouncements from Somalia on the Kenyan territorial issue and the fledgling beginnings of a rapprochement between Kenya and Somalia.

In short, it would be difficult for the United States to expand its role in Kenya and Somalia without becoming enmeshed in volatile regional politics. As part of a quid pro quo with Kenya, the United States has increased its military and economic aid both to Kenya, in exchange for access to its naval base in Mombasa and adjacent airfields, and to Somalia, for use of the former Soviet base at Berbera.

Concerned that weapons supplied to the Somalian government by the United States may be used against Kenya, Nairobi is also alarmed that an alliance between the United States and South Africa against the Soviets will make it difficult or impossible for Kenya to draw too close to the United States. The Kenyan government believes that such an association could isolate Kenya from the rest of Black Africa, which sees Pretoria, not Moscow, as the greatest threat to African security. Kenyan officials have warned the United States that in its haste to teach the Soviets a lesson, Washington should not run the risk of alienating its moderate friends in Africa by too close a public identification with white South Africa. It would be ironic if, in the course of protecting allied access to Persian Gulf oil, the United States adopted policies toward South Africa that caused a confrontation with Nigeria, a major trading partner and (at 900,000 bd) its second largest supplier of oil, and Angola, which at 130,000 bd is also a relatively important oil source.

Somalia and Kenya both have serious economic and political problems. The Kenyan economy is deteriorating, and Kenya is experiencing major food shortages. As many as 1.5 million refugees from Ethiopia have fled to Somalia, a country with a total population under 4 million. In pro-Western Sudan nearby, the number of refugees is 500,000. The chief danger of a large American military presence in Somalia is that renewed conflict in the Ogaden would make it difficult to avoid a confrontation between superpowers, especially if Ethiopian aircraft flown by Soviet, East German, or Cuban pilots were to strike Berbera.

The danger of current U.S. strategic policy in the Persian Gulf and Indian Ocean regions is that the Reagan administration, in designing a "cooperative security framework" to protect Persian Gulf oil, has not paid enough attention to potential sources of political instability in the region. The United States should be very careful that its military build-up not intensify regional instability by blurring the distinction between regional animosity and superpower confrontations fought through surrogate states.

Before it cements an irrevocable agreement with either Kenya or Somalia the United States should conduct a thorough risk assessment to identify the local political difficulties affecting positioning a RDF force in Kenya or Somalia or both. In the meantime the United States should explore the possibilities for other land-based facilities or a sea-based defense capability. The United States should particularly consider how to improve its security relations with Pakistan, Egypt, and the Sudan.

For too long U.S. policymakers have ignored the pivotal importance of Pakistan to the defense of both the Gulf and the Indian Ocean. U.S. access to port facilities in Karachi and Pakistani Baluchistan would enhance the U.S. strategic position along the Arabian Sea and in the Gulf, at the same time reducing political pressure on the Arab Gulf states that do not want a highly visible U.S. presence in the Middle East itself. Reopening air facilities and intelligence-gathering facilities at Peshawar would make it easier for the United States and Pakistan to encourage a withdrawal of Soviet forces from Afghanistan or at least to notify the Soviet Union that any further such activity in the region will be more costly.

Improving our relations with Pakistan presents problems, however. Many senior Pakistani officials regard the Persian Gulf and Afghanistan as separate areas of tension. Pakistan is willing to cooperate in the Gulf but is reluctant to take aggressive or provocative actions regarding Afghanistan. Thus it is far more likely to increase its naval cooperation than to reopen the Peshawar facilities for American personnel. Moreover, to gain Pakistan's confidence, the United States must provide Pakistan with two squadrons of F-15 fighters, (or possibly F-16s), a sale the Ford and Carter administrations vigorously opposed as a threat to the stability of the Indian subcontinent. The United States will also have to review its nonproliferation policy with Pakistan; any policy change could adversely affect Indian-American relations, especially if the United States proceeds with its plan for a $3 billion assistance program for Pakistan.

Despite these obstacles the United States should give priority attention to constructing a new security relationship with Pakistan. With access to bases in Pakistani Baluchistan the United States would be better positioned to thwart a Soviet thrust from Afghanistan to the Indian Ocean through either Pakistani or Iranian Baluchistan. Should the Soviets intervene in northern Iran, the United States must be ready to move against the Iranian port of Chahbahar, potentially one of the best in the Indian Ocean.

Originally planned under the shah of Iran, the Port of Chahbahar is designed to handle Spruance-class destroyers and U.S. diesel submarines and has superb air cover. Whoever controls the port has first-class antisubmarine warfare and surveillance capabilities. As A.J. Cottrell and colleagues note, control of Chahbahar allows "a patrolling of sea lanes and routes of access and egress to and from choke points and other strategic passages east and south of the Persian Gulf."[6] From bases in Pakistan, it is possible to prevent Chahbahar from falling under Soviet control.

Although both Egypt and Israel have serious political reservations about having U.S. forces stationed in their territories, neither has ruled out the possibility of allowing the United States to position some equipment and materials and to improve existing facilities that could prove vital to moving an RDF into the Persian Gulf region. A U.S. basing agreement with Israel might cause U.S. relations with the oil-producing states of the Gulf to deteriorate, however. Only in the event of a major direct confrontation with the Soviet Union should forces be deployed from Israel into even friendly Arab countries.

Instead, the United States and Egypt should try to improve the facilities at Ras Banas, across the Red Sea from Jubail and Yanbu, to allow positioning of military supplies and to extend the site's air facilities to accommodate large-scale U.S. air transports. This should be a priority task in U.S. Persian Gulf policy. Access to these facilities will not only aid U.S. and Egyptian efforts to protect the Gulf oil fields but could prove invaluable as part of Egypt's defense commitment to the Sudan.

Because Sudan initially supported the Camp David accords, has a defense treaty with Egypt, has adopted a leading role in countering Libyan and Soviet-backed adventurism in the Sahara, and is intricately involved in the politics of the Horn of Africa, it is essential that the United States be especially aware of the effects that a political destabilization of the Sudan might have on Egyptian national security. Although the Sudanese government later stopped supporting the peace process because it was opposed by fundamentalist Islamic sects in the Sudan and broke diplomatic relations with Egypt, relations have been restored and Sudan has expressed its willingness to join any nation fighting Soviet, Libyan, and Cuban adventurism.

There is disturbing evidence that Libya, having annexed Chad, is now trying to destabilize the Sudan, which may soon become Qaddafi's testing ground for the encirclement of Egypt. The Arab leaders of the Gulf, especially of Saudi Arabia, are concerned by these events—and their counsel should be heeded.[7] The Numeiry government in the Sudan has recently offered the United States RDF basing rights in exchange for increased military equipment sales to fight Soviet and Libyan aggression. This offer merits consideration as an element in U.S. Gulf security strategy. However, the Sudan faces serious economic and political problems and before the United States constructs an RDF basing facility in the country it should make a timely assessment of the Sudan's political stability and decide to what extent strategic considerations could make it necessary to bolster the Numeiry regime against an Islamic fundamentalist opposition.

The United States has also expressed an interest in acquiring access to RDF military facilities in Turkey. From Turkey it would be easy to monitor Soviet access to the Mediterranean and to control the most direct air and overland routes between European Russia, the Middle East, and Africa. When he was supreme allied commander of NATO forces, General Alexander Haig noted that if a war began, bases in eastern Turkey could be vital to protection of Western petroleum sources in the Middle East and the Persian Gulf.[8]

Turkey poses unique problems as a location for RDF facilities. Turkey is a member of NATO, but NATO's strategic umbrella does not extend to the Persian Gulf and there is concern in European NATO circles that the presence of U.S. RDF facilities in Turkey could provoke the anger of the OPEC oil producers or, in the event of U.S.-Soviet conflict in the Gulf, provoke air strikes against Turkey that might subsequently extend to the rest of Europe. Denmark, Belgium, and the Netherlands are particularly concerned about this possibility.

Turkey is beset with problems that threaten its political stability. The state's acute dependence on insecure sources of oil (Iraq, Libya, and the USSR), combined with poor fiscal and monetary policies, a staggering foreign debt, and sky-high inflation, has caused recurring financial crises. Turkey is also plagued by right- and left-wing terrorism, and military intervention is a constant threat to its civilian governments.

Moreover, short of a major military conflict between NATO and the Soviet Union, Ankara would like to avoid antagonizing Moscow. While Turkey is wary of the Soviet Union, showing interest in increased cooperation with the USSR gives Turkey some diplomatic leverage with the other NATO countries regarding its territorial dispute with Greece. What is more, Turkey is the largest single recipient of Soviet foreign assistance in the Third World, and the USSR, which provides about 10 percent of Turkey's oil, is Turkey's sixth largest trading partner.

As a member of NATO Turkey is theoretically protected against a Soviet invasion, but many Turkish military leaders question whether NATO would come to its aid if the Soviets invaded its eastern frontier. They especially question how the West would respond if the Soviets assisted Kurdish separatists.

Turkey is also concerned about the regional implications of playing a more active role in the defense of the Persian Gulf. Although it is a Moslem country, Turkey has diplomatic relations with Israel as well as with most of the Arab states in the area. The Turks are sensitive to Arab animosity toward them because of their domination of the region earlier in history but are especially concerned not to alienate Iraq and Libya, the major sources of oil. Since both Iraq and Libya want to keep the superpowers out of the region, Turkey wants not to appear closely associated with U.S. Middle Eastern policies. For this reason Turkey refused the United States the use of its facilities to resupply Israel during the 1973–74 Arab-Israeli war and has annnounced that it will not permit any use of its bases for direct combat or logistical support of Israel.

With so many uncertainties the United States should not consummate a bilateral agreement for RDF facilities with Turkey but should negotiate with the Turks in the broader NATO context to extend NATO's sphere of action to include the Persian Gulf. This policy, however, may be opposed by most of NATO's members.

The United States' major allies have a fundamentally different perception of U.S. efforts to effect a "strategic consensus" in the Middle East than does Washington. Not only are Western Europe and Japan well aware of the difficulties of militarily repelling direct Soviet intervention in the Gulf, they also believe that the Soviets will not move against the Gulf in a military way. Rather, they think the Soviet Union will try to increase its influence as local political events give them the opportunity to do so, a strategy for which a unified allied counter-strategy is probably impossible. Many European and Japanese strategic analysts believe that a continued impasse on the Arab-Israeli conflict provides the USSR continued political openings to extend its sphere of influence. If this is true, U.S. failure to adopt a more balanced policy toward the Arab nations could increase political tension in the Persian Gulf region.

Western Europe's perception of Soviet policy in the Gulf makes it difficult for the allies to unequivocally support a tough allied response to the Soviet intervention in Afghanistan and the U.S. boycott of Iran. Because of their greater dependence on oil supplies from the Middle East, their interest in preserving trade relations with the Communist bloc, and their genuine fear of a new cold war, many Japanese and Western Europeans have serious reservations about the current direction of U.S. policy. The United States must exhibit a greater willingness to consult Western Europe and Japan on policies affecting their vital interests, or relations with the allies will become increasingly strained.

THE SOVIET ENERGY PROBLEM

One of the most complex issues the allies face is how to deal with the energy problem that the Soviet Union and Eastern Europe are certain to face, in a way that minimizes the danger to European and Middle Eastern security. No one doubts that the Soviet petroleum, coal, and nuclear industries face formidable problems, and no one knows if the Soviet Union can solve these problems quickly enough. That the Soviets will experience a shortfall in domestic oil production is almost certain. How large a shortfall is a matter for intense speculation. Energy analysts disagree about whether the critical problem in the Soviet energy system is a bottleneck in the pipeline and transportation network, engineering difficulties with enhanced recovery techniques, poor drilling equipment and procedures, or the rigidities of the Soviet planning system.[9]

The critical policy questions confronting the U.S. government and its major allies center on what actions they should take if the Soviet energy situation transforms the USSR from a sizable oil exporter (3 mmbd) to a net oil importer: Should the Western world provide the

USSR with oil technology to reduce political and economic pressures on a tight world oil market? Will such technology reduce Moscow's need to move into the Persian Gulf either commercially or militarily to ensure its access to energy supplies? With aid from the industrialized world, would the Soviets be more likely to concentrate capital in domestic energy production than in military expenditures? Will technical assistance convince the USSR to abandon political and military solutions to its energy problem? Will the extension of technology aid give the industrialized nations more political leverage in their dealings with the USSR? How much will aid to the USSR benefit U.S. exports?

At the same time, considering the enormity of the USSR's energy resources, the United States and its allies must consider the geopolitical implications of helping to make the Soviet Union energy self-sufficient at a time when the industrialized world, especially Europe and Japan, remain overwhelmingly dependent on imported energy. Finally, the United States must consider what will happen if, instead of following U.S. policy directives, Europe and Japan establish separate energy relationships with the Soviet Union.

According to Central Intelligence Agency estimates, the Soviet Union has vast reserves of energy and mineral resources, including proved oil reserves of 33.5 billion barrels, roughly the same as proved U.S. reserves.[10] Probable and possible Soviet reserves far exceed U.S. potential, although they lie mostly deep offshore on the Arctic continental shelf and in other reservoirs from which recovery would be difficult.

Soviet natural gas reserves, the largest in the world, amount to an estimated 630 trillion cubic feet (Tcf), approximately a 52-year supply at current production levels.[11] Much of future gas production is to come from West Siberian fields and offshore regions. The Soviets have abundant coal resources as well, enough to last 400 years at present levels of output,[12] but problems with labor, technology, capital, mine depletion, and transportation plague the industry and will continue to do so for some time, and the coal is of poor quality. Use of nuclear power for electricity generation is slated to increase rapidly, especially west of the Urals, but the problems that plague this sector make it questionable whether the ambitious targets set in the eleventh five year plan will be met. Peat, oil shale, firewood, and hydroelectric power now collectively contribute almost eight times as much energy nationally as does nuclear energy.[13]

The Soviet Union is the world's largest oil producer. In 1980 it pumped 12.1 mmbd, 3 mmbd of which were exported to Eastern and Western Europe (1.6 mmbd to Eastern Europe, the remainder to Western Europe and non-European Soviet satellites). Oil exports to the West have accounted for over half of Soviet hard currency earnings since 1977.[14] These export earnings are critical since hard currency allows Moscow to import needed grain and advanced technology and lessens the need to divert scarce rubles from other sectors (including the military) or to effect major changes in the Soviet agricultural sector. Gas export revenues, although growing in importance, do not begin to approach the revenue potential of oil exports.[15]

In a series of reports that began in 1977, the CIA startled the international energy community by projecting that the Soviet Union would cease being a sizable net oil exporter and become a sizable net oil importer by 1985.[16] Although the CIA projections are not easily verifiable, it appears that the CIA's prognosis played a key role in the December 1977 Communist party's central committee plenum adoption of a crash program to conserve energy resources, to accelerate production of the West Siberian oil fields, and to begin substituting other fuels for oil wherever possible.

As Jonathan Stein has noted, asking a populace that lacks adequate heat much of the time and has only one automobile for every forty to fifty people to conserve energy can have only a marginal economic and perhaps a negative political effect. Soviet domestic oil prices are still well below world prices, which encourage industrial oil use rather than conservation. Industries heavily dependent on oil feedstocks stiffly resist scheduled price rises; the heavy Soviet industries (such as steel) use significantly more oil per unit of output than do their Western counterparts. Because of this a constant level of military purchases requires a larger ruble expenditure, so the influential ministry of defense has an incentive to intervene in order to moderate increases in fuel prices.[17]

Even with vigorous conservation programs, it will be difficult, as Stein notes, to shift industrial priorities enough in the 1980s to save very much energy. The growth rate of energy consumption will continue to outpace the GNP growth rate.[18] The eleventh five year plan calls for fuel substitution, but because of financial and logistical bottlenecks an energy crunch is expected west of the Ural Mountains. Two-fifths of the population lives in this central belt and consumes 55 percent of Soviet fuel.[19] While the USSR has enough coal and gas to make up for shortfalls in oil demand, the energy demand mix west of the Urals poses problems for Soviet energy planners not unlike those posed in certain regions of the United States.

The western USSR uses massive quantities of fuel oil and other heavy products and much smaller quantities of gasoline.[20] Even with major changes in the western infrastructure in the next five years, delays installing large-diameter gas pipelines may retard progress. Seventy percent of Russia's natural gas reserves lies in Siberia, another 13–14 percent in the central Asian deserts. Installation of compressor stations has fallen behind schedule[21] as negotiations about large-diameter pipe and compressor stations (two-thirds of which are imported) are stalled over financial details and strategic issues. As a result these large new gas projects will not begin to make up any shortfall in oil production before the late 1980s.

Production of natural gas will increase yearly but not as fast as projected. Furthermore the major petroleum shortfall will be for light distillates (gasoline, jet fuel, and diesel fuel), so the potential for natural gas substitution will remain limited. There is not enough refining capacity to convert large volumes of residual fuel oil into lighter products,[22] where gas could substitute for residual fuel oil. Natural gas production at the giant Tyumen fields is beset with technological, financial, and other problems, such as inadequate staff housing, insufficient railroad tank cars (for storage and shipping), and delays in equipment servicing.[23] As a result, much gas is flared.

The production and use of coal to produce electricity and to fire industrial boilers west of the Urals has not increased as rapidly as forecast by Gosplan,[24] the state planning agency because of the large distances between the Siberian coal fields and the consuming centers in European Russia. Generating power at the mine site and transmitting it cross-country is a technological dream the USSR will not realize until at least 1990. The quality of Siberian and central Asian lignites is not suitable for existing industrial boilers.[25] The coal target for 1980 was scaled down from 805 million tons to 745 million tons,[26] and the legion of problems plaguing the coal sector forced this production level down to 712 million tons.

The energy situation poses terrible problems for the Soviet economy. With economic growth nearly stagnant since 1978 and with energy consumption rising, the USSR faces a dilemma: A policy of curtailing economic growth to save energy may be only partially successful, and a decline in economic activity may slow down production in the intermediate industries that service the petroleum sector.

Thus, it is very unlikely that energy conservation, fuel substitution, or a forced decline in economic growth will solve the USSR's near-term energy problems. Indeed, Soviet energy problems in the 1980s will probably be exacerbated by bureaucratic rivalry among the various ministries responsible for energy and by inadequate exploratory drilling, outmoded drilling techniques, and poor-quality equipment.

The nation's energy problems were so serious that in 1978 Moscow embarked on a crash effort to explore and develop the supergiant and giant fields of Tyumen Oblast, especially Samotlor. Soviet leaders decided to accelerate production in these older fields when it became apparent that the newer fields would not reach their targets. As a result, output from Samotlor peaked in 1980; after 1981 production from the older fields is expected to decline rapidly.[27] To reverse this decline the newer West Siberian fields must come into production quickly, but these fields are smaller, more remote (many lying in vast swamp pools), and therefore harder to develop.[28] Development of an infrastructure of pipelines, powerlines, roads, and housing lags far behind schedule.[29] Half of Western Siberia remains unexplored, and future exploration will occur at depths of 2.5 to 5 kilometers, for which Soviet seismographs and turbodrills are inadequate.[30]

Many people do not realize that simply keeping oil production at 1980 levels will require a massive industrial effort. To replace reserves produced during the tenth five year plan (1976–1980), 21 billion additional barrels of oil would have to have been discovered, almost twice the level of discoveries in 1971–1975.[31] Petroleum production, which grew an average of 10 percent a year in the early 1960s, grew only 6.8 percent from 1970 to 1975 and a mere 2.4 percent between 1978 and 1979. Annual increments to production peaked in 1975 and have since declined.[32] This falloff in the reserve/production ratio is even worse when you consider the higher percentages of very heavy (often nonflowing) oil found in most new large discoveries. Water-flooding releases only a fraction of this oil,[33] making recent large finds far less valuable than they might seem.

Despite a new Spring 1981 CIA estimate, which revised prior 1985 "low-range" output figures from 8–10 mmbd to 10–11 mmbd, and more recent DIA analyses projecting stable or increasing production, it is difficult to see how the Soviets can reverse the declining reserve/production ratio. The latest CIA effort points to greater investment and more exploratory drilling in West Siberia; the DIA analysis refers to the "very large" Salym Field which DIA believes will be a major producer in five or six years. In fact, the Salym uplift is part of a

". . . vast and complex bituminous shale formation present over a large part of Siberia . . . the oil was found to be contained in the fractures of the shale and producing rates quickly dropped as the fracture systems were brained."[34] In addition, the West Siberian Fedorovo field, while very large, cannot provide sufficient production to offset the dwindling output of the remaining supergiant reservoirs.

The deterioration of the petroleum sector affects the Soviet economy, foreign policy, and national security. It is increasingly apparent that the USSR will have to import more technology and industrial equipment from the West to solve its energy problems. During the tenth five year plan Soviet large-diameter pipe production met only a portion of the oil and gas industries' needs; 4–5 million tons of imported pipe were essential to complete the plan.[35] In payment for this pipe, Austria, Italy, West Germany, and France received, respectively, 60, 22, 17, and 12 percent of their natural gas from the Soviet Union.[36]

Responding to the Soviet intervention in Afghanistan, the United States in early 1980 imposed a ban on high-technology exports to the USSR, urging its European and Japanese allies to follow suit. Simultaneously, Deutsche BP announced that it was negotiating an $15-billion gas deal that would bring 40–50 billion cubic meters of gas from West Siberia to West Berlin, West Germany, France, Austria, Italy, Belgium, and the Netherlands.

The West German government was embarrassed by the timing of the announcement, but Western Europeans reject the Reagan administration's view that enhanced gas trade, by increasing dependency on Soviet energy resources, will threaten Western European or NATO security. European leaders argue that imported energy always entails political risk and that the alternative is greater dependency on politically insecure liquid national gas (LNG) sources or pipeline gas from Libya, Algeria, and Nigeria or oil from the Middle East. They note too that the element of barter trade involved will raise employment and stimulate their ailing economies.[37]

The Western European governments argue further that Soviet gas will supply only 3–8 percent of the total energy used by the major industrialized countries, on average. The Federal Republic of Germany emphasizes the many obstacles that remain before the agreement is final, pointing out that the pipeline will not be built before 1985 at the earliest and probably not before 1987–88. Therefore the Germans see little reason for U.S. concern about Europe's short-term energy security. The United States, on the other hand, believes that the Europeans are vulnerable to energy embargoes and that because capital they have invested in joint development projects could be nationalized or hard-currency debts from the USSR and Eastern Europe renounced, their foreign policy or economy could be held hostage.[38]

Alliance debate on this issue demonstrates how differently the links between energy and national security are perceived on the two sides of the Atlantic. Europe sees Middle Eastern politics as the paramount threat to oil supplies. The United States too often perceives energy as tangential to national security, the chief threat to which it views as the Soviet challenge.

The United States often fails to analyze the strategic problems the Soviet Union faces because of its energy problems. It is urgent for the Soviet Union to develop an adequate energy transportation network; without it even new energy discoveries will not help the situation. Although the dual-capacity "friendship" pipeline system extends 3,000 miles from the Volga-Urals region to Poland, Czechoslovakia, the German Democratic Republic, and Hungary, most refined products and crude are carried by rail because the Soviets do not have adequate compressors and pumping stations.[39] Without Western technology the system seems certain to remain unreliable. Furthermore before the Iranian crisis natural gas imports from Iran allowed the Soviets to export more natural gas to the West for hard currency. With imports from Iran curtailed, not only have there been energy shortages in Armenia, Azerbaijan, and Georgia but the Soviets have also had to divert revenue to build expensive pipelines to areas previously served by cheap foreign imports from Iran and Afghanistan. The loss of this gas has reduced the USSR's ability to ship gas west of the Urals to Eastern and Western European markets to substitute for declining oil reserves. Although this lost natural gas could be replaced by 1990 if nuclear and coal electricity-generating capacity reach target levels and oil output holds at peak production levels, none of these events is likely to occur.

To understand what this means for foreign policy, one must analyze energy relations between the Soviet Union and Eastern Europe. Coal represents 26 percent and oil 44 percent in the Soviet energy mix. In contrast, 53 percent of Eastern Europe's energy comes from coal and only 28 percent from oil, although oil's share of the energy mix is increasing faster than the share of other fuels.

In 1980 the Soviet Union supplied 80 percent of Eastern Europe's oil import needs, or 1.6 mmbd.[40] This percentage figure will increase, however, as Romania's oil output declines and Romanian consumption increases. Hungary and Yugoslavia, which produce less oil than Romania, are currently experiencing serious oil production problems. Polish coal exports have suffered as a result of Poland's political upheaval, as strikes have delayed mine and port operations.

A severe blow was dealt the Eastern European countries at the meeting in June 1980 of the Council for Mutual Economic Assistance (CMEA). Premier Alexsis Kosygin announced that oil supplies would increase only 8 percent during the eleventh five year plan, in sharp contrast with the 53 percent increase under the ninth five year plan (1971–1975).[41] The price per barrel was increased for *all* Soviet customers, though at prices far below world levels. Several months after the CMEA meeting, Oleg Bogomolov of the Institute of World Socialist Economics promised a 20 percent increase in energy deliveries under the eleventh five year plan, but added that "almost none of the projected increase would be in oil." The Communist bloc partners were warned to *"rely more on development of their own oil deposits"* (italics added).[42] Since Eastern Europe's meager oil deposits are declining, statements like this suggest the seriousness of the Soviet oil problem. Increased exports of gas and electricity can help alleviate the oil shortfall, but nuclear power generation in all of the CMEA countries (including the USSR) is short of the original 1980 target by one-half.[43] Even if all of the nuclear powerplants currently planned are built, they could not offset the Soviet bloc's oil problems until the early to mid-1990s.

Natural gas imports via the Orenburg pipeline, which has been operating since November 1978, will supply 2.8 billion cubic meters of gas per year to Czechoslovakia, Poland, the German Democratic Republic, Bulgaria, and Hungary and 1.5 billion cubic meters annually to Romania.[44] The Soviet natural gas sector will have to expand, however, for the USSR to implement the stated intention of exporting more gas instead of oil. The 1980 natural gas target was met, but a slowdown may well be in the offing. Production and transport delays suggest that the Soviets will be hard-pressed to meet their internal gas needs, increase Eastern Europe's supplies, and at the same time increase their hard-currency export market to Western Europe.

Meanwhile in 1980 the non-European partners in the Council on Mutual Economic Assistance (CMEA) (Cuba, Mongolia, Vietnam, and North Korea) imported nearly 250,000 barrels of Soviet oil per day; in 1985 Cuba alone (with roughly 80–85 percent of the total) may import that much.[45] Vietnamese oil exploration has yet to yield sizable returns and will do little more than satisfy domestic demand for the rest of the decade.

Thus, the Communist bloc's energy future is uncertain; much will hinge on primary Soviet production. If the USSR produces as much as planned, Eastern Europe's oil needs will be strained but manageable. Eastern Europe will seek oil from OPEC and other non-Communist sources, preferably on barter terms (such as arms-for-oil swaps, although barter deals beyond a minimal level will probably not be very popular with most OPEC governments). Under a "high" Soviet oil production scenario, the need for further imports will be low, but the East Europeans could still experience a shortfall.

Should the Soviets experience a rapid production shortfall, as much as 2–4 mmbd by 1985 (leaving Soviet output at 8–10 mmbd), things will be much worse. At a production level of 10 mmbd, the Soviets would need to import 1 mmbd of oil for domestic consumption and at least 2–3 mmbd for their allies; at 8 mmbd the Soviets may need to import 4–4.5 mmbd for Communist bloc consumption. If Moscow were to foot the bill at 1980 averaged world oil prices, $37 per barrel, the annual import bill could at worst exceed $60 billion. The Soviet Union would probably not be able to acquire that much oil without using military strength or extreme coercion; the extra production will simply not be available in those quantities. Furthermore to assume a $60 billion petroleum debt Moscow would have to restructure its economy and curtail its military expenditures, currently estimated at about $130–160 billion a year.

The USSR would view the prospect of a $60 billion import bill gravely. Asking Eastern Europe to pay its share of oil import expenditures, which it would probably have to do, could provide an economic crisis in Eastern Europe of such magnitude that major political unrest would occur and the reliability of Warsaw Pact units (especially Poland, Hungary, and Romania) would be doubtful enough to hamper Soviet crisis contingency planning. In any case Western banks might be unwilling to finance escalating debt levels or OPEC might demand hard currency, two possibilities that pose unprecedented challenges for Soviet economic policymakers.

To meet the energy crisis in Eastern Europe, Moscow has the following bleak options, each with its own pitfalls:

1. Reduce exports to Western Europe and incur shortfalls in hard currency;
2. Curtail oil supplies to Eastern Europe;
3. Require reduced domestic consumption;
4. Obtain oil from the Persian Gulf;
5. Expand domestic production by using Western technology.

Of course, if the industrialized world curtails sales of oil technology, it may drive the Soviets toward the Persian Gulf out of desperation.

The announcement by the USSR that 1981 oil exports to Western Europe would be reduced by 20–25 percent[46] was a clear indication of a desperate energy situation. Rising world energy prices could soften the impact of this curtailment on hard currency earnings, but as world energy demand continues to decline in response to the 1979–80 doubling in the price of oil sagging prices will exacerbate the crisis.

With a sizable shortfall of oil, Soviet leaders might maintain the reduced level of exports to Western Europe at the same time tightening their grip over Eastern Europe's economic policy by enforcing strict austerity measures. This could provoke major political disturbances in the satellite countries, however, precipitating a crisis that could jeopardize valuable East-West trade if the West in response to that country's political repression were to curtail trade with the USSR.

Even if the Communist bloc's oil shortfall is smaller than predicted, the USSR could still face difficult choices. Unless it cuts domestic consumption by 20 percent, the best it could hope for in a shortfall would be severe curtailment of Eastern European demand through low economic growth and greater use of non-oil fuels. However, the political risks lower economic growth would entail and the huge sums that would have to be diverted from the military to the civilian economy to effect fuel substitution make a policy of "guided" or forced demand restraint most improbable. Seen in this light, it is understandable that the USSR would refute CIA projections of a shortfall. The implications of a projected output of only 8 mmbd are too staggering for the Soviet planner to contemplate publicly.[47]

The level of Soviet energy production in the 1980s will greatly affect global security. The Soviets will perceive that a crisis exists when they have to import oil to meet *both* Soviet and Eastern European requirements at the same time that shortages of hard currency and barriers to barter trade foreclose payment options. At 10 mmbd production, the USSR will no longer earn hard currency, because exports to the West will have to be diverted to Eastern Europe, unless Eastern European energy demand is severely curtailed.[48] Considering demand projections for the industrial and agricultural sectors, the limited possibilities for conservation and fuel substitution, and reports that Soviet tank crews, aircraft, and other military units do not have enough fuel for their exercises, the USSR will undoubtedly be forced to enter the world oil market.

As oil production falls, the Soviets will have to assess the political and economic value of their different export markets. Loss of their West bound oil exports will cost the USSR tens of billions of dollars (including the opportunity cost of supplying Eastern Europe below world prices). These losses could be partially recouped by the end of the decade if natural gas sales through the new Yamal pipeline to Western Europe begin by 1986 or 1987 or if electricity sales between the EEC and COMECON begin. Natural gas revenues will not match oil revenues, however, and it is uncertain when or if the Yamal pipeline will be built. Loss of most or all Western export sales would not only slow economic growth below current low levels, but would make import costs a greater burden proportionately. The sale of mineral and gold reserves, diamonds, military equipment, and natural gas could offset the trade deficit somewhat, but there would still be an unbreachable gap between modest export receipts and expanding import costs. By 1985 escalating foreign trade debt in the Soviet Union and Eastern Europe may make the international financial community reconsider Soviet creditworthiness and extend fewer new loans.

Under no circumstances will the Soviets allow Eastern Europe, an essential element in the Soviet security system, to collapse economically. Rather than risk military intervention in Communist bloc troublespots after an energy-related breakdown, Soviet strategy will probably be to ameliorate energy shortages before economic disaster. Eastern Europe countries will be required to make major concessions in the energy sector at a time when they are having trouble remaining economically solvent. The USSR will not push its allies to the brink, but it will demand sacrifices (greater investment in Soviet energy projects, manpower aid, and payment of world prices) and will do everything possible to ensure at least low levels of growth.

The Eastern bloc could reach this point by late 1983 if, as appears likely, Samotlor and other major fields fail to hold peak levels beyond mid-1982. Timing is important, particularly for Moscow; in the mid-1980s the military balance will appear to favor the Soviet Union as never before and probably never again. In terms of quantity, NATO's defense industrial base will not catch up to the Soviet advances of the 1970s until the late 1980s; technologically Soviet armaments are now equal in many ways to those of the West and perhaps superior in others (tanks, antisatellite weapons), though this is open to debate.

Some time during the 1980s the Soviet Union will assess the risk of more active political involvement in the Middle East. Although it appears unlikely that the Soviets will actually move to occupy oil fields in the Persian Gulf region, U.S. contingency planning has to provide for such a scenario. The United States has to anticipate that a hawk in the Kremlin might pose the following question: Why should the Soviet Union strain all its resources to pay exorbitant oil import bills when the possibility exists of procuring such supplies at an acceptable level of risk? Military intervention need only be threatened: subversive activity, internal unrest in one or two key oil states such as Iran or Iraq (whose output could make up the USSR's shortfall) or the use of proxy forces could put enough political pressure on key oil producers that they would sign special oil deals for Soviet currency rather than hard currency, in effect providing the Soviet Union with oil at a fraction of its market price. Behind the political maneuvering would be the veiled threat of direct military intervention. The United States would not send in rapid deployment forces; it could not easily counter a threat that appeared to originate in the Persian Gulf area itself. NATO allies would never agree to U.S. led intervention in a Gulf state civil war; fearful that OAPEC would retaliate by cutting off its oil supplies, the Atlantic Alliance would be paralyzed. In this situation, the Soviet Union might consider a power play. With foreign debt escalating, world oil production falling, the domestic energy situation deteriorating and Soviet military forces surrounding the Gulf (in Ethiopia, South Yemen, Afghanistan, and Syria), even a cautious Soviet leadership might be tempted to adopt a more adventurous policy. If this debate occurred in the Politburo during a Soviet succession crisis, the danger posed to the world could be incalculable.[49]

Against this backdrop, the Western allies and Japan will soon confront tough political choices. Should the major industrialized countries help the Soviet Union and Eastern Europe reduce the need for greater Soviet involvement (peaceful or otherwise) in the world petroleum market and the Middle East, or is the Communist bloc's energy problem such a threat to the Soviet empire that Moscow should be forced to divert resources from the military to the civilian sector to solve it?

As oil production in the USSR slides toward 10 mmbd, Western intelligence services should expect increased covert activity in the Persian Gulf region and North Africa and gradually increasing Soviet naval movements in the northwest quadrant of the Indian Ocean. Acting as opportunities present themselves, the Soviets will move not to cut off OECD supplies but to ensure access to their own. One of their major concerns is to maintain the flow of oil to the Soviet Far East in the event that war with China cuts off the Trans-Siberian railroad, thus cutting the USSR's vital oil lifeline to the Far East.

Beginning a war in the Indian Ocean or on the Arabian peninsula is no more in the national interest of the USSR than is spending $40–60 billion yearly for oil imports. With World War III and billions in import expenditures equally unacceptable, Soviet policy will lie somewhere between the two extremes. The task for U.S. contingency planners is to consider the options from the Kremlin's vantage point.

Western contingency planning must deal with the central question of whether the industrialized nations should provide advanced technology to help the Soviet Union out of its energy crisis and whether providing such assistance will make the Soviet Union less adventurous in the Middle East.

The industrialized world should not provide the Soviet Union with this kind of assistance unless major political concesisons are made in return, for example withdrawing from Afghanistan or reducing arms spending. The allies are likely to remain dependent on imported oil for the rest of the century, so making the Soviet Union energy-independent would unfavorably shift the global strategic balance.

Western Europe is unlikely to agree with a U.S. policy of denying assistance to the Soviet Union, on whom it depends for energy supplies. Therefore, the United States should demonstrate to Western Europe that it will offset any losses in energy supplies from the USSR by a massive increase in coal exports to Western Europe, as well as valuable export-related employment. The difficulties would be prodigious, but the expansion of coal exports must nonetheless become a paramount item on the U.S. national security agenda.

The United States must convince its allies that it is not trying to isolate the Soviet Union but that that nation must be put on notice that the economic climate will improve only when it abandons its aggressive military program and embarks on a program of peaceful economic coexistence.

THE UNITED STATES AND CANADA

The United States tends to view energy relations with Canada in terms of Canada's abundant energy resources, often assuming that many of those resources will eventually find their way to U.S. customers. Indeed it is tempting to perceive a "continental logic" at work, with energy flowing naturally along north-south lines. However, technical, economic, and political factors may well limit development of Canada's energy resources, and the basic economic and political ground rules for Canadian energy development are currently very unsettled. Unless the U.S. and Canadian governments take steps to avoid it, conflict over joint energy projects is more likely than a major expansion of exports between the two countries or even continental cooperation.

Supply relations between the two countries have changed considerably in the last ten years. Before the 1970s both Ottawa and Washington adopted policies to ensure access to oil and gas markets and to encourage domestic production. In Canada this meant a policy of exporting to the United States; in the United States, it meant that the quota system designed to limit oil imports was not applied to Canada until 1970. In 1973 the peak year of Canadian oil exports to the United States, Canada supplied 17 percent of gross U.S. oil imports. The Canadian share of U.S. oil imports had fallen to 5 percent by mid-1979 and continues to fall as Canada phases out oil exports.

In the 1970s both countries were concerned primarily not with access to markets but with access to supplies. Canada's recent strategy has been to displace foreign oil supplies with domestic ones if necessary by reducing exports. Oil exports have been dramatically reduced, except for heavy oil that could not find a market in Canada itself. Gas exports have held steady and new exports were authorized in 1980. This gas must clearly be surplus to Canadian needs; if domestic gas is ultimately diverted to the Maritime provinces (New Brunswick, Nova Scotia, Prince Edward Island) to reduce their dependency on imported oil, then gas exports to the United States could be reduced.

Not only have supply relationships changed, but links between energy and other issues, such as trade and investment, have also become more apparent. Canada's desire for greater access to U.S. markets for processed raw materials, such as petrochemicals, and for reduced U.S. ownership of the Canadian oil and gas industries, are potential sources of conflict. Increasing Canadian concern about the long-range transport of acid rain to Canada from coal-fired power plants in the United States could become a major issue in U.S.-Canadian relations.

Canada clearly cannot solve the problem of U.S. dependence on insecure oil imports, but energy-related policy, especially investment policy, will occupy a prominent place on the U.S.-Canadian agenda. The dependence of some U.S. regions on Canadian gas, the construction of the Alaskan gas pipeline across Canadian territory, the treatment accorded U.S. energy investment in Canada, and the importance of energy in Canadian politics make it imperative that the United States pay close attention to the energy policies and problems of its northern neighbor.

Perspectives on energy resources changed fundamentally on both sides of the border in the late 1960s and early 1970s, as a growing concern over scarcity of energy resources was reinforced by the dramatic transformation of the international oil market in October 1973. Canadian energy planners accorded increasing importance to energy self-sufficiency and import reduction, a policy that led to sharp reductions in oil exports. Canada's leaders, who must cope with both sharp economic disparities between regions and a growing political battle over the division of power between the federal and provincial governments, have not been completely successful in dealing with the problems that have emerged.

Data on Canada's energy resources, particularly in the frontier regions, vary in uncertainty, and the federal government tends to be conservative in its appraisal of these resources. One thing is fairly certain, however: Future exploration and production will tend to concentrate in the so-called frontier areas of the Beaufort Sea, High Arctic, and Labrador Shelf, as well as the Alberta tar sands, where lead times on development will be substantial and where significant climatic, technical, and transportation problems must be overcome, generally at considerable cost.

Oil and gas exports to the United States were important to Canada until the 1970s, but production from new sources will take so long to develop and involves so many uncertainties that it is unrealistic to expect imports from Canada to be a significant source of future U.S. supplies of oil and gas during the remainder of this century. The United States is likely to import more electricity and uranium from Canada in the 1980s and to export more coal to Canada's eastern provinces.

Oil and Gas

Prospects for oil exports from Canada are particularly slim. In 1980 Canada produced 1.4 mmbd of oil from conventional oil fields south of the sixtieth parallel and from frontier areas north of the parallel and on the Labrador Shelf. Official estimates, which place total recoverable conventional crude at over 11 billion barrels, do not include frontier resources, partly because they are so uncertain and partly because the absence of transport links makes them inaccessible. Conceivably oil exports could increase if syncrude, Beaufort Sea, and Labrador Shelf oil projects all reached their full potential by 1990, but there is little evidence that this will happen.

Industry and government officials agree that frontier resources will be the key to Canadian energy self-sufficiency. The potential of Canada's Beaufort Sea (30–40 billion barrels of oil and 250–350 TCF of natural gas), for example, is often compared with that of the North Sea. So are its development problems and costs unfortunately. Similar difficulties make it unlikely that significant quantities of oil will be produced from the Labrador Shelf before 1990, and development of tar sands and heavy oil in Alberta and Saskatchewan, the largest relatively untapped sources of crude, have been delayed pending a final clarification of Prime Minister Trudeau's new energy program.

No matter which political party is in power, Canada's federal government will probably feel political pressure to strive for energy self-sufficiency, which will leave little if any room for additional exports. Light crude is available only through exchanges, at approximately 100,000 bd, each way and occurs only where the economic benefits of such swaps reduces transportation costs. Continuation of these exchanges may prevent a shortfall for refineries (historically dependable on Canadian crude) in the so-called Northern Tier of the United States (Michigan, Minnesota, North Dakota, Montana, Washington), but they represent only a temporary solution. Exports of heavy crude, which have been exempt from Canada's general phaseout of exports, may gradually decrease through the mid-1980s as Canada invests in refinery conversions that allow it to use heavy oil. It is imperative that the United States develop an alternative way of supplying the Northern Tier, such as a pipeline from its own West Coast.

Prospects for exports of natural gas are somewhat more optimistic. Gas exports will probably remain at about 1 trillion cubic feet (Tcf) through 1990, then decline under existing licenses. Development of large proven reserves in the High Arctic (16–18 Tcf), Mackenzie Delta (250–350 Tcf) area, and Deep Basin area of Alberta and British Columbia, plus additions to existing reserves, could increase Canada's export potential, but at the very most Canadian gas will satisfy only 5–6 percent of total U.S. gas needs. Of course, the importance of this gas to the Northern Tier will be far greater.

Canadian gas fields are located in the same general region as the oil fields, but gas appears to be more abundant than oil in the frontier regions. In December 1979 the National Energy Board revised its estimate of discovered conventional reserves in western Canada upward, from 66 Tcf to 72 Tcf. Ultimate potential is estimated at 147 Tcf in conventional areas and 96 Tcf in the frontier region.

The level of gas exports beyond 1990 will depend on several factors, among which the development of High Arctic resources will be one of the most important. The means of delivery chosen—pipelines or LNG tanker—will also be important. Pipelines are profitable only if large volumes can be shipped to a large market. Transport by LNG tanker makes it possible to seek smaller markets anywhere, but could lead to renewed controversy over the sovereignty of Canadian arctic waters. Failure to develop the Alaskan gas pipeline through Canada could hinder development of the Mackenzie Delta reserves since without large volumes of Alaskan gas it would not be profitable to develop a pipeline to transfer the smaller gas reserves of the Mackenzie Delta.

Canada's gas industry has argued that exports, by increasing the market for gas, might make early production more feasible. The Trudeau government, however, has taken the position that Arctic gas is Canada's safety net and has cautioned that development may be slower than the industry would like if faster development entails substantial new exports and thus involves the government in political controversy.[50]

At the very least, new export applications will be carefully scrutinized, and licenses may be valid for shorter periods than in the past, possibly for less than ten years. This possibility, plus the general volatility of energy politics in Canada, make planning difficult for American gas utilities and their customers, so the possibility of an all Alaskan gas route for North Slope gas that bypasses Canada by moving LNG either to the continental United States or the Far East is being discussed once again.

The Canadian national energy plan projects only a modest increase in Canadian gas demand over previously projected levels, since Canada has already emphasized substitution of gas for oil for several years and since eastern Canada, where fuel substitution is being pushed hardest, is at best a small market for natural gas. In considering the prospects for Canadian gas exports, however, U.S. energy planners must acknowledge the political importance in Canada of maintaining the commitment to expand gas sales in eastern Canada.

Although the U.S. market is important for Canadian gas exports, at present only about 75 percent of gas export volumes Canada's National Energy Board has authorized are in fact being taken by U.S. consumers owing to the current availability of cheaper gas in the United States as well as a fall in demand in response to higher prices. Most of the shortfall in demand is occurring in California and the Pacific Northwest, where the gas market is fully saturated. Imports could increase somewhat in the Northeast, where gas accounts for as little as 6 percent of total energy consumption (the U.S. national average is 27 percent) and where Canadian gas, which is cheaper than residual fuel oil, could offset shortages in domestic oil supplies. A change in U.S. gas pricing, to allow the "rolling in" (averaging) of higher prices for Canadian gas with lower prices for indigenous U.S. supplies, could also make high-cost imports more attractive relative to the cost of imported residual fuel oil.

The government of Prime Minister Pierre Trudeau discourages any U.S. thoughts that Canada could become once again a major U.S. supplier, let alone participate in a North American common market, a proposition that administration roundly rejects. Intent that exports neither drive Canadian energy policy nor dominate corporate investment decisions, the Trudeau government is willing to use its taxation authority to discourage or eliminate exports, which from the viewpoint of the corporations are extremely attractive owing to the fact that oil and gas prices in the export market are substantially above those in the domestic market.

How this policy will affect development of new projects remains to be seen, although there are preliminary indications that oil and gas rigs are fleeing Canada in great numbers. It is very doubtful that private corporations will be willing to withhold production until a strictly

Canadian market is available, and if they do not go along with Trudeau's policy, frontier exploration and production may either slow down or be increasingly assumed by Petro Canada, the Canadian national oil company. Given Petro Canada's limited financial resources, the timing of oil exploration and development in the frontier areas could be delayed.

U.S. energy planners should expect Canada to seek international prices for its exports to the United States. Oil exports have been priced at world levels since 1973, and gas is priced at a Btu parity with crude oil imported into Canada. Lower prices will be offered, or scheduled price increases postponed, only if doing so is necessary to make the commodities competitive in the U.S. markets they serve. These supplies will be made available only if they remain surplus to Canada's needs.

Oil and gas dominate the U.S.-Canadian energy agenda, but prospects for bilateral trade in the electricity sector, defined here as including bulk power, coal, and uranium, are far brighter, bounded far less by constraints of supply and demand, and, with the possible exception of trade in uranium, less likely to be politicized in the way oil and gas trade have been.

Electricity, Coal, and Uranium

American utilities have been a major consumer of Canadian electricity. Currently, 100 transmission lines, capable of handling 8 gigawatts of power, link the two countries. The addition of new high-voltage electricity lines will raise cross-border transmission capacity by 1985 to 11,000 megawatts (Mw), which represents 1.4 percent of American generating capacity and 10 percent of Canadian capacity. Regional trade, especially in the Northwest, should increase as a result. Canadian utilities have often sold surplus electricity to U.S. utilities on an interruptible or seasonal basis. Now however utilities in Quebec, Manitoba and Alberta are investigating the possibility of building new hydroelectric or coal-fired powerplants dedicated primarily to markets in the United States.[51]

Prospects for expanding Canadian electricity sales are not unlimited though. Canada does not yet have a fully interconnected power grid, and developing one is a major goal of Canadian nationalists, who might well be expected to support imposition of a federal export tax on electricity. Export sales may also be constrained by increasing use of air-conditioning in Canada and of a seasonal peaking pattern similar to one common in the United States. Finally making surplus capacity available for export is one thing, but dedicating new capacity to the U.S. market is another, one that could encounter public resistance if Canadians see themselves as bearing the environmental costs for projects that benefit Americans.

Canadian uranium resources, which rank second to U.S. supplies in the non-Communist world, should find a market among U.S. utilities now that the United States is lifting its ban on uranium imports. Theoretically, U.S. utilities should be able to get as much Canadian uranium as they want. At best, Canadian nuclear capacity will reach 14,445 Mw by 1990, and the Canadian uranium industry will produce five to seven times the amount of uranium Canada needs in the 1980s. Most of this surplus will be available for export.

U.S. satellites may not regard this Canadian supply, or the prices for it, as secure, however. Despite declining real prices for uranium, Canadian uranium contracts since December 1976 have contained a clause specifying that prices be renegotiated annually. In theory, Canadian uranium should sell at the prevailing market price, either the current spot price or an escalating floor price, whichever is higher. In practice, Ottawa sets the price each year, leading some customers to believe that the contract is virtually worthless before the ink dries.

A second problem is that U.S. antitrust law applies to Canadian subsidiaries of U.S. firms that participated in the international uranium cartel in the 1970s. To the extent that these firms follow Canadian government pricing policy, they could be charged with price-fixing under U.S. law. Finally goverment action at the provincial level may impede Canadian production, especially if excessive severance taxes or royalty rates are imposed or mining bans are levied for environmental reasons. There is a five-year ban on uranium mining in British Columbia, for example.

One fuel for which bilateral trade should prosper—with Canada the buyer and the United States the seller—is coal. The National Coal Association expects U.S. coal exports to Canada to increase by 2 million tons by 1983, up from 17 million in 1980.[52] Ontario will probably continue to find U.S. coal exports less expensive than Western Canadian coal, because of lower transportation costs. Transportation costs will not affect coal users in the prairie provinces, where utilities are likely to build up coal-fired capacity using local coal, particularly the low-sulfur coal from Alberta. Canada itself has an estimated 5.2 billion tons of economically recoverable coal.

Continentalism

When the idea of creating a North American common market for fuels and other goods came up during the 1980 U.S. presidential campaign, the federal government in Ottawa rejected it. The idea of a "continental" framework for energy trade had been of considerable interest to Canada in the 1960s, when Canadian authorities tried to integrate the two markets. Canadian access to U.S. oil and gas consumers had been threatened by the U.S. Mandatory Oil Import Program established in 1959, and Canada gained an exemption from the import quotas only through hard lobbying. Although a continental approach to energy trade was never the declared aim of the Canadian government and was in fact criticized by Canadian nationalists, it was implicit in attempts to remove market impediments to the flow of oil and gas as well as investment funds and manpower. U.S. officials were unwilling to consider a continental arrangement so long as domestic U.S. oil producers found it difficult to compete with imported Canadian crude in the upper Midwest.

Even before the Arab oil embargo of October 1973, however, changes in Canadian energy policy began to reflect Canada's increasing pessimism about its resource base and a growing awareness of how rising international oil prices would affect the Canadian economy. The emphasis in Canadian energy policy switched from protecting its market in the United States to protecting its own consumers from expensive imports and expanding the domestic market for Western Canadian oil and gas—indeed, making expansion of that domestic market a precondition to approval of new export contracts. Using its powers to tax and regulate the nation, the Canadian government tried to dominate energy policymaking, and in exercising direct jurisdiction over pipeline construction in the territories caused a rift in federal-provincial relations on the question of how to resolve pricing and marketing issues that continues to confound Canadian politics today.

Without consulting the United States, Canada's National Energy Board announced in October 1974 that it would phase out oil exports by 1981 and gas exports by 1979. (The policy curtailing gas exports was modified in 1977–78 once it became apparent that a gas supply surplus to Canadian needs would be available. Oil exports, except for heavy oil exports, which are exempt from legal restrictions, were to be completely phased out in 1981, with the exception of crude oil exchanges.) Nevertheless, the concern of both countries about the adequacy and security of supplies slowly brought into focus the areas where case-by-case cooperation between the two countries was possible: chiefly on aspects on the energy infrastructure that would benefit both countries, including methods of transporting supplies such as the Alaskan Highway and the Mackenzie Delta gas pipeline.[53]

The Alaskan Pipeline

Although Canada and the United States are both interested in completing the Alaskan gas pipeline, their principal motives are different. The United States, which is interested chiefly in the gas itself (which represents 13 percent of proven U.S. reserves), has focused on the cost of the gas to the consumer. The Canadians have been most interested in benefiting economically from the pipeline construction and in the process developing a pipeline industry capable of handling the difficult pipeline projects needed to carry Arctic resources to market.

The commitment of the federal government in Ottawa to the project is most evident in the controversial procurement arrangements designed to maximize participation of Canadian industry in construction of the Canadian part of the pipeline. The symbolic importance to the Canadians of timely completion of the ANGTS project should not be underestimated. Start-up of pipeline construction was delayed for several years because of financial, organizational, and environmental problems affecting the Alaskan portion of the pipeline. Although this impasse was broken in 1981 by congressional, and executive branch action, the Reagan administration should reassess the serious questions of potential cost overruns before it gives a final green light to the project. For one thing, current estimates place the cost of the pipeline between $40–50 billion, with the cost of gas delivered to the customer estimated at $12 to $14 per thousand cubic feet (mcf), compared to current rates of $6 to $9 per mcf for most high cost domestic gas. If the decontrol of natural gas prices is accelerated before 1985, there is a distinct possibility that enough gas could be discovered in the lower forty-eight states to make it difficult for the higher priced Alaskan gas to compete in terms of price in the U.S. market.

One alternative that should be examined seriously is to abandon the Canadian pipeline route for an all-Alaskan gas pipeline paralleling the oil pipeline from the North Slope to Valdez, with an LNG export terminal at Valdez from which gas could be shipped to the lower forty-eight states when market conditions permit. Alternatively, while the cost of the pipeline would be high ($25 billion), the gas could be exported to Japan and elsewhere in the Far East as part of a broader U.S. strategy to maintain or improve relations with the nations of the Pacific Basin, especially Japan. When and if market conditions create a need for the gas in the lower forty-eight states, it could begin to serve the U.S. market.

Another possibility worth considering is to abandon the idea of LNG exports and develop an Alaskan world-scale petrochemical facility using Alaskan natural gas (especially methanol and ethanol) as feedstock. The low cost of the natural gas feedstock could effectively undercut the cost of oil-derived petrochemicals in the Far East, and the sale of petrochemicals to Japan and other Pacific Basin countries could improve the U.S. balance of payments. The problem is that abandonment of the Canadian route for Alaskan natural gas would not only antagonize Canada but would also create specific difficulties with at least one energy project of considerable importance to both countries.

Although American firms have Canadian energy contracts running into the 1990s, Canada's National Energy Board has not approved any new export licenses since 1970. However, recent discovery of a gas bubble in Alberta has revived interest in Canadian sales to the United States, and a number of ways are being considered to augment exports: to increase volumes under existing contracts, to provide Canadian gas now in exchange for Alaskan gas in the future, or to create entirely new contracts. All of these arrangements would tax current cross-border transmission capacity, a problem that could be resolved by early construction of the southern (Alberta) portion of the Alcan line.

Until July 1980 Ottawa was reluctant to move ahead on construction without U.S. assurance that the entire ANGTS pipeline could be financed and would be constructed. Despite misgivings about President Carter's assurances on this point, Ottawa finally softened its position and decided to permit building of the southern portion of the pipeline prior to completion of the Alaskan part. In December 1979 Canada's National Energy Board authorized new exports of 3.75 Tcf over the next eight years, of which 1.9 Tcf were allocated to the southern section of the ANGTS system. These new exports will increase by 50 percent the amount of gas Canada exports to the United States, reducing by several billion dollars Canada's chronic trade deficit with the United States.[54] The whole project would be jeopardized if the United States were to abandon the ANGTS pipeline.

The United States also needs Canadian cooperation on an oil pipeline linking Alaska and the Northern Tier states, so that refineries hurt by Canada's phasing out of oil exports can replace Canadian oil with crude from Alaska or other sources. In 1980 President Carter endorsed the all-U.S. Northern Tier pipeline, the major competitor of which is the U.S.-Canadian Trans-Mountain project, which would cross from Washington state into British Columbia and then into Alberta, where it would tie into existing pipeline networks serving both Canada and the United States. In July 1981, the Trans-Mountain project consortium dropped out of the competition citing increasing costs and the current oil glut as the chief factors in their decision. Until the Northern Tier pipeline is built, changes of crude oil with Canada, averaging 100,000 bd in each direction in 1980, must be relied upon to handle the deficit.[55]

In the past talks between Canada and the United States concerning energy usually focused on supply and price, especially on how to increase exports from Canada to the United States. Although Canada may export more electricity to the United States and U.S. coal exports to eastern Canada are certain to increase substantially, in general U.S. policy toward Canada should not be predicated on the assumption that new U.S. energy initiatives will elicit substantially higher imports of Canadian resources. The political battles that are being waged in Canada over energy policy and the framework in which it is to be developed go to the very roots of Canadian sovereignty. The United States must avoid intruding on this struggle. U.S. energy planners must resign themselves to the fact that despite its rich resources, Canada is not in a position to help the United States out of its energy predicament in this decade.

This is not to say that energy will not dominate the agenda on bilateral discussions, but the terms of discussion are likely to change and so are the terms of trade. The Canadians are seeking greater control over investments in their economy; the National Energy Plan's provisions regarding foreign investments have already drawn protests from Europe and the United States. Both the United States and Canada may be warier about long-term supply arrangements in the future—Canada to avoid a long-term supply commitment, the United States to avoid a commitment from an increasingly unreliable source.

It is important that the United States develop realistic expectations about Canadian supplies, because as Canadian oil and gas exports dwindle, new energy sources must be found for the regions affected most by Canadian cutbacks: California, the Pacific Northwest, and the Northern Tier states. Completion of the Alaska pipeline, construction of a Northern Tier oil pipeline, and development of other oil and gas supplies take on added importance in this context. The United States must particularly recognize the importance to U.S.-Canadian relations of completing the Alaskan Natural Gas pipeline through Canada. Although there is some justification for considering alternatives to the pipeline, Canada has proceeded with its portion of the line on the basis of assurances from President Carter and the U.S. Congress that the Alaskan portion would be completed and despite great political controversy about the project within Canada and the United States. The United States will bear the onus if this project collapses.

As oil and gas exports from Canada to the United States decline, it is important that the two countries coordinate their efforts to develop new supplies from unconventional and frontier sources, making the most efficient use possible of productive capacity and taking maximum advantage of transportation facilities that will benefit both countries. Apart from cooperation on the pipeline, the two countries can cooperate more on energy research and development, particularly in situ recovery projects for tar sands and oil shale as well as coal gasification and the joint development of the resources of the Alaskan and Canadian Arctic. A joint strategic petroleum reserve in Newfoundland and Nova Scotia could aid oil-import-dependent New England in the event of a crisis. These projects, however, have so far foundered over technical and political problems. U.S. cooperation on such matters as across-the-border transmission of airborne pollutants should not hinge on the expectation of increased exports in return. Rather, the United States, while watching out for its own needs, should do what it can to help Canada further its goal of energy self-sufficiency, if for no other reason than to free Canada's oil imports for the world market and to show the world that an industrial state can become energy-dependent.

U.S. RELATIONS WITH MEXICO

If 1981 reserve estimates prove correct—that Mexico's proved petroleum reserves (oil and gas) are 72 billion barrels and potential reserves are as much as 250 billion barrels—Mexico should become one of the major oil-producing and exporting countries in the world. Not surprisingly, many officials in the United States have come to view these large Mexican reserves as a natural way to reduce U.S. dependence on insecure supply sources in the Middle East. Such a view is unrealistic. Few issues have caused as much trouble between Mexico and the United States as those related to energy. Negotiations on energy matters are complicated by the fact that in Mexico the state owns the natural resources.

U.S.-Mexican energy relations cannot be understood without realizing how strongly Mexicans feel about the way their country was exploited by foreign powers before all foreign energy assets in the country were nationalized in 1938. Perhaps no event in Mexican history has unified the nation as much as nationalization of its resources. The anniversary of the nationalization remains an important national holiday. To Mexicans, Petroleos Mexicanos (PEMEX), the Mexican national oil corporation, means that Mexico can make its way in the world without foreign assistance. Not only has PEMEX become essential to the nation's economic development, but many regard it as the chief guardian of Mexico's national sovereignty. Mexico views with deep suspicion any attempt by foreign energy interests to gain access to or control of Mexico's natural resources on any terms except those dictated by Mexico.

Since 1938 many events have made Mexico apprehensive about the United States and the international oil companies. In the wake of the nationalization, oil companies halted equipment sales to PEMEX, boycotted its petroleum products, and lobbied against the U.S. loans for Mexican petroleum development. On the whole, the oil companies were supported in these actions by U.S. government policies, which, then as now, reflected a disturbing failure to understand the realities of Mexican politics, particularly the view prevailing in Mexico that it is better for the country to develop its oil and gas revenues slowly, even if the economy suffers, than to compromise its sovereignty over its own resources.

From 1955 until the early 1970s, Mexico had no negotiations either with U.S. government agencies responsible for petroleum imports or with the major international oil companies, and Mexico abrogated existing contracts with a few independent oil companies during this period as well. In the 1950s and 1960s, when Canada was seeking assurances about access to U.S. markets for oil and natural gas, Mexico was trying to avoid dependence on foreign markets. PEMEX Director General Bermúdez explained why:

> It is illusory, and would be harmful to pretend that petroleum produced and exported in large quantities could become the factotum of Mexico's economy or the panacea for Mexico's economic ills. Mexico does not wish ever to be forced to export such an indispensable energy and chemical resource. Neither does it wish to compete with or join a world oil combine which does not and could not have Mexico's best interests at heart.[56]

Bermudez's views were echoed by all of PEMEX's directors general until the giant oil discoveries of the early 1970s. By then PEMEX and the Mexican economy were in serious trouble.

Before the giant Reforma oil and natural gas reserves were discovered in 1972, total Mexican oil exports, which peaked at 38,000 bd in 1951, were minuscule. Falling reserve/production ratios, increasing oil imports, and rising world oil prices precipitated a major economic crisis in the country. PEMEX responded by embarking on an aggressive development program that added enough oil to Mexico's resource base by the fall of 1974 to restore domestic self-sufficiency and to allow Mexico to resume exports.[57]

However, Mexico's problems were far from over. Pyramiding foreign debt threatened to offset all economic gains, private capital was fleeing the country at an alarming rate, economic growth rates were declining, incidents of political terrorism were occurring with repeated frequency, and the peso was plunging on international markets. Despite much political opposition, in 1976 the Mexican government had to go to the International Monetary Fund to stave off financial collapse. Upon election that year, President Lôpez Portillo announced that the country would have to modify its petroleum policy to survive.

Awareness that Mexico might once again become a major petroleum exporter rekindled U.S. interest in Mexican production of both oil and natural gas. However, Mexico, which in 1974 was still profoundly suspicious of U.S. motives and fearful of domination by the "colossus of the north," categorically rejected proposals for direct U.S. participation in development of Mexico's oil-rich southeastern region. Mexico is always extremely cautious when U.S. companies offer economic assistance to develop the border regions. Mexican nationalists want to develop the economy and to see Mexico become a world power, but they believe that Mexico (and Mexico petroleum production) should develop at a slow enough pace that the Mexican economy can absorb the change.[58]

Some Mexicans fear that too rapid a development of the country's oil potential will overheat the economy, accelerate inflation, speed up migration from the countryside to the cities, and create structural imbalances between the agricultural and industrial sectors of the economy—increasing dependency on food imports and exacerbating the maldistribution of income between regions and groups of Mexican people.

Even more important, many Mexicans fear that if PEMEX becomes too powerful in the state bureaucracy, it might rival the controlling Partido Revolucionario Institucional (PRI) political party and the military, historically the twin guardians of Mexican sovereignty and national independence. Many Mexicans believe that the hydrocarbon industry or even PEMEX itself could in the name of economic development become mere extensions of foreign economic interests. The 1977 natural gas negotiations with the United States confirmed the worst suspicions of those who have such fears.

That year PEMEX, in an effort to boost revenues, began building an 800-mile large-diameter natural gas pipeline to connect the Reforma Basin (rich in both oil and natural gas) with the industrial centers of northern Mexico as well as the U.S. border. Construction was scheduled to be completed in 1979; the initial export capacity of 1 billion cubic feet per day (Cfd) was to be increased later to 2.2 billion Cfd. In August 1977, PEMEX signed a letter of intent with six U.S. companies, specifically selected by PEMEX to ensure the widest possible distribution of natural gas in the United States, to the east (north and south) and to California.[59] After the U.S. and international financial community had shown great interest in financing the line and the U.S. Export-Import Bank had tentatively approved its first loan to PEMEX (for $590 million), the U.S. government, having shown few signs of opposing the terms of the sale during the negotiations, withheld approval.

development, law enforcement, migration, border cooperation, and tourism. To demonstrate the degree of its interest, the United States appointed an ambassador-at-large to coordinate the activities of various U.S. agencies that impinged on Mexican affairs. The natural gas negotiations that resumed in June 1979 culminated in an agreement to export 300 Mcf at a cost of $3.60 per Mcf, a 38 percent increase over the price U.S. officials had argued a year earlier was too high. Likewise, the final volume of gas made available to the United States was only about one-seventh the amount Mexico was originally willing to sell.

It would be comforting to think that the United States had learned something from the natural gas negotiations; apparently it had not. It was difficult, for example, for Mexico to accept the U.S. Department of Commerce's complaint in January 1980 that Mexico was unjustified in increasing oil prices to $32 per barrel. Not only did the Commerce Department seem to be implying that the United States has the right to dictate Mexican pricing policy, but shortly thereafter Washington auctioned off its equity oil from the national petroleum reserve at Elk Hills at prices over $40 per barrel.

U.S.-Mexican relations have not been improved by the following events: pollution of the South Texas coast by the Ixtoc oil spill; Mexico's failure to readmit the shah of Iran for medical treatment, thus forcing the United States to admit him; U.S. opposition to Mexico's civilian nuclear power program, which led to U.S. delays in signing an enrichment contract with the International Atomic Energy Agency to provide for Mexico's needs; Mexico's recent decision to abrogate its fishing treaty with the United States; Mexican support of revolutionary groups fighting the right-wing regimes of Central America. Actions on both sides of the border continue all too often to be governed by prejudice and stereotypes.

In an era of insecure energy supplies, the United States and other oil-consuming nations have an interest in seeing Mexico and other oil producers develop their energy resources as rapidly as possible. Moreover Mexico, to whom the United States exported $7 billion trade in capital goods in 1979, is currently the United States' third largest trade and investment partner and could in a few years become second, after Canada. Total U.S.-Mexican bilateral trade has risen from $12.8 billion in 1978 to $27.6 billion in 1980. Traditionally the United States has a trade surplus with Mexico; in a few years this could become a deficit. It is in the U.S. interest to keep that trade in balance.

What the U.S. government and private industry have not yet faced up to is that there is a quid pro quo for such trade. The United States regularly offers less-favorable sales terms to Mexico than are offered by such industrial nations as Germany and Japan. Because of domestic political opposition greater volumes of lower priced Mexican capital and agricultural goods have not been allowed into the United States. Until the United States realizes that both it and Mexico can benefit from better trade relations, Mexico will show little interest in aiding the United States. The challenge confronting the Reagan and Lôpez Portillo administrations is to remove trade barriers that hurt both nations, despite predictable opposition from powerful entrenched interests in both countries.

One of the most formidable obstacles to improved relations between the two nations is the difficult issue of undocumented workers. The unemployment rate in Mexico is at 40 to 50 percent, and 800,000 people enter the labor force each year, so there is massive migration not only inside Mexico but also to the United States, often illegally. Although it will take some time and involve extremely complex negotiations to institute a "guest worker" program for Mexicans in the United States, it is urgent that the two governments consider this option seriously.

A major debate is brewing in Mexico over whether to raise oil production from around 2.5 mmbd to 4.5 mmbd, or even higher. The decision to raise production to 3 mmbd in 1981 raised critical economic, social, and political issues. The oil boom has already produced serious inflation, massive migration to the cities, congested ports, and sagging agricultural production. The Mexican economy is experiencing serious structural imbalances, and the plight of the poor is worsening. Raising oil production to 4-5 mmbd will have momentous implications, both inside Mexico and abroad.

To reach this level Mexico will also have to expand its natural gas infrastructure, because oil and natural gas often occur in the same reservoir so that releasing the oil releases the gas as well. If Mexico does not have the infrastructure to capture the natural gas, it must be flared; to avoid flaring it, Mexico must first have a market for the gas, so even greater quantities of gas would have to be sold to the United States. Although the Mexican government is under continued pressure to keep the U.S. share of total oil export sales at less than 50 percent, the decision to limit sales to the U.S. market might make the United States less willing to negotiate seriously on the outstanding trade and immigration issues. Similariy, to the extent that Mexico links crude oil and product sales, the U.S. refining industry—already in a difficult financial position—could see more of its market eroded.

There is little reason to believe, given Mexico's burgeoning internal oil consumption, that Mexico will make enough oil available to the United States to substantially reduce dependence on Persian Gulf oil or that increased independence of Middle East sources will automatically reduce the need for a forceful U.S. military presence in the Persian Gulf. Not only should the United States continue to protect Western European and Japanese access to oil, it must also discourage the Soviet Union from thinking that in the absence of U.S. power it can move toward dominating the region by subverting regimes friendly to the United States.

After years of neglect and political and economic conflict with the United States, most Mexicans are concerned that under the guise of a hemispheric or North American energy and security accord, promoted by many presidential candidates, including Reagan during the 1980 presidential campaign, they will once again see their resources exploited by their giant neighbor to the north with little or no benefit accruing to Mexico.

For the time being, the United States should discard the notion that Mexico offers even a partial solution to the U.S. energy crisis. Because of its proximity the United States is clearly a more logical market for Mexican oil than Europe or Japan, but Washington should not try to prevent greater energy trade between Mexico and the other major industrialized nations. Indeed, increased trade between Mexico and Japan might eventually make possible a tripartite arrangement under which Japan could sell Mexican crude oil to the United States in exchange for Alaskan oil being shipped to Japan. Such transactions could result in large transportation cost savings as well as allow Mexico to diversify its markets, thus reducing political pressure against excessive dependence on the United States. However, it should be noted that in the wake of U.S. legal restrictions on the export of Alaskan crude, the North Slope oil producers have commenced alternative investments in the Four Corners Pipeline project and a pipeline across Panama that could be jeopardized by the change in law. Mexico must be an active partner in deliberations on such an arrangement, of course.

Although many obstacles hinder enhanced U.S.-Mexican cooperation on energy matters, in some areas cooperation would benefit both nations. The idea currently generating the most interest is the exchange of electricity.[60] On both sides of the border there are a number of communities and industrial facilities that could be supplied at less cost by the other country. In some cases such exchanges would allow communities in isolated areas, especially in Mexico, to receive for the first time electrical power that could create jobs and attract new industries.

Similarly both countries would benefit if the United States provided the technical expertise needed to bring appropriate alternative energy technologies to Mexico's outlying areas. The United States should reassess its decision to curtail federal research and development in this field because Mexico has great interest not only in passive and active solar applications but in advanced energy conservation methods and applications. By the end of the 1980s exports of unconventional energy technology could contribute as much as $1–2 billion toward the U.S. balance of payments, which could help offset the trade deficit with Mexico projected for that time.

Mexico and the United States, working together with Venezuela, could also embark on cooperative ventures of benefit not only to themselves but also to the developing nations of the Caribbean. One possibility is to either expand or create free trade zones (FTZs) in South Texas and Louisiana, from which Mexico and the Caribbean islands could be provided with desperately needed petroleum products. A U.S. free trade zone is an area designated as duty-free; any material or merchandise brought in is not considered an import as long as it is used to make a product that is then exported. Under the proposed arrangement, Mexican or Venezuelan crude oil would be brought into an FTZ, processed into petroleum products, and exported.

Such an arrangement could help Mexico and Venezuela meet their countries' escalating demand for petroleum products without their having to invest the large sums required either to upgrade existing refineries or to build new ones. The arrangement would also improve the U.S. balance of trade. Almost 2.7 mmbd of the total 18 mmbd U.S. refinery capacity is currently idle, and nearly 90 percent of U.S. refineries are located where foreign crude can be shipped by sea, or by a pipeline connection to the sea. If a sizable proportion of idle capacity for processing foreign crude were located in the FTZs, U.S. exports under this arrangement could add billions of dollars to the positive side of the balance-of-trade ledger.

In the proper political climate, which does not currently exist, Mexico might be persuaded to develop an emergency production capacity for oil and natural gas[61] (to aid the United States in the event of a supply disruption) or to increase its oil, gas, and electricity exports to the United States. In return, the United States could enact a guest worker program or offer trade concessions. Both areas should be explored in discussions between the two countries, although quick action is unlikely.

In summary, U.S. relations with Mexico are at a crossroads. Opportunities exist that would benefit both nations, but their different perspectives on energy, trade, fishing, immigration, and foreign policy may preclude a speedy improvement in relations. Indeed, considering how much Mexicans tend to fear U.S. domination over their economy and how sharply the two nations disagree on current U.S. policy in El Salvador, with the 1982 Mexican presidential election looming in the horizon, it may be politically impossible for the Lôpez Portillo administration to move closer to the United States.

Recognizing that its paramount national security interest in Mexico is Mexican political stability, the United States must also finally acknowledge that accelerated petroleum production is not in the best interest of either country in the long run. In its own best interests and certainly in Mexico's, the United States should do everything it can to help Mexico develop its energy resources at a pace that will also allow such major social and economic reforms as redistribution of income and greater employment. In the process Mexico might come to view its northern neighbor with less suspicion and more trust. Conversely, a U.S. decision to encourage Mexico to produce oil as rapidly as possible without first enacting major economic and social reforms could lead to a major political convulsion in Mexico, posing grave problems for both nations.

U.S. POLICY TOWARD VENEZUELA AND THE CARIBBEAN NATIONS

Just as the United States has never developed a coherent policy on energy relations with Mexico, so it has never developed one for South America and the Caribbean. Partly this is because the nations involved are so different from one another and partly because the United States government tends to think of the region as under its sphere of influence and ignore economic activities there. Nowhere is failure to develop a comprehensive policy more evident than in U.S. relations with Venezuela and the Caribbean islands (the Bahamas, Netherlands Antilles, Puerto Rico, Trinidad, and the Virgin Islands) that provide the United States with so much of its crude oil and petroleum products.

Reliable supplies of petroleum from Venezuela have been extremely important to the United States, especially during periods of international tension. During World War II, the Korean conflict, the Suez crisis, the 1970 Libyan crisis, the 1973–74 oil embargo, and the 1979 Iranian crisis, Venezuela helped the United States by accelerating oil production to reduce pressure on world oil supplies and prices. Yet U.S. policies, especially the Mandatory Oil Import Program in effect from 1959 to 1981, have regularly discriminated against oil imports from Venezuela. The fact that this has occurred during a period of increased concern about the availability of reliable oil supplies is especially ironic, since on numerous occasions beginning in the late 1940s Venezuela has offered to make long-term supply agreements at specified volumes in return for guaranteed markets in the United States. Continued rebuffs to these initiatives greatly influenced Venezuela to assume a key role in the formation of OPEC in 1960. Even since 1960, however, Venezuela on at least five occasions has continued to seek a bilateral deal with the United States.

The importance of Venezuelan and Caribbean refineries to the U.S. market grew in the postwar period. Responding to the surge in demand for gasoline after World War II, many U.S. refineries restructured their refinery capacity to maximize gasoline production. Utilities plagued by coal strikes and the high cost of coal began using more and more residual fuel oil, a cheap by-product of gasoline production. Responding to the new market that was thus created, U.S. multinational firms expanded their refineries in Venezuela and the Caribbean islands so that they could process heavy Venezuelan crude oil into residual fuel oil ("resid"), which they then shipped to utilities on the East Coast. To protect themselves, the coal and railroad industries launched a vigorous campaign to limit imports of oil products. A key argument in the national debate that followed was the danger to national security of increasing dependence on foreign crude oil and products. Concern about escalating imports led Congress to enact the Mandatory Oil Import Program in 1959. Imports continued to climb nonetheless, not only because "overland" imports from Canada and

Mexico were exempt from the import restrictions, but also because so many special exemptions were granted, including exemptions for petrochemical products from Puerto Rico and oil products processed in the Virgin Islands (largely from Middle Eastern crude oil). Venezuela was deeply angered by these loopholes for Mexican and Canadian crude, especially since Caracas's view was that it had always been a staunch ally of the United States.

By 1966 the import restrictions were also removed for residual fuel oil, after several oil companies with refinery interests in the Caribbean argued successfully not only that Caribbean and Venezuelan refineries were as secure as those in the United States but also that imports of their residual fuel oil held U.S. consumer costs down because foreign crude oil at the time cost less than domestic crude. As the United States became more concerned with environmental questions in the late 1960s and early 1970s, the Caribbean refineries had an additional cost advantage; free of U.S. environmental restrictions, they could turn out cheaper petroleum products. The Venezuelan and Caribbean refineries had the further advantages that they could benefit from the economies of scale offered by the availability of deepwater ports for supertankers and lower taxes. Finally, because they were exempt from the Jones Act, Venezuela and the Caribbean islands reaped additional economic benefits through lower transportation costs even for small ships to the U.S. market.

With the lifting for all practical purposes of import controls on residual fuel oil in 1966, there was a surge of refinery construction in the Caribbean, which was further encouraged by the exemption of home heating oil from the import restrictions. Refinery capacity in the Caribbean increased from 2.4 mmbd in 1966 to 4.8 mmbd in 1981, when the major export refineries could handle the following volumes of crude oil:

Bahamas	500
Netherlands Antilles	
Aruba	420
Curacao	362
Puerto Rico	284
Trinidad	456
Venezuela	1,349
Virgin Islands	728
Total	4,099 mmbd

Development of the Caribbean's refinery capacity was not without drawbacks. Since residual fuel oil was cheaper than coal as a fuel for utilities and industrial boilers, coal production continued to decline owing to a lack of market demand. The sagging market for coal did not provide enough capital for the railroad industry to revitalize the coal transportation network. Thus began the deterioration in the U.S. railway network that continues to hamper accelerated coal development to this day. Imported residual fuel oil increasingly replaced natural gas as a boiler fuel as clean-burning natural gas was diverted into higher-priority uses. This led to an accelerated U.S. dependence on oil imports, especially in New England and the Middle Atlantic states. Because U.S. refineries concentrated on developing light-end-of-the-barrel refinery capacity to meet the burgeoning U.S. demand for these products, they got themselves into their present position of being unable without sizable capital investments to process the huge volumes of heavy OPEC oil that is increasingly shipped to the United States.

Furthermore, increased dependence on cheap North African and Middle Eastern crude oil left certain refineries vitally exposed at the time of the 1970 crisis in Libya, the 1973–74 OAPEC oil embargo, and the 1979 Iranian crisis. Finally, because residual fuel oil was exempt from the Mandatory Oil Import Program, resid prices increased 472 percent between 1969 and 1974, while gasoline prices rose only 126 percent.[62]

By 1980 63 percent of U.S. product imports were from the Caribbean, about 58 percent of them residual fuel oil. Although product imports accounted for only about 9 percent of total product demand, imports from the Caribbean accounted for about 37 percent of total resid demand and almost 70 percent of resid demand on the East Coast. In terms of volume, the United States imported about 900 mmbd from the Caribbean in 1980.

While U.S. government policies were encouraging the development of offshore capacity and thereby increasing oil imports, Venezuela was taking another course. Caracas had been incredulous when the U.S. Congress, despite Venezuela's ready response to OAPEC's 1973–74 oil embargo, had in November 1975 failed to grant Venezuela trade benefits under the general system of preferences and had excluded it from the provisions of the Trade Reform Act simply because Venezuela was a member of OPEC. Since in addition the United States had not responded to Venezuela's suggestion that they establish a special relationship, Venezuela began diversifying its markets. Until 1976, the year it nationalized all foreign oil, Venezuela was the United States' main supplier of crude oil and petroleum products; that year, Saudi Arabia and Nigeria became the main U.S. suppliers, and Venezuelan exports to the United States began a decline that has continued to this day.

As the leading force behind the formation of OPEC and as a frequent defender of high oil prices, Venezuela has often pursued policies that did not endear it to the United States. In wresting control of its oil industry from the multinational oil companies in January 1976, Venezuela became, in the eyes of the U.S. government (particularly the Departments of State and the Treasury), an adversary of the United States, an image that political developments in the Caribbean have served only to reinforce.

The four main objectives of Venezuelan foreign policy are to safeguard democracy, guarantee Venezuela a long-lasting oil income, defend nationalism while fighting imperialism (not surprising, given the historical domination of Venezuela by foreign economic interests), and provide constructive leadership to Amazonian and Andean Latin America, the Caribbean islands, and Central America. Unfortunately, Venezuela's foreign policy is often at odds with U.S. foreign policy. For example, Venezuela has assumed a prominent leadership role in Caribbean and Central American development problems precisely when U.S. policy toward the states in these regions is being expressed in a neo-cold war mode. Moreover, the former government of Venezuela strongly supported the democratically elected government of Salvador Allende in Chile, the Sandinista political movement in the Nicaraguan civil war, and the reincorporation of Cuba into the hemispheric system. Although relations have improved under the more conservative COPEI (Christian Democratic Party) government, the two countries, while desiring better relations, remain deeply suspicious of each other.

Without arguing the relative merits of U.S. and Venezuelan foreign policy, it is safe to say that the United States would benefit as much from closer cooperation between the two countries as Venezuela would. Their trade relations are of growing importance to both nations. Venezuela ranks fourth in the amount of air traffic to the United States and seventh in tourist trade. More important, the United States cannot afford to ignore the enormous development potential of the Orinoco Tar Belt, which contains perhaps 3 trillion barrels of very heavy poor-quality crude. Even though only about 10 percent of this reservoir may be recovered, the Orinoco could surpass the entire Middle East in potential volume of oil. It will take years and cost billions of dollars to develop the region's full potential, but the Orinoco will clearly play a major role in the future world economy.

Although U.S. interests in the Orinoco resurrects strong expressions of Venezuelan nationalism, which has a large anti-American component, Venezuelan officials realize the pivotal role that foreign capital could play in assisting the timely development of the Orinoco Basin. However, every Venezuelan politician realizes the political explosiveness of appearing to move close to foreign economic interests. As a result, development of the Orinoco will proceed more slowly and in a manner commensurate with Venezuelan political sensibilities.

Despite Venezuela's nationalistic concern, in March 1980, Venezuela's Energy Minister Humberto Calderon Berti proposed an energy alliance among the countries of North and South America to develop energy supplies and to moderate future demand.[63] The United States has ignored Venezuela's proposal, but the Reagan administration should respond to this initiative as part of its new comprehensive Caribbean policy.[64]

Over 50 percent of the crude oil shipped to the United States passes through the Caribbean and adjacent waters. Yet the region is beset by acute economic difficulties that are a clear threat to U.S. national security. The United States simply must join Mexico and Venezuela in helping the poorer nations of the Caribbean solve their problems. To start with, a Caribbean energy conference should be convened to address not only the problems of the island refineries but also the broader energy and economic problems of all the states in the Caribbean basin.

Whether the United States will decide to offer the region development assistance and whether domestic politics will allow it to make major trade concessions remains to be seen, yet it is with this kind of policy that the United States can help the region deal with unemployment levels that average 30–50 percent. Failure to enact such policies, especially bilateral and multilateral renewable energy programs, may produce the very reaction the United States fears most: a serious drift toward leftist authoritarianism in the Caribbean.

Only economic assistance can relieve the endemic social and economic instability that make this region a perfect target for leftist subversion. To a great extent energy problems are at the heart of the economic crises confronting the troubled regions of the Caribbean. The United States, Mexico, and Venezuela working with the major international financial institutions (the Inter-American Development Bank, the World Bank, the Caribbean Development Bank, and the International Monetary Fund) must accelerate dispersion of technology to develop the region's energy potential and, where possible, help develop new renewable energy technologies. The Reagan administration should reverse its policy and support the creation of the World Bank energy affiliate and increase the level of its support for all of the lending institutions just named to demonstrate the seriousness of its commitment to solving the problems of the region.

In addition, the United States must deal with the following policy issues in the next few years:

1. It must decide what policy to adopt in response to demands from Venezuela and Mexico that we import more of their products and less of their crude oil.

2. Now that oil prices are decontrolled in the United States, the percentage of oil products from the Caribbean under completely free market conditions could increase. Increased competition from Caribbean refineries, which offer the many economic advantages noted over U.S. refineries, could pose severe problems for some small and independent U.S. refineries as well as make the United States more dependent on imported oil. On the other hand, if the U.S. program to convert boilers to coal use ever accelerates, the reduced demand for Caribbean resid could cause serious economic and political problems on the islands where the giant export refineries are located. These problems could be exploited by our adversaries. Effecting a delicate balance between our policy goals to reduce oil imports and to stabilize the Caribbean could prove very difficult.

The changing nature of oil-product demand and the deteriorating quality of available crude oil imports will require U.S. refineries to invest sizable sums to modernize their refineries to increase their desulfurization capacity, in order to be able to process more heavy, high-sulfur crude oil. U.S. refineries have desulfurization capacity of only 288,000 bd compared with desulfurization capacity in the Caribbean of 870,000 bd. To install comparable capacity in the United States that meets environmental standards would be extremely costly. The federal government should enact tax measures that allow U.S. refiners accelerated depreciation on the necessary capital investments and should adopt more liberal capital-formation policies for all manufacturing industries, including the refining industry. Applying the new accelerated-depreciation and capital-formation policies to all major refineries (whether they belong to large domestic oil companies, multinational oil companies, independent refiner marketers, or long-standing small refiners serving isolated markets) would allow them to compete better under normal market conditions. Small refineries that were built after 1973 only because of DOE regulations with a "small refiner bias" should receive no special tax treatment.

However, the government must be careful that any policy it adopts to reduce dependence on the Caribbean refineries not be so extreme that it weakens the financial stability of the island economies to the point that extremist forces are able to gain political power. It is equally important to U.S. national security to maintain a strong refining industry, on the one hand, and to promote stability in the Caribbean, on the other. The fact that most of the offshore refineries are owned by U.S. companies will add to the intractability of problems surrounding U.S. refining policy. Again, U.S. policymakers must walk a fine line between conflicting policy goals.

3. In the absence of a coherent policy on the Caribbean, the federal government must determine what policy it will adopt toward expansion of refinery capacity in areas serving the U.S. market. Should free-market conditions be allowed to prevail even if they undermine some domestic refiners? In particular what should U.S. policy be toward the refining and petrochemical industries in the Virgin Islands and Puerto Rico? Should these regions receive special treatment because of their unique historical ties to the United States? Should we be concerned about the great dependence of refineries in the Virgin Islands on crude oil from Libya?

4. Except for the Hess refinery on St. Croix, which processes some Alaskan crude, the island refineries depend almost entirely on foreign crude, almost 1.3 mmbd of which comes from North Africa and the Middle East. The U.S. Department of Defense is considering to what extent refineries should be rated "more" or "less" secure, in terms of whether they process crude from Arab or non-Arab sources. However, congressional action on domestic refining policy responding more to domestic economic interests may work at cross-purposes with policy planning in the executive branch, where national security concerns often predominate. It is urgent that the executive and legislative branches of U.S. government begin coordinating their work on national refining policy.

Specifically, the federal government must figure out how to determine what security risks are in the Caribbean and what to do about them. Are some export refineries politically more secure than others (apart from the question of where they get their crude oil), owing to existing political conditions on the islands? What criteria should the government use to determine relative political security? Even if the federal government formulates no coherent policy on Caribbean refining, should it take any actions to protect the sea lanes in the Caribbean?

GLOBAL ENERGY SECURITY: FUTURE DIRECTIONS FOR U.S. POLICY

Events unleashed by OAPEC's 1973–74 oil embargo have transformed the geopolitics of energy. The prospect of a world petroleum shortage in the 1980s generates fear not only of armed conflict between the superpowers over the flow of oil but also of potential social, economic, and political chaos. Traditional political alliances are in a state of transition, and every nation is faced with complex energy and foreign policy problems.

The problems of ensuring access to energy supplies and preserving national security and internal stability will be linked more critically than ever in the 1980s. Yet at a time when the world must become more interdependent to meet the energy crisis, there is a dangerous trend toward economic protectionism and political isolationism. Diplomatic approaches to political crises are often complicated by considerations of how a solution to a problem will affect access to energy supplies. Foreign policy is often buffeted in the crosscurrents of conflicting political and economic goals. Eight years after the oil embargo, the United States still has not perceived access to energy supplies as a paramount element of U.S. national security.

In analyzing the foreign policy challenges the United States faces in the future, we on the Energy and National Security staff are struck by the government's failure to link issues and to see that without effective assistance from stronger nations, many nations in the world have been so adversely affected by the energy crisis that their political, social, and economic stability are endangered. If the United States does not help them address their problems, they will have little choice but to look elsewhere for assistance.

The United States needs to formulate a new strategic doctrine relating energy policy to national security concerns. Today, our fundamental energy problem is to develop an energy policy that faces the future rather than the past. The age of plentiful oil supplies is gone. The era of insecurity in world oil supplies is just beginning, not ending. The nature of the challenges posed to the global community by the energy crisis makes it impossible to view our energy dilemma exclusively as a domestic political and economic problem. However, despite the need for greater bilateral and multilateral international initiatives to deal with the energy crisis, there are disturbing indications that the Reagan administration may be retreating into an Energy Fortress America.

Although the domestic relationship between energy and environmental goals are discussed in the Reagan administration's National Energy Plan III (NEP III) with the recommendation that environmental restrictions be weakened, there is no discussion of the critical international implications in doing so. A weakened U.S. environmental policy could exacerbate existing conflicts with Canada over the pollution of Canadian resources by acid rain moving in from the United States. The U.S. Government Accounting Office issued a report in 1981 detailing the very serious effects of acid rain on U.S.-Canadian ecosystems.

Likewise the NEP III is singularly silent about how the accelerated development of the outer continental shelf by Canada, the United States, and Mexico may lead to increased levels of tension as a result of incidents such as the Ixtoc oil spill and what can be attempted to deal with such. The administration should give urgent attention to joint research with Canada and Mexico on the potential for developing new technologies for controlling oil spills.

The NEP III also gives no attention to ways in which to deal with the problems of hazardous nuclear wastes, nor does it indicate concern over the long-term global consequences of the greenhouse effect arising from accelerated fossil fuel utilization.

Moreover, in encouraging multilateral development of alternatives to oil, the administration's record is spotty. It scrapped the joint Solvent Refined Coal II liquefaction facility with Germany and Japan; it relied upon the "free market" to speed up U.S. coal exports to Europe and Japan; and it has not sought to lift the ban on the export of Alaskan oil to Japan. The Alaska gas pipeline project is still left to the financial market, but if the market cannot assume the cost, the pipeline may lose its national security importance, as has already been acknowledged by the president. The administration's strident opposition to increased energy trade between Europe and the USSR has raised concern in the capitals of member nations of the International Energy Agency (IEA) about the degree of sophistication of the Reagan administration on a range of international energy and political issues.

As noted, the energy crisis has exerted a considerable impact on the global economy. What has not been noted is that among the greater departures of the Reagan administration from the policies of the past three administrations is the comparative lack of commitment to meet the energy needs of the Third World. Although the Reagan administration is correct in noting the positive contribution that the private sector can play in assisting Third World energy development, the administration's philosophical opposition to bilateral governmental or multilateral energy initiatives for Third World energy development does not address the following weaknesses:

1. The lack of interest by big companies in developing marginal energy deposits that may be very important to local economies but not to international energy trade;
2. The lack of viability of many Third World nations to adopt full market pricing of petroleum products and keep their governments in power;
3. The frequent lack of local expertise in energy matters to deal equitably and in an informed manner with multinational corporation negotiators;
4. The discontinuity in a U.S. Caribbean policy that announces a new attack on problems in the region and at the same time scraps twenty bilateral reforestation and renewable energy programs with the island nations of the region;
5. The failure to note the major role that energy assistance could play in U.S. aid policy, and the contribution that U.S. exports of renewable energy technology could make to the U.S. balance of payments.

In light of these problems and the devastating impact that the energy crisis is having on Third World social, economic, and political stability, it is urgent that the United States government reverse its policy and lead an accelerated effort through private, bilateral, and multilateral initiatives to assist the Third World nations in solving their energy problems.

The NEP III will also need to be rethought in terms of international nuclear policy. First, by encouraging a third tier of states allowed to have sensitive nuclear technology (non-weapon-holding advanced industrial states), the entire fabric of the Nuclear Nonproliferation Treaty may be undermined. Second, despite its commitment to a breeder reactor program, the NEP III makes no mention or provision for an international plutonium regime as part of an effective nonproliferation strategy. Third, despite a firm commitment to global nonproliferation, the Reagan administration has not yet offered details as to how the spread of nuclear weapons can be contained. Fourth, the Reagan administration appears to have no policy for stopping a nation not a party to the Nuclear Nonproliferation Treaty from acquiring a nuclear weapon, any more than did earlier administrations. It is of utmost importance that the president assign the very highest priority to addressing these matters to ensure that the benefits of the peaceful uses of atomic energy not be further clouded by global nonproliferation concerns.

Despite the need for new energy initiatives in many arenas, the energy realities that must be confronted today are that OPEC will continue to dominate global oil trade throughout the rest of the century, and the United States will depend on oil imports to satisfy a significant proportion of its demand for crude oil and product oil. The challenge to the United States is to develop a policy that both recognizes these constraints, and works to enhance flexibility for energy use in the marketplace. Energy resources must be developed and an effective response to any future oil disruption must be prepared.

The United States can foster a stabler energy environment. The risks of political instability in the developing countries and of an international financial crisis can be minimized by less reliance on the commercial banks in the recycling process. The resources of the International Monetary Fund and the World Bank for coping with structural problems of the less-developed countries must be strengthened. This can be done by drawing on additional resources from the Organization for Economic Cooperation and Development and from OPEC. The United States should also encourage OPEC's economic dependence on the United States, including OPEC investment in U.S. assets, because such dependence gives the oil exporters a more potent vested interest in a healthy U.S. economy. The United States needs to work more closely with the major oil importers. Acting in concert, the ability of the oil consumers to influence OPEC would be vastly enhanced. It is impossible not to observe how closely all these problems are interwoven. Yet, this means that the possibilities for constructive change are also intertwined. This can be clearly seen in the issue of Third World energy development.

The plight of the oil-importing developing countries has been noted before: Crushing international debt, shortage of fuel wood, resulting famine and migration to urban centers all add to already extant poverty. What has not been heard so clearly are the benefits accruing to U.S. security in improving the lot of these countries most seriously affected. By helping them develop their own energy resources, the United States not only helps the countries, it also helps itself, for by diversifying its energy suppliers the United States lessens its dependence on OPEC. The United States also fosters an enlarged export market for its energy-related goods and services.

Washington should support the multilateral development efforts such as the World Bank's proposed affiliate lending agency for energy development. The United States should also provide more bilateral assistance for the development of conventional and unconventional energy resources in the LDCs. Such assistance will remove strains on the global economy as well as reduce pressure on the global oil supply/demand balance.

It is imperative that the United States develop a cooperative relationship with the developing countries in energy before the era of "resource wars" is really upon us. The Third World is the fastest growing consumer of energy. According to Exxon's latest projections, Third World energy demand will grow at greater than 5 percent annually through 2000, increasing their share of total world energy demand from 12 percent in 1979 to at least 20 percent by the end of this century. This change in energy trade has important political implications for international relations: The industrial and developing world will be competing for the same scarce resource.

Continued cooperation among the major industrial oil-importing nations also is imperative. It is especially important that multilateral energy relations—through the IEA—be strengthened at a time when bilateral relations are becoming increasingly contentious. Given the current state of U.S. bilateral relations with Canada, Western Europe, and Japan discussed in this volume on energy issues, it is extremely dangerous to rely exclusively on bilateral ties.

Without a doubt the IEA is at a crossroads in its development. Renewed attention must be given to its improvement. What needs to be strengthened is not the organization itself—we do not want to see another international bureaucracy develop—but the commitment of the member states to using the IEA as a forum and as a tool for coping with common energy problems. The importance of the IEA as a political forum and as an economic tool has been neglected.

It is a political forum providing the structure within which the member states can agree on a common strategy toward OPEC, the oil-importing developing countries, and the Communist bloc. It is an economic tool that can be utilized to formulate approaches to managing an energy disruption and to accelerate the exploration and development of conventional and unconventional energy resources.

It is fundamental to the future stability of the international system that the industrial states develop a trilateral approach to the world's energy problems, embracing the West, OPEC, and the Third World. The IEA can be an essential part of this approach only if it is given sufficient diplomatic and financial support.

Too often critical attention has focused on the Emergency Sharing Program (ESP) of the IEA, the part that would attempt to allocate supplies worldwide in the event of a disruption. Certainly there are problems with the ESP; as many analysts believe, the system as presently constituted is unlikely to work adequately in a disruption. The very fact that the system has never been used despite several close calls indicates that member states also fear it will not operate promptly.

There are several problems with the program: Since 1974 substantial changes in the oil market may have reduced market flexibility; the increasing use of oil-destination clauses by producing countries may hinder the system's ability to respond, for example. A second problem is that allocation system presumes some type of price controls, whereas with no price controls the free market would equilibrate supply and demand and thus there would be no need for a sharing program. The IEA has established a dispute settlement center to resolve pricing differences, but major difficulties will have to be overcome to achieve price agreement in an emergency. The permutations of the allocation methods (intra- and intercompany shifts, company-to-state agreements) provide considerable opportunity for pricing controversies. It is hard to understand why, if the free-market system is the most efficient allocator of supplies domestically, it should not be so internationally.

The need for an allocation program remains, but the approach must be rethought in light of the changes to world petroleum markets since 1974. What is forgotten is the guiding purpose of the IEA. The IEA was not designed just to allocate supplies; rather, it was to be the basis for a unified response to OPEC from consumer nations, which in time would counterbalance producer power, placing downward pressure on oil prices. From the outset IEA was to be a visible symbol of allied solidarity. This should still be the raison d'etre of the organization. How can this purpose be achieved?

1. The United States needs to reiterate its support for the principles of the IEA agreement. The stated preference of some officials of the Reagan administration for letting the free market operate even in the event of a crisis has cast doubt on whether or not the United States will support the IEA allocation system in the event of a crisis. Such doubt should be dispelled.

2. The member states should reopen producer-consumer negotiations with OPEC to discuss the stabilization and predictability of world oil price increases while at the same time ensuring the steady development of the oil producing countries. Such an initiative would be a clear signal to Saudi Arabia that the major industrialized nations not only support Saudi efforts to stabilize global petroleum prices, but will also act to protect and assist the OPEC nations' long-term development objectives.

3. The IEA needs to demonstrate a greater concern with the energy problems of the Third World nations, especially those eight nations that account for the major part of LDC oil consumption. It might be in the IEA's eventual interest to bring some of the large LDC oil-consuming states into the emergency oil-sharing program once the difficulties of effecting their participation could be worked out, but in the interim, it is manifestly in the West's and Japan's interests to create an institutional forum to help assist the LDCs in their energy problems.

4. A common policy needs to be developed on cooperation in Communist energy development trade. U.S. policy has been ad hoc, reduced at times to jawboning our allies on avoiding dependence on Soviet energy imports while we could not decide what, if any, energy technology to sell them. At the same time, American companies have been encouraged to invest in energy development in the People's Republic of China. Unless the

Secretary of Energy James Schlesinger, supported by the U.S. Department of State, opposed the sale on the grounds that at $2.60 per thousand cubic feet (Mcf) the price was too high. The U.S. and Canadian governments had just concluded lengthy negotiations over a Candian export price of $2.16 per Mcf, and U.S. officials argued that acceptance of the Mexican price would reopen the Canadian negotiations. Some officials also worried that because the Mexican gas was priced so much higher than price-controlled U.S. domestic gas (which was $1.46 per Mcf), approval of the deal would worsen U.S. inflation (an argument not prominently featured in negotiations with Canada). U.S. officials also opposed linking the price of Mexican gas to the price of no. 2 home heating fuel, because if Mexican gas prices increased at the same rate as world oil prices they would be giving de facto parity equivalence to oil and gas prices, a principle the administration was opposing in its negotiations with the Algerians for supplies of liquefied natural gas.

As if technicalities in both countries' arguments were not complex enough to block an early agreement, key U.S. congressmen intervened publicly in the debate and U.S. officials remarked intemperately that sooner or later Mexico would have to sell its gas to the United States, since Mexico could earn more that way than by exporting LNG to overseas markets. Nothing could have fueled the flames of Mexican nationalism more effectively.

Despite some merit to the U.S. negotiating position opposing linking the price of Mexican gas to the price of no. 2 residual fuel oil delivered in New York Harbor, the Mexican perception that Washington was trying to dictate terms to Mexico and the introduction in Congress of measures designed to punish Mexico for its intransigence made it impossible for PEMEX to calm critics of the deal who already feared that the contract represented too much dependence on the United States. Indeed some Mexicans suspected that if the United States were one day to demand unacceptable terms that Mexico would have to refuse, the United States might intervene militarily. With Mexico bitter about the breakdown of negotiations in 1978, President Lôpez Portillo reaffirmed the dedication of Mexican gas resources to domestic consumption despite the lost opportunity cost. Psychologically the damage to U.S.-Mexican relations was incalculable.

In an attempt to improve relations, President Carter went to Mexico in February 1979. As a result, the United States and Mexico established a consultative group to study outstanding issues between the two countries related to energy, finance, industrial technology and

United States sits down soon with its allies and coordinates a common approach toward Soviet energy development, this issue will have grave effects on the cohesion of the Atlantic alliance.

5. The time has come to encourage France to drop its long-standing opposition and to join the other industrial nations in the IEA. The election of President François Mitterand provides an opportunity for a change in French policy. This opportunity cannot be lost. At the same time, discontinuities between the EEC's energy emergency sharing system and that of the IEA need to be coordinated to ensure that they do not work at cross-purposes in the event of a crisis.

These are general policy prescriptions but more specific work also needs to be done. The United States needs to support sub-trigger (below 7 percent) responses to supply shortfalls. Such responses need not entail the implementation of the allocation system but might require coordinated governmental stockpile or inventory drawdown policies that could not be left solely to the operation of the free market. It is also important that common strategic stockpile programs and implementation policies be adopted and that the difficult issue of pricing allocated supplies be addressed without delay. These efforts may require changes in U.S. antitrust restrictions on corporate cooperation with the IEA secretariat.

Every effort should be made to improve the quality and quantity of information flowing to the IEA. The United States should reevaluate its policy of monitoring oil company participation in the IEA and analyze how much federal antitrust law inhibits the free flow of information to the secretariat and hence IEA's ability to monitor and allocate oil supplies in a crisis.

Great effort needs to be made as well on a program of demand restraint—that is, conservation. Demand restraint has been so liberally interpreted that no real program has developed. Its success depends on the disposition of each member state to restrain domestic demand; IEA has done little to determine if these programs have real teeth or are paper tigers. Even current U.S. measures are astonishingly inadequate; those that have been considered would save little energy in the short run, when the need for conservation may be greatest. The recent rejection by the Reagan administration of several of the Carter energy emergency curtailment measures means that the new administration must put forth its own energy emergency program as soon as possible.

Very little has been accomplished in energy research and development, what should be a vital part of a reinvigorated international energy program. Limitless opportunities exist for facilitating technical cooperation among the major industrial states for the exploitation of conventional and unconventional energy resources, including renewable energy. It is dismaying that despite the urgings of the Venice Summit, the United States has drastically curtailed government research and development of renewable energy sources and advanced conservation technologies.

In the course of the investigation of which this book is a result we have concluded that the U.S. government's executive branch's arrangements for coordinating international energy policy are inadequate. In the past, bureaucratic rivalries among and within the Department of Energy (and some of its predecessors, the Federal Energy Administration [FEA] and the Energy Research and Development Administration [ERDA]), the CIA, the Treasury, Defense, and Commerce departments and the National Security Council (NSC) have made formation of a coherent energy policy so difficult that it has never been given the attention it deserves in the foreign policy community. For this reason, a new post, under secretary for international energy policy, should be created in either the State Department or the Department of Energy, to serve both as the principal international energy official of the U.S. government and as the coordinator of interagency energy policy. Creation of such an office may finally help place international energy questions at a level of policymaking where the nation's attention can be focused on the critical energy issues that must be faced in the 1980s.

The outlook for international energy cooperation is bleak because the United States appears paralyzed to act. Rather than moving forward and articulating a renewed approach to international energy policy such as was launched during the Ford and Carter administrations, this country seems to have retreated to an earlier era that predates the 1973 oil embargo, in which the United States could largely have its own way in internal politics owing to its energy self-sufficiency.

The Reagan administration may yet effect a comprehensive energy program that more fully recognizes areas in which government must play a larger role, often in support of the private sector. Still, time passes. If one argues that the current "oil glut" is here to stay, then NEP III may suffice for domestic purposes. But with the specter of renewed hostilities in the Middle East, the prospect of further economic shocks to the international financial system, growing divisions in the Western alliance in many areas, continued uncertainty over the Eastern Bloc's energy future and the implications for its foreign policy, the political implications on Saudi oil production policy and on U.S.-Saudi relations of a congressional denial of the AWACS sale to Saudi Arabia, and the threat of new political upheavals in some of the major oil-producing countries looming before us, there is little reason to be sanguine. It is time the Reagan administration embark on pragmatic directions that address these problems. Let us hope it will do so and demonstrate the forceful leadership that will ensure U.S. and global energy security for the remainder of this century.

NOTES

1. Jonathan P. Stern, "U.S. Intervention in the Middle East," *Defense, Communications and Security Review* 80/1 (1979): 3.
2. Ibid., p. 4; see also, *Oil Fields as Military Objectives: A Feasibility Study,* Special Subcommittee on Investigations of the Committee on International Relations, Congressional Research Service, August 21, 1975, p. 42.
3. John M. Collins and Clyde R. Mark, *Petroleum Imports from the Persian Gulf: Use of U.S. Armed Forces to Ensure Supplies,* Issue Brief no. IB79046, Congressional Research Service, July 24, 1979.
4. Stern, "U.S. Intervention in the Middle East," p. 8.
5. See Chapter 8.
6. Alvin J. Cottrell, Robert J. Hanks, and Frank T. Bray, "Military Affairs in the Persian Gulf," in *The Persian Gulf States,* ed. Alvin J. Cottrell (Baltimore: The Johns Hopkins University Press, 1980), p. 158.
7. Interviews at Saudi Arabian and Sudanese embassies, Washington, D.C., March 1981.
8. Melvin A. Conant, "The Challenge to Turkey," *Geopolitics of Energy* 1 no. 8 (August 1980).
9. See Howard Bucknell, *Report of the Seminar on Soviet Energy,* Energy and National Security Project, Ohio State University, Mershon Center, Columbus, Ohio, June 1980.
10. U.S. Central Intelligence Agency (CIA), *Prospects for Soviet Oil Production: A Supplemental Analysis,* ER 77-10425, July 1977, p. 32.

244

11. Ellen L. Stein, *The Dynamics of Soviet Oil and Natural Gas: Access to Future Energy Sources,* 1979, p. 3. Jonathan P. Stern of Conant and Associates estimates an 80-year gas supply at current production levels, "The World Oil Market in the Years Ahead—A Commentary on the Soviet and East European Section," cited in *Intelligence on the World Energy Outlook and Its Policy Implications,* Permanent Select Committee on Intelligence, U.S. House of Representatives, 1980, p. 99.

12. Friedman Müller, "The Energy Sector Status to the Soviet Union with an Eye to the 1980s," translated from *Osteuropa Wirtschaft,* no. 1 (1979) and reprinted in *Soviet and Eastern European Foreign Trade* (Spring 1980): 13.

13. Leslie Dienes, "Modernization and Energy Development in the Soviet Union," *Soviet Geography: Review and Translation,* March 1980, p. 123. The Soviet energy mix as of 1978 stood at 43.9 percent petroleum; 23.9 percent natural gas; coal/lignite 26.2 percent; peat, oil shale, and firewood, 2.4 percent; hydro 3 percent; and nuclear 0.7 percent.

14. Marshall I. Goldman, "Is There a Russian Energy Crisis?," *The Atlantic* (September 1980): 56.

15. Marshall I. Goldman, "The Changing Role of Raw Materials Exports and Soviet Foreign Trade," in *Soviet Economy in a Time of Change,* U.S. Congress, Joint Economic Committee, vol. 1, 1979, p. 188.

16. CIA, *Prospects for Soviet Oil Production,* Washington, D.C., April 1977; *Prospects for Soviet Oil Production: A Supplemental Analysis; The World Oil Market in the Years Ahead,* ER 79–10327U, August 1979; *The Soviet Economy in 1978–79 and Prospects for 1980,* ER 80–10328, June 1980.

17. Jon Stein, *The Soviet Energy Outlook in the 1980s: Implications for U.S. National Security Policy,* unpublished manuscript, March 2, 1981, Georgetown University School of Foreign Service, Washington, D.C.

18. Ibid.; see also CIA, *The World Oil Market in the Years Ahead,* p. 40. Oil consumption in the USSR has increased every year since 1970, jumping from 5.15 mmbd to 8.9 mmbd in 1979. CIA, *International Economic and Energy Statistical Review,* December 11, 1980, p. 25.

19. Dienes, "Modernization in the Soviet Union," p. 133.

20. Ibid., p. 124.

21. Ibid., p. 147.

22. J. Richard Lee and James R. Lecky, "Soviet Oil Developments," in *Soviet Economy in a Time of Change,* pp. 585–586, cited in Stein, *Soviet Energy in the 1980s,* p. 8.

23. CIA, *The World Oil Market in the Years Ahead,* p. 39. The Urengoy gas fields are reportedly lagging behind schedule. "Concern for Soviet Energy Problems," *Petroleum Economist* (June 1980): 230; Ellen Stein, *Dynamics of Soviet Oil and Natural Gas,* pp. 17-18 and also p. 18, where the author says, "In Tyumen, the set-up is difficult; the gas contains considerable water, and there are no dehydration facilities"; Yu. Permiken, "Tyumen Needs Special Oil, Gas Machinery," *Pravda,* November 14, 1980, reprinted in *Current Digest of the Soviet Press,* December 17, 1980; "Soviet Union—Labour Shortages and Problems," *Petroleum Economist* (July 1980): 312; cited in Jon Stein, *Soviet Energy in the 1980s,* pp. 8-9.

24. Dienes, "Modernization in the Soviet Union," p. 141.

25. CIA, *Central Siberian Brown Coal as a Potential Source of Power for European Russia,* p. 39; Jonathan P. Stern, "Soviet Energy Prospects in the 1980s," *The World Today* (May 1980): 191.

26. CIA, *The Soviet Economy in 1978-79 and Prospects for 1980,* ER 80-10328, June 1980, p. 21.

27. CIA, *The Soviet Economy in 1978-79 and Prospects for 1980,* p. 19; CIA, *The World Oil Market in the Years Ahead,* p. 38.

28. Dienes, "Modernization in the Soviet Union," p. 145.

29. Lee and Lecky, "Soviet Oil Developments," p. 591.

30. Dienes, "Modernization in the Soviet Union," p. 145.

31. Lee and Lecky, "Soviet Oil Developments," p. 586.

32. Dienes, "Modernization in the Soviet Union," p. 144.

33. Lee and Lecky, "Soviet Oil Developments," p. 587. "Soviet production practices make it difficult to implement tertiary recovery procedures, because their massive water flood techniques adversely affect oil-reservoir permeability" (CIA, *Prospects for Soviet Oil Production: A Supplemental Analysis,* p. 2).

34. Joseph P. Riva, Jr., *Soviet Oil Prospects,* Congressional Research Service, April 6, 1981, pp. 22-23.

35. Herbert L. Sawyer, "The Soviet Energy Sector: Problems and Prospects," in *The U.S.S.R. in the 1980s* (Brussels: NATO, 1978), pp. 35-36.

36. Jonathan P. Stern, "Western Technology and the Soviet Energy Situation II," *Geopolitics of Energy* 2, no. 3 (March 1980).

37. Melvin A. Conant, "The Consequences of Choice: Energy Options for Germany," *Geopolitics of Energy* 2, no. 11 (November 1980).

38. Stern, "Western Technology and the Soviet Energy Situation II."

39. Ellen Stein, *Dynamics of Soviet Oil and Natural Gas,* pp. 9-11.

40. "Soviets Apparently Lift Oil Charges Sharply for Eastern Bloc Allies," *The Wall Street Journal,* February 4, 1981, p. 31; CIA, *The World Oil Market in the Years Ahead,* p. 41. The OECD projects

1990 East European oil imports at 2.6 mmbd. Richard F. Staar, "Soviet Policy in East Europe," *Current History* (October 1980): 77, note 15.

41.   "Russia Sends Its Allies Scrambling for Oil," *Business Week* (July 7, 1980): 20.

42.   *Facts on File,* October 3, 1980, p. 753.

43.   Stern, "Soviet Energy Prospects in the 1980's," *The World Today* May 1980, p. 192. Installed nuclear generating capacity in CMEA countries (1980) was 13,000 megawatts.

44.   Ellen Stein, *Dynamics of Soviet Oil and Natural Gas,* p. 30; "Concern for Soviet Energy Problems," *Petroleum Economist,* p. 231; Robert L. Pfaltzgraff, Jr., *Energy Issues and Alliance Relationships: The United States, Western Europe, and Japan,* Cambridge, Mass.: Institute For Foreign Policy Analysis, April 1980, p. 46.

45.   CIA, *The World Oil Market in the Years Ahead,* pp. 41–42.

46.   "Soviet Union—Lower Exports to the West," *Petroleum Economist* (August 1980): 352. In 1979, oil imports (crude and product) from the USSR accounted for over 60 percent of Finnish and Icelandic oil imports; 21 percent of Austrian imports; 17 percent of Swiss imports; and less than 10 percent of West German and Italian imports (Marshall I. Goldman, "The Role of Communist Countries," p. 128). Also see *Soviet Union Daily Report,* Foreign Broadcast Information Service, February 5, 1981, p. G2.

47.   Stern, "Soviet Energy Prospects in the 1980's," pp. 31–33.

48.   Lee and Lecky, "Soviet Oil Developments," p. 582.

49.   Jon Stein, p. 37 ff.

50.   Ministry of Energy, Mines and Hydrocarbons, *The National Energy Program,* Ottawa, October 1980, p. 44.

51.   *Energy Daily,* July 28, 1980.

52.   *Coal Week,* October 29, 1979.

53.   This discussion draws upon Paul Daniel and Richard Shaffner, "Lessons from Bilateral Trade in Energy Resources," in *Natural Resources in U.S.-Canadian Relations*, ed. C. Bergie and A. Hero, vol. 1 (Boulder, Colorado: Westview, 1980).

54.   National Energy Board of Canada, *Reasons for Decisions,* Ottawa, November 1979, chap. 9.

55.   U.S. Department of Energy, *Petroleum Supply Alternatives for the Northern Tier and Inland States through the Year 2000, Draft Report,* February 21, 1979, chap. 5.

56.   Daniel and Shaffner, "Lessons from Bilateral Trade in Energy Resources," vol. 1.

57.   David Ronfeldt, Richard Nehring, and Arturo Gandara, *Mexico's*

Petroleum and U.S. Policy: Implications for the 1980's, RAND, Santa Monica, Calif., June 1980, p. 55.

58. Sevinc Carlson, *Mexico's Oil: Trends and Prospects to 1985,* Center for Strategic and International Studies, Georgetown University, Washington, D.C., July 1979.

59. Ronfeldt et al., *Mexico's Petroleum and U.S. Policy,* p. 59.

60. Carlson, *Mexico's Oil,* p. 23.

61. *Electricity Exchanges, United States/ Mexico,* report prepared by the U.S. Department of Energy and the Comision Federal De Electricidad Mexico, D.F., DOE/RG-0033, May 1980.

62. Ronfeldt et al., *Mexico's Petroleum and U.S. Policy,* pp. 85–87.

63. G. Henry M. Schuler, *The National Security Implications of Increased Reliance upon Importation of Refined Products,* Conant and Associates, Washington, D.C., 1979, p. 135.

64. Interview, Venezuelan Embassy, April 7, 1980.

INDEX